At the Side of Torture Survivors

At the Side of Torture Survivors

Treating a Terrible Assault on Human Dignity

EDITED BY

Sepp Graessner, M.D.,
Norbert Gurris, and
Christian Pross, M.D.

TRANSLATED BY

Jeremiah Michael Riemer

The Johns Hopkins University Press
BALTIMORE AND LONDON

Translation prepared with the generous assistance of Inter Nationes.

Originally published as *Folter: An der Seite der Überlebenden, Unterstützung, und Therapien*

© C. H. Beck'sche Verlagsbuchhandlung, Munich, 1996

2 4 6 8 9 7 5 3 1

The Johns Hopkins University Press

2715 North Charles Street

Baltimore, Maryland 21218-4363

www.press.jhu.edu

Library of Congress Cataloging-in-Publication Data

will be found at the end of this book.

A catalog record for this book is available from the British Library.

ISBN 0-8018-6627-8

Contents

Contents

Foreword

Man's capacity for inhumanity is beyond normal comprehension. Yet there is within each one of us a potential for evil to dominate and possess us. By the grace of God, there is also in each of us a potential for overflowing love. This is the well that those who are victims of torture need desperately to find. This book is an important addition to a growing library of guidance and healing for those who are traumatized. Tragically, there are thousands of broken people in the world. This book documents the experiences of a group of caregivers helping victims to learn to trust and love themselves and those around them. I commend it to all those who are involved in this important ministry.

May it also encourage those who are concerned for human rights to an even stronger commitment and zeal to oppose oppression.

God bless you.

Desmond Tutu
Archbishop Emeritus

Foreword

The goal of torture is to destroy personality and annihilate identity. Torturers know that people without identity—people with shattered personalities—lose their capacity for resistance and give in to the demand that they reveal secrets and practice betrayal. In order to reach their goal, torturers go about their business in a systematic fashion. They know that wearing people down has to proceed step by step. It is a precisely calculated process, carried out cold-bloodedly and in accordance with the character traits of an individual prisoner. It would not make much sense to begin immediately with the harshest measures. The victim has to be allowed enough time to experience the torments and humiliations, to identify with them, and to lose the will to resist bit by bit. So long as the victim has not lost the last inner hold on—the last tip of—self-confidence, the goal has not been reached.

Torturers are often trained in psychology, yet they may be distinguished from psychotherapists because their task is to destroy rather than heal the human psyche. They try to perform this task through physical violence. Blows to the soles of the feet with whips made from barbed wire, pulling out nails, burning body parts with cigarette embers and hot plates, rape, and fake executions are the common methods in international use. Beyond that, there is an infinite variety of bestialities. Here torturers have proven how inventive they can be. An Iranian prisoner told me that he was forced by his torturers to eat his own hair that had just been cut off.

Victims need to counter this strategy of total humiliation with a strategy of their own, their own defense technique, a technique for sustaining self-confidence and resistance. The victim cannot afford to show any weakness, to give way to self-pity, to start reflecting on the torture or the torturers. Whoever does not want to be at the mercy of the torturer dare not attempt to distract his thoughts from what is happening, to ignore the crime. The strategy of tuning out sense perceptions may prove useful after the first slap in the face, but as soon as the soles of the feet are struck by whips and testicles are stomped on, the prisoner begins to learn how useless this method is. The person being tortured has to look the beast in the face, has to experience, live through, and understand the sin, the crime, down to the last detail. Feelings, sense perceptions, and comprehension must all become interchangeable, must form a single entity fused together in order to concentrate on the event. Any lack of concentration or discipline, any slipping away into other thoughts, wears away the power of resistance. The victim has to see, smell, taste, and apprehend the torture.

One prisoner wrote: "The blows don't just strike your body; they strike much more at your soul, your spirit, your reason. Pain and emotion bore their way through the entire body until they reach your soul, your ego. The torment is not merely perceived, it penetrates consciousness, it is apprehended. You want to scream. The screams come from the gut and push through to the throat, but they are held back by reason, self-consciousness, pride, so that you nearly suffocate. It is a struggle between body and soul, a struggle between body and spirit."

Enduring torture requires not just a physical but, above all, a kind of mental peak performance. That is why most victims fall into a deep silence after the torture is over, a silence that turns what was experienced into a secret even after the victim's release. If a victim has failed, has revealed secrets, has committed treason, then life in the open becomes torture, an eternal plague of conscience. But even those who put up resistance continue the silence. Whether it comes from a feeling of shame or from an incapacity to summon up the power to recount what they experienced, they are usually not ready to relate their experiences to those closest to them. Even if the physical scars should heal at some point, the psychic wounds will remain for life in the absence of outside help and treatment. Victims often suffer from intense depression, and they are often pursued by nightmares and anxieties. Amnesia, agitation, delusions, feelings of powerlessness, a constant shift between aggressive overreaction and apathy are among the victims' observable attributes.

Many victims remain under their tormentors' control even after their release. They are constantly in danger of being incarcerated again. Only a few of them succeed in escaping abroad. But the path to freedom is bound up with a new torment: if the refugee succeeds in gaining entry to a country of sanctuary—an enterprise that is frequently life-threatening—what commences next is a procedure that seems endless to the asylum seeker. Life in a "camp," where extremely difficult and degrading circumstances are the rule, reawakens memories of time spent in prison. Being together with foreigners whose language one barely understands can also drive refugees into indescribable loneliness. Each hour becomes an eternity. One has to kill time in order to get through the restless, sleepless nights.

Add to this the hearings before the asylum authority. The old survival strategy—of keeping silent about what was experienced, mentally burying the past, banishing the torture from memory—can prove disastrous for the refugee. For the investigating officials, the decision makers upon whose judgment the refugee's fate now rests, are now demanding precise information together with credible proof. The refugee is forced to recall to mind what had been laboriously repressed. Even an insignificant contradiction in testimony can lead to an application for asylum being denied. Permanent anxiety about deportation is like a sword of Damocles. Life in a camp can last for years.

The Treatment Center for Torture Victims in Berlin is one of the few facilities in Germany that concerns itself with the fate of people tortured like this. The reports submitted here testify to how much empathy, patience, and dedication are required to heal the destroyed identity and shattered personality of each "patient" and to make life appear meaningful again to the victims. I imagine that the therapists who work there can actually only help the patients if they dedicate a portion of their very own being, of their soul, to each individual victim. How can one thank them for this selflessness?

Bahman Nirumand

Introduction to the
English-Language Edition

Survivors' Silence and the Difficulty of Knowing

"Enduring torture requires not just a physical but, above all, a kind of mental peak performance. That is why most victims fall into a deep silence after the torture is over," writes Bahman Nirumand in his foreword to this book. I want to begin with an exploration of this "deep silence," a silence that still constitutes an enigma for us all. What are its origins, its manifestations, its implications? How can it be addressed or even partially resolved? Johan Lansen, one of the contributors to this book, offers a model based on psychoanalytic object-relation theory for the comprehension of the sequelae of severe traumatization (chapter 12). A profound regression is induced during the process of torture, in which the person reexperiences the earliest childhood imagery of fantasized horrors of helplessness, worthlessness, and castration. This regression, this damage, is not completely reversible, and it persists as an ego deficit that continues to shape later interpersonal experiences. Thus an altered, deformed internal representation of the world and of people comes into existence and continues to shape future life experience.

In this altered internal world, there is no "other," no empathic companion who is willing to listen and to respond to one's needs. After those moments of mental "peak performance," nourished by fervent hope and yearning for an eventual human response, are over, the survivor of torture feels completely alone. He—or she—no longer believes in the very possibility of human communication; he envisages no one who will be present to him and for him if he returns in his mind to the places of horror, humiliation, and grief from which he barely emerged and which continue to haunt him. He is too terrified to face them alone, and his inner companion / witness, summoned for survival, is gone forever. The torture survivor therefore falls into a deep silence because there is no one to tell; and the traumatic experience itself is muted, it has

no voice except for recurrent nightmares, flashbacks, and unconscious reen-
actments. It is the function of the therapist to bring back that lost voice. According to Ferdinand Haenel, another contributor to this book, psychotherapy
leads to an enhancement of the patient's self-awareness through a correction
and enhancement of the parental images (that failed to protect) by the additional internalized image of a new healing object—that of the psychotherapist.
This correction of the deformed internalized world representation may reopen
the possibility of dialogue and of telling, setting the frozen memories back in
motion.

But is the survivor alone in perpetuating this silence? Frank Merkord, in his
contribution to this volume, describes in detail the painful journeys, trials, and
tribulations traversed by those who seek asylum in refugee camps. The long-
awaited moment of liberation from torture does not bring them back home.
Like Holocaust survivors, they land in D.P. camps. And even if they return to
their homeland, they may never feel "at home" again. The testimony of a
mother and her (by now middle-aged) offspring, both Holocaust survivors, is
illustrative. While she recounts with pride how her son, upon his arrival home
after two years in a camp, first ran to his toy closet and found all his toys there,
the son contradicts her, remembering that what he found was an empty closet.
Despite the mother's longing—the liberation she yearned for, hoped for, imagined—the reality is the empty closet. Most excruciating, however, is the desperately yearned-for encounter with friends and family, or even fellow Jews. One
cannot wait to tell them what one endured—only to meet with disbelief and
lack of interest. Primo Levi reports an almost prophetic dream that he had in
the camp—a nightmare that other inmates also experienced. He was home
with his family, telling them what he had undergone. One by one, they left the
room until he found himself alone.

The general public is even less interested in knowing. Peter Novick, in a
recently published book, *The Holocaust in American Life* (1999), documents
how little interest the general American population—and even the American
Jewish community—demonstrated in the mass murder of European Jews while
the Holocaust was occurring and for several decades afterward. Neither was
there much interest in the "liberated" survivors who reached American shores
after the war or in what they had to tell. Addressing the situation in the Netherlands after World War II, Christian Pross, in his contribution to the present

book, interprets this apparent lack of interest. He states, "It seems to be a general phenomenon that nobody likes the victims of a dictatorship, since they keep alive the bad conscience of the silent majority." I would go further in interpreting as *normative* this public inattention, this lack of interest (and at best prolonged latency in the acknowledgment of contemporaneous atrocities, thus rendering them "nonevents"). To empathically know, recognize, and acknowledge ongoing atrocities is to experience the very fragility of the structures of our civilization, our very proximity to destruction. More recent genocidal events in Cambodia, Bosnia, Rwanda, East Timor, and many other places reemphasize the reluctance of governments and world public opinion to know, acknowledge, confirm, and most of all to take a stance and to respond to massive violations of human rights—even ongoing mass murder. This holds true even when information is readily available and prevention through resolute intervention possible. Atrocities thus remain essentially unknown, unwitnessed, and unanswered. Is it a wonder, then, that survivors of torture fall into deep silence? It is the various voices in this book—therapists, torture survivors, case workers, storytellers—that try to unlock the silence—to recapture the lost reality of the unwitnessed event.

The German Context

The context in which this trauma work is done and in which this book was written is of utmost importance. The book is a study of the psychotherapeutic work carried out with victims of political violence and oppression from thirty countries around the world (including the former Yugoslavia, the Middle East, Southeast Asia, North Africa, the former GDR, etc.) The work takes place in Berlin, in unified Germany—the locus par excellence of political violence and large-scale warfare for the first half of the twentieth century. The authors of the various essays in this book are clinicians who live and work in Germany, who are cognizant of the atrocities committed by Germans during World War II, cognizant also of the complicity of the German healing professions in carrying out these atrocities. As is mentioned repeatedly throughout this book, the healing professions have never acknowledged such complicity and have never been held accountable by society for their deeds. The authors who have consciously chosen to do this work are, on the other hand, fully aware of the ways in which it is informed by their legacy. Coming from family and societal backgrounds marked by the devastations of twentieth-century barbarism, they have chosen to know it and to confront it. This choice shapes their listening, interacting, and intervening on behalf of their patients; it makes them better attuned to what their patients have to say. The patients in turn sense this preexisting knowledge and the readiness to hear it (again), and they are willing to take risks in naming what terrifies them most. It is also possible that torture refugees arriving in Germany can experience and remember more, because the host culture and society (if it is willing) is more informed by its own history and therefore more open to their experience. Both sides, patients and therapists alike, speak of something that really happened on their respective soils and that affected them intimately and profoundly.

By contrast, the American context is so very different. No major war has ravaged this country's territory since 1865, and no political dictatorship has ever ruled it. American expeditionary forces have waged wars and witnessed (and perhaps even carried out) atrocities on foreign, distant shores on other continents. The veterans who returned from these conflicts—except for those from Vietnam—have usually remained silent about what they saw and experienced. Refugees by the millions were invited to join the American dream, to rebuild their lives in a new country and not look backward. Americans typically experience political, state-sponsored and state-perpetrated atrocities as unreal in spite of graphic and vivid TV reportage, because these things happen so far away. This form of atrocity can only be imagined, not really remembered. American mental health professionals hear directly about trauma either as related to situations of military combat (involving mostly Vietnam and Desert Storm veterans) or related to physical, emotional, and sexual assaults perpetrated by criminals or by abusive family members.

For many professionals in the United States and Canada, no cultural, familial, or personal reservoir of experience exists into which they can delve in order to authenticate—to experience—the reality in themselves of the traumatic torture experiences reported by their refugee patients. Countertransference feelings and the ability to empathize are inevitably affected by the level of reality that the therapist experiences while listening to memories of traumatic experiences. We Americans are both innocent and naive. It doesn't really exist for us. That is not to say that we are not a very violent society—violence in North

America, however, is perpetrated by individuals or at most by criminal gangs, not by agencies of the state. That is also not to say that a European therapist more intimately acquainted with the destruction of war and associated atrocities, will not defend himself or herself from hearing such accounts. Such defensiveness is rampant, particularly in Germany. If the therapist does, however, make the decision to open himself, the potential for hearing the patient's reality more readily exists.

It is perhaps this unreality of state-perpetrated torture and atrocity in the American context that promotes the emergence of a rather neatly packaged clinical entity like posttraumatic stress disorder. This diagnostic label does not recognize the shattered individual, familial, and communal lives of torture victims—a shattering that goes far beyond the specific clinical syndrome of a single individual (and for which such categories as "complex PTSD" or "DES" are at best halfhearted attempts at formulation).

It would be historically incorrect, of course, to maintain that state-perpetrated atrocities have never occurred in the American context. But the liquidation of Native Americans, the enslavement of Africans, the Civil War prison camp at Andersonville—all of these are historical examples, mostly relegated to the distant past. Massive traumatization continues in the present—among the approximately two million prison inmates in the United States (among the highest per capita in the world), and among the 600,000 homeless adults who spend their nights on the streets of our major cities or in urban homeless shelters. We have become habituated to their existence only out of self-protectiveness; we have trained ourselves not to see them, not to perceive their plight.

Shifting Spaces, Protective Places

The treatment of torture survivors can be a horrendous undertaking. To quote Ferdinand Haenel, it is "as if the victim takes her prison cell from the past and keeps carrying it along with her." Consequently, the goal of the treatment, according to Norbert F. Gurris, is "the conscious internalization of the entire traumatic reality into the patient's self-concept, so that at some point he can say: Yes, I really did experience that; it happened to me, but it's history. I am no longer a victim; I'm a survivor instead." All this has to be accomplished while the war in Bosnia drags on, the persecution at home continues, family members there remain endangered, the oppressive regimes at home persist in their denial of atrocities they committed, and the new host countries refuse to grant asylum or even the most basic support. It is as though the torture machine has never stopped and the "new" reality rests on ever-shifting sands. It takes a resolute and well-grounded therapist to say to the patient, "It's the situation, the torture, that's crazy, not you. The way you react to it is normal and completely human" (Ferdinand Haenel).

It also takes a highly unorthodox, flexible, creative, and above all multidimensional therapeutic approach to effectively address such situations. It is essential to keep in mind that a whole person, a person whose life has been shattered on multiple levels, is in treatment. First and foremost, a past reality, that of torture, needs to be acknowledged and confirmed; and a present reality, that of exile, fear for loved ones, and dire need, must be addressed by whatever means one has. In view of the reality of evil, only real advocacy is a meaningful intervention, a possible counterforce to that reality of evil. Because the psychological regression induced by torture is never completely reversed, the survivor is left with a propensity for regression to such an extent that the therapeutically induced regression can become a mere repetition and reenactment of the torture experience in the transference-countertransference relationship. That is, the patient can experience the therapist as a torturer, and the therapist can inadvertently fulfill such a projected role. Therefore, it is an important safeguard for both patient and therapist to keep reality, and especially the helping reality, in mind.

The level of the therapeutic intervention needs to shift continually to the locus of the patient's most urgent need. Treatment cannot be limited to a *specific* syndrome (PTSD), memory (torture), behavior pattern (unconscious reenactment, substance abuse), physical injury, unconscious fantasy, or damaged family, community, and economic-material status. All of the above have been profoundly affected by the severe persecution and the atrocities committed and must therefore be addressed. The therapeutic approaches illustrated in this book range from straightforward case work and psychoeducation to pharmacotherapy, pastoral counseling, family therapy, cognitive-behavioral therapy, psychodrama, body movement and art therapy, Gestalt therapeutic dreamwork (to enhance ego resources), hypnotherapy, simple storytelling, and more traditional psychoanalytic depth psychotherapy.

A shattered life needs multiple levels of intervention in striving to become whole again, especially in a situation in which real-life tragedy continues and can never be reversed, can never be made whole again. Such holistic life intervention will never happen if the victim is treated merely for a clinically defined syndrome such as PTSD that limits its focus to pathological symptoms; if treatment is defined (and controlled) by the policies of health insurance companies that dictate what is (and what is not) a medical necessity; or if treatment is governed by ideological rigidity of any kind—be it psychopharmacological, behavioristic, psychodynamic, or social rehabilitation.

Many of the interventions described in this book achieve only partial relief for the patient and promote a therapeutic experience that is somewhat removed both from oneself and from the "real." Psychodrama reenacts the traumatic event on a make-believe stage; art therapy finds a new medium for its indirect expression. That is first and foremost because of the impossibility of full and direct reconstruction of an atrocity in memory, in shared testimony, or in the therapeutic transference. The cognitive, linguistic, and emotional capacities of normal human beings are simply not commensurate with such a task. Thoughts cannot focus; concepts are inadequate; words are missing; feelings cannot be sufficiently contained to permit expression. Consequently, various therapeutic interventions can create partial truths on improvised stages on which it can all happen again, but this time around in relative safety and distance, with a therapist-gatekeeper who can regulate it, stop it when needed, and always guarantee a safe exit when it becomes too much.

Although these partial truths can function as defensive screens, they are nevertheless essential for coping. They create transitional holding environments that provide protection not only to the victim but also to the listener—therapist or testimonial witness—and even to the average citizen, who is better able to accept and absorb certain truths when a playwright or screenwriter dramatizes it (e.g., *Schindler's List*) than when a journalist reports it directly through pictures or words.

The various therapeutic modalities illustrated in this book engage and capture the many aspects of the destruction of the human fabric inherent in the torture experience by creating such safe (transitional) spaces that permit the healing process, driven primarily by the therapeutic relationship, to unfold and proceed. Although lies are toxic and truth is considered healing, the latter may never be achieved, and healing may remain incomplete. The courtroom and the truth commission constitute the boldest attempt to restore truth. Their potential for healing, however, remains to be proven. Whatever healing is possible may entail a process of grieving wherein what cannot be restored, what cannot be mended, is accepted as is—never to be whole again.

Dori Laub, M.D.

Preface

Torture, described as the "plague of the twentieth century," is still widespread throughout the world. Whoever wants to know about it can find out in the media on a daily basis, in dispatches from Turkey, from Iran, from the former Yugoslavia—a complete list of the countries would be alarmingly long. Amnesty International's annual reports name more than a hundred countries in which prisoners are tortured and mistreated. Torture is meant to deter the populace from rebelling against a dictatorship. People are not tortured only to elicit information and force confessions; torture aims especially at disorienting the person, to the point where personality is destroyed. Rehabilitating torture victims has the goal of restoring dignity to human beings—and this also always means resistance against the torturers and their regimes.

The idea for setting up the Behandlungszentrum für Folteropfer (Treatment Center for Torture Victims) emerged from a confrontation with the practice of medicine under National Socialism, when doctors participated in violent crimes and mass annihilation. After 1945, large sections of the medical profession refused to face up to the Holocaust survivors and offer them help. As the place where National Socialist genocide once had its central office, and also as the former headquarters for East Germany's State Security Service, Berlin has a special moral obligation to foster rehabilitation for victims of human rights violations.

Since it was founded in 1992, the Berlin Treatment Center has offered medical, social, and psychotherapeutic assistance to people who have been tortured. It is constructed like a polyclinic where different disciplines—general medicine and psychiatry, psychotherapy, physiotherapy, and art therapy, as well as social work—work closely together. Those seeking help (in 1999 they numbered over four hundred) now come from more than thirty countries.

The Treatment Center is politically neutral; it is bound only by the UN

Convention against Torture and Other Cruel, Inhuman, or Degrading Treatment or Punishment, the Madrid Declaration of the European Medical Profession banning physician participation in torture, and the conventions of the European Parliament on human rights. It is supported by an advisory council that includes Duchess Soscha zu Eulenburg, vice president of the German Red Cross; Professor Dr. Ulrich Venzlaff, former director of the Psychiatric State Hospital of Lower Saxony in Göttingen; Professor Dr. Georges M. Fülgraff, former director of the Federal Health Authority and Coordinator of the Berlin Public Health Research Network; Professor Dr. Thomas Dieterich, president of the Federal Labor Court; Dr. Jürgen Kühling, a justice on the Federal Constitutional Court; members of the German Bundestag; Professor Dr. Herta Däubler-Gmelin, Minister of Justice (member of the Bundestag, SPD); Dr. Heiner Geißler of the CDU/CSU parliamentary group; and Cem Özdemir, from the Alliance 90/the Greens parliamentary group.

The Treatment Center cooperates closely with the German Red Cross and is sponsored by the Federal Ministry for Family, Senior Citizens, and Youth, by the United Nations, and by the European Union. Approximately 50 percent of its budget has to be raised from donations. The donors include private citizens, firms, and such foundations as the Alfried Krupp von Bohlen and Halbach Foundation, the Dr. Joseph and Sibylle Krettner Foundation, the Heinrich Böll Foundation, and the Deutsche Bank Foundation in honor of Alfred Herrhausen.

This book documents the center's very difficult and complicated therapeutic work without hiding the limitations and failures that often accompany this kind of work. It tells of the burdens imposed on those providing aid and about the difficulty of diagnosing the symptoms of torture, as well as about the problems impeding the establishment of therapeutically effective contact with torture victims.

The chapters in this book take stock of our experiences in our first four years in operation, which we want to pass on to those doing work at similar institutions. The book is not only addressed to a professional reading public. We are attempting to report concretely and vividly, in a language that is generally intelligible, about the everyday world of treatment. Accordingly, some concepts are described in detail in the Glossary.

It was not easy to pour contributions from so many authors into a mold that is appropriate for this book. We thank the editor at C. H. Beck Verlag, Dr. Stephan Meyer, for helping us to master this assignment. We also thank our librarian, Leyla Schön, for compiling the Bibliography and for technical assistance in preparing the manuscript's final draft.

Berlin, summer 2000

At the Side of Torture Survivors

CHAPTER ONE

Foreign Bodies in the Soul

Ferdinand Haenel

We often observe that people who come to us seem to live under the tension of two extremes, spanning completely contradictory feelings, perceptions, thoughts, and values. Many seem to lack drive and vitality, appearing numb and tense, but they can also be excessively irritable and lose all control over themselves as they succumb to rage. Some experience just one extreme of these contradictions: they have completely turned their backs on their emotional world, notice nothing at all, and act as if anesthetized. Others, in turn, threaten to sink into anxiety, despair, and grief. Some have little recollection of the things that happened to them while they were being mistreated, while others retain sharp memories in which all the events are photographically captured.

It is as if the downward slope from power to powerlessness experienced in relation to the perpetrator has ripped apart the victim's ego and world into two or more pieces—as if the victim's ego could now only exist in tension-filled categories of two polarities, moving sharply and mercilessly between the extreme horizons of an either-or situation: either omnipotent or powerless, either fantasy or reality, either black or white. Shadings, the degrees of gray that lend intensity of depth perception to a photograph, are often not perceived initially.

Fantasy or Reality

Thirty-year-old Ms. S. arrives at our facility for an initial admission interview. During the greeting and introductory explanations, I am struck by her caution and reserve. She comes from a Southeast Asian country and has been in Germany for two years, where she has applied for asylum. Tearfully she describes her biggest problem at the moment, which is that the officials and the courts have refused to believe her so far. Since her arrival in Germany she has been trying to suppress the psychological problems she has had since a roughly one-year incarceration in her native country. At first it actually seemed to work. For several months now, however, nightmares keep waking her, drenched in sweat and heart pounding. But in the daytime, too, in ordinary, everyday situations—for example, in a packed subway that reminds her of her narrow confinement in overcrowded and overheated jail cells, or when she accidentally encounters pedestrians on the street whom she imagines recognizing as her torturers—she is assaulted by vivid memories of that time and by panicky feelings of anxiety. She is constantly under the strain of an inner overexcitability and irritability, and she easily breaks out in fits of rage at trivial provocations.

Even meditation techniques, in which she is well versed, were only able to provide relief that was provisional; it was hardly sustainable for the kind of psychic pressure she has been enduring. She has been totally beside herself since her appeal for asylum was rejected by the administrative court. Now she fears losing what little remains of her inner control, and she contemplates taking her life.

Under my cautious questioning she provides the following account of her life. In her homeland she had been a sales clerk in a large textile firm. One Monday morning when she came to work, she was extremely surprised to find no one at the office. She had had no inkling that there had been a secret coup attempt against the government over the weekend, an attempt that had been suppressed and in which the entire management of her firm was suspected of being involved. A short time after she arrived at the office, the police showed up and began to ask her questions that she could not answer. They took her away and continued the interrogation at headquarters. She was repeatedly hit, repeatedly raped, and tortured with electric shocks and with cold, hard jets of water. For nearly a year she remained in prison, at times under the most humiliating circumstances in a narrow, dark, overheated isolation cell without enough to eat. Thanks to family connections and assistance, she managed to get out after a year and leave her country for Germany.

Her story is repeatedly interrupted by moments where she loses control and can no longer hold back tears and despair. Initially, shock and empathy make it hard for me to maintain my equanimity.

Ms. S: "All these things are now two years behind me. In the meantime, I've even managed to banish them from my consciousness. From experience, I know it's possible. But now my despair and my anger that no one seems to believe me has reopened the old wounds."

I reply: "We are well acquainted with the psychological problems that you're relating. Unfortunately, almost everyone who comes to us suffers from ailments similar to yours. We're familiar with this. What you see as your suffering or your sickness is actually something completely normal, a completely understandable reaction to the abnormal and incomprehensible experience you had in jail. It's the situation, the torture that's crazy, not you. The way you react to it is normal and completely human."

Her facial expression brightens up a little. "Torture?" I say provocatively. "Actually, there's no such thing." Irritated and distraught, she looks up. "I mean," I go on to say, "there's hardly a country where the government will publicly admit that torture goes on. A simple, politically quite routine general denial, and the result is that torture doesn't exist in most people's minds, at most maybe on the fringes of the news or in some Amnesty International statistics. Consequently—and this is also a strategy of the perpetrators—it's hard for the victims to gain credibility about what happened to them. No one is willing to listen to the victims; no one wants to have anything to do with torture. The reality of everyday life runs right past the secret, disavowed reality of the torture pit, without anyone from the first reality wanting to take cognizance of the second."

Ms. S. is now listening very attentively to me. I seem to have touched on something that is preoccupying her profoundly. As the conversation proceeds, I notice that the subject of no one believing her keeps coming back, and we are apparently traveling around in circles. So I ask her: "Can it be that you sometimes experience exactly what the officials do, that you also doubt whether these things happened in jail back then, and that you yourself can't trust your own recollection any longer?"

Then she starts crying violently. I had put it into words. For, secretly, she doubts whether she really was tortured and raped in jail. Two years later, she would no longer believe it herself if it were not for the nightmares, the thoughts, and the images, the constant inner tension and the agitated sense of unrest. She was never like that before her time in jail. Sometimes she also thinks she only imagined it back then, and that now she has turned into someone who is "simply just crazy."

The story of Ms. S. offers an example of how a massive existential trauma is followed by a string of new, small traumatic experiences. In spite of all her efforts to forget, this is what keeps alive the memory of jail and everything that happened there. Like sexually abused children, she confronts a world that either discounts or does not believe her statements and declarations, with the result that she herself begins to regard her story as a fantasy and explain it as "crazy" or "sick." At the end of this process, she is the one who feels guilty and ashamed: as a result, her withdrawal from her fellow human beings and from the world increases. She starts drawing into herself, enclosing and absorbing her memories of the violence she experienced. This intensifies her feeling of isolation and of being excluded from the world. It is, as I could see in most cases, as if the victim takes her prison cell from the past and keeps carrying it along with her.

The psychiatric interventions I have portrayed above need to be understood as attempts to find the right key for opening this inner prison door.

Incapacitation or Militant Self-Assertion

Another patient, Ms. T. from South America, complains about constant headaches and shifting pains all over her body, as well as about panic attacks that crop up sporadically with palpitations, chest pains, shortness of breath, faintness, and anxiety about death. Since her arrival in Germany five years before, the nightmares—with their detailed sequence of scenes involving torture by giant-sized policemen—have ceased. Today, however, she still suffers from disturbances of memory and concentration, depression with frequent crying, and severe lack of motivation.

In her homeland Ms. T. was once a prominent trade union functionary.

Many years ago she lost her husband, who had also been incarcerated and had died as a result of torture. After the loss of her husband, she had to care for her two children on her own.

In November 1985, like all trade union leaders, she was fired by the military dictatorship. During one of the ensuing protest and letter-writing actions that she led, she was arrested. She was severely tortured. Following her release from prison after two months, she resumed her political and social activities. After being put back in jail, she was again tortured. And following a second release from jail she was put under open surveillance and constantly threatened, so that she felt compelled to flee to Germany with her two daughters.

Ms. T. and her daughters were given asylum in Germany five years ago. During these five years in exile, Ms. T. had been constantly ill. When she was not spending the day at home in bed, depressed and apathetic, her daily schedule was filled with medical appointments: from orthopedist to internist, from gynecologist to neurologist, and so on. There was nothing wrong with her, some doctors said before sending her on. Others administered medications and shots for a while, at least until the futility of these efforts led to a rupture in the doctor-patient relationship. There were serious problems with the children. On the one hand, they were driven at an early stage into adult roles by their mother's helplessness and frailty. On the other hand, they felt ashamed of their invalid mother before schoolmates and friends.

Thus, our first conversation for orientation purposes took place in the presence of her daughters, since the mother felt unable to carry out an appointment with the doctor on her own. The daughters looked after their mother, and as a result of this role reversal, their mutual relationship was bad. The daughters made no bones about their aggressiveness toward the mother; they criticized her and treated her as if she were a helpless child. The mother, for her part, spoke very broken German and used the daughters as her dictionary. She let herself be made into a victim by her daughters, be treated as if she were the minor and not they.

I did not have more than a total of eight individual sessions with Ms. T., but even in our second session, something she had been carrying around inside for what must have been five years or longer burst out of her: she dissolved into tears and related her story. The interpreter also lost her composure, so much so that she was no longer able to translate certain shocking details. But the important thing was ultimately not *what* Ms. T. told; it was *how* she told it. She was reliving a large portion of the humiliations and insults; these were present in the room, and they took hold of the interpreter and of me as well: being completely powerless and at the mercy of others; the physical and psychological insults; despair, but also rage. All of that was present, as if these things had taken place just now and not five years ago.

In the following three sessions, Ms. T. became increasingly vigorous and self-confident. Another side of her—different from the humiliated victim, the helpless child of her own daughters—now came to light: that of the militant politician and former trade union leader. As she now related her story, she appeared more cheerful, energetic, and dominant. She imagined how she might become mayor of her hometown, in case there should be an amnesty allowing her to return, since even today she remained very popular there and would certainly be elected.

At the start of the fifth session, she became overwhelmed by the glare of the sun shining through the window as she sat down. Without hesitation she simply moved to another spot. She said that the sun in her face reminded her of the attempt to blind her with an electric light during interrogation. Conversely, she was also having anxiety attacks when it got completely dark, and in small, narrow rooms. The previous sessions had done her good. She actively attempted, without any prompting from me, to try out or test how long her subjective perception of improvement might last in case she should deliberately subject herself to some of the triggering mechanisms that had previously elicited such unbearable anxiety in her. Her children, she continued, were also happily confirming how things were improving for their mother, how she looked more secure. Ms. T. now started coming to the Treatment Center on her own.

After eight sessions Ms. T. decided to end the treatment. For the first time after five years of illness and constant visits to the doctor, she had found a job. For the first time in years, she felt strong and self-confident. Finally, she was able to earn enough money for her daughters, and also to be there for them more than she used to be. It was certainly clear to her that she still had a lot of unsolved problems. But she also sensed (so she told me) that continuing our sessions threatened to impair her newfound confidence, so that for a while she wanted to do without them altogether, in order to be able to enjoy her new experience of life fully and completely.

During these eight individual sessions, the patient succeeded in getting reacquainted with those once strong and powerful parts of her ego that had become completely buried under the wounded ego's powerlessness. It looks as if a blockade has been broken, as if recovering access to Ms. T.'s own strong ego stake has put her in a position where she can continue on the path toward overcoming her trauma on her own. My part in all this was to listen, and to establish from the very outset that what Ms. T. suffered from was well known to us as one of torture's psychological effects. This distinguished me from some colleagues who had previously treated her by telling the patient—out of desperation and annoyance at her unaltered state of health, in spite of all their efforts—that there was nothing wrong with her. As in the case study described before this one, not recognizing torture and its effects means an additional, renewed traumatization of the person affected by trauma, in whose eyes society already seems more inclined to side with the perpetrators, who are also denying what happened.

Powerlessness and Omnipotence

I recall an older man from Turkey who had already lived in Berlin for a long time and was arrested without a warrant and severely tortured while on vacation in his homeland. Since, on his release, he was threatened with rearrest if he should ever tell anyone else about this, fear of further persecution by his tormentors kept him from daring to confide in anyone, even his next of kin. His relatives noticed his depressive state and his apathy, which led to psychiatric treatment—initially inpatient, but periodically (because of suicidal tendencies) also in confinement. Later on, he managed to recover a little, especially because he had a job in which he was valued as an extremely hardworking and energetic colleague. An accident on the job put a sudden end to this compensatory coping strategy. In the clinic where he had to be admitted and treated several times following this accident, the doctor was struck by the big discrepancy between the relatively minor x-ray findings and the severity of his clinical ailments, which repeatedly led her colleagues to take diagnostic steps, producing no satisfactory results. Finally the patient, after persistent questioning, confided in the admitting physician. Early on in the course of the patient's numerous physical exams, this doctor had noticed body scars for which the patient had so far offered no satisfactory explanation.

A positive course of treatment is fundamentally handicapped by the way in which the omnipotence of the perpetrators and the powerlessness of their victims lives on in the inner psychic reality of the latter. The treatment can completely collapse when, as in the case of Kurds from Turkey, persecution continues against fellow countrymen and close relatives remaining at home. Thus, in the two years I have spent at the Treatment Center so far, I have had to experience how, bit by bit, several extended families—men, women, and small children from the same village in southeast Anatolia—fled to Berlin. Most recently, two third-generation children, aged 4 and 2, arrived without their parents. And so I became a witness to the gradual depopulation and destruction of an entire village and of a community that had grown up over centuries.

The individual consequences of persecution, torture, uprootedness, and an insecure residential status in Germany include a breakdown in the community's patriarchal values. At an age where children still understand little or nothing about politics, they do notice that the fathers they experience as omnipotent cannot maintain home and hearth. Beyond that, they also notice that their fathers have become physical and psychological invalids under the impact of losing physical and mental integrity. The results are quarrels within the younger generation and family units that can no longer be settled by a binding word from the elders. The loss of the family head's authority then links up with a feeling of individual and political powerlessness, intensifying the helplessness and disorientation of everyone involved. During therapy sessions in this kind of situation, questions about God and the meaning of this suffering often surface, questions that seem to ask why God is testing them. What have we done? What aim does this help God to pursue? Of course, this also puts us therapists at wits' end. In moments like this, the only option seems to be making it apparent to the patient what I would only wish for myself in a similar situation: Maintain your bearings, and be as dignified as you can about accepting things you can't immediately change. Maybe this will succeed in restoring strength and authority to the elders vis-à-vis the younger generation.

An Excursion into Theory

What really happens in psychotherapy with people who suffer from the after-effects of torture? How does therapy take effect, and what is the nature of its deeper meaning? A good way to start answering these questions is by taking a closer look at the process of general psychological development. From the moment of our birth we experience the world primarily in relation to, and in contact with, people from our immediate surroundings. In general, these are mother, father, maybe siblings, grandparents, other relatives, friends, and close acquaintances. The sum total of all the events and situations in the relationship connection—along with the "how" of this connection—are what shape the breadth of inner experience, the self-image, and the personality inside the developing ego of the growing child and later of the adult. A happy child will have experienced love, esteem and affection, sympathy and emotional involvement, reliability, and parental interest (or interest from parental figures). The way we experienced our parents is how we now experience the world and ourselves. Whoever was allowed to experience love and esteem from parental figures is later able to love, respect, and esteem others, and to develop a relationship with the world in which he can develop talents and aptitudes undisturbed.

Images of parents and other close acquaintances as teachers and guides remain inside us for life. We have internalized them, and even later in life, when we are grownups, they can serve (consciously or unconsciously) as internal advisers when we are making important life choices. There are, of course, early experiences with parents that are frustrating and full of conflict, that leave behind ruptures and shadows on the smooth, glowing surface of the positive parental images, and that are bound up with feelings of rage and sadness, and with abandonment anxieties. Tempering or fusing the highly idealistic "good" with the "bad," frustrating, and rejecting side of internal parental images to create a single, more realistic picture is a distinct task for a special phase of development around the age of 3–5 years (Kernberg 1989; Blanck and Blanck 1989).

Inner images like this, reflecting early experiences with parents and close acquaintances, are labeled "object representations" (in shorthand: "internal objects") in professional jargon. They represent not just persons but also the spatial environment and landscape. The house in which we grew up, the village or city, the landscape, climate, and nature—all this finds representation, mirror image, and resonance within the inner psyche. Depending on the emotional climate, these things also possess the coloring of the pleasant or unpleasant, of "good" or "evil." Situations we experience, encounters, persons, and our associated sensations, feelings, and wishes form the larger part of our conscious ego. Others are bound up with the impulses and tendencies in us that are censored by the superego and that remain unconscious, since they are capable of awakening oversized feelings of shame, guilt, and anxiety. The sum total of all internal objects, consisting of all the good and bad life experiences, whether conscious or unconscious, is (so to speak) the software of the psyche. It determines our feelings, thoughts, values, and motives; in brief, our self-image. It differentiates us from Caspar Hauser, the boy raised by wolves and the human model for a pure, unprogrammed hardware system.

What is decisive for psychological health and stability are experiences with close parental figures from childhood, experiences that shaped internal images, the above-mentioned inner objects or object representations. If experiences with these people clash too strongly with each other or with individual needs and instinctual wishes, this can lead to mental symptoms.

And, with some oversimplification, one may say that psychotherapy means nothing more than the expansion of one's own ego-consciousness by way of correcting or expanding these internal parental images via an additional internal image, through a new, healing internal object, namely the psychotherapist.

In psychoanalysis, the path leading in this direction is called regression—or, better yet, regressive transference. This means (depending on the type of treatment) that the phenomenon of a relationship appears (slowly or rapidly) between patient and doctor where the patient is unconsciously taken back to the developmental stages of early childhood. There the patient develops feelings and attitudes vis-à-vis the doctor like those he had as a child vis-à-vis parents and other important parental figures.

Most psychotherapists encounter people who seek psychotherapeutic help for a variety of ailments, for example, anxiety attacks, depression, phobias, and obsessive-compulsive disorders. But when we look at people who have had to live through a life-threatening situation (whether an accident, natural disaster, kidnapping, robbery, or imprisonment and torture), the first thing we notice is that, in addition to the variety of psychosomatic ailments that are possible, all those affected complain about the more or less burdensome symptoms of posttraumatic stress disorder (PTSD). These include recurring mental stagings of the traumatic events in nightmares and daydreams as well as in thoughts and images linked to states of anxiety and accompanying physical symptoms such as a racing heart, intensive sweating, and trembling. The internal level of agitation can be raised to a permanent state of tension with a feeling of aggressiveness that can barely be controlled; conversely, it can also be reduced to the point of apathy and complete insensibility. Most often, one also finds a pattern of symptoms resembling classic phobia (pseudophobia) as well as a cognitive capacity diminished by disturbances in attention, apprehension, and memory. If these ailments are taken at their word, as expressions in a psychosomatic language, one might translate them this way: the threat from the past is not over, but is still with us.

In the case where the external factor occasioning the threat has disappeared, this can only mean that the traumatic experience has planted itself in the persons affected, that the trauma has an immediate presence for them as an internal image, which has been joined by other internal objects from earlier life developments. The trauma contains situations, people who took part, and especially the experience of suffering from powerlessness, of being at the mercy of others, of profound insults and humiliations. And it is possessed by a kind of psychic energy against which all previous inner objects become pale, void of meaning, and devalued by comparison.

And indeed, the persons affected complain that they become overwhelmed by these events—in dreams during the night, in thoughts and daydreams by day. Depending on the severity of the trauma, the countervailing force of the personality and life history from an earlier time tends to fade into the background. In addition, memories and images from the trauma are experienced as something alien to the ego. It is as if a foreign body is resting in the soul. The rupture within the person's continuum of existence brought about by misfortune, catastrophe, or the trauma of torture and incarceration generates a new internal image or object. This new image or object cannot be brought into harmony with the previous conception of the ego because it summons up feelings of shame, guilt, and anxiety that are too strong. The ego can apparently only live with this if it views this object as something not belonging to the ego, as a foreign body, which the ego can cut off and encapsulate (Dreyfuss 1941; Jacobson 1959).

Picking up on the above reflections about how internal objects are formed during childhood development and changed or corrected by psychotherapy, we have to ask ourselves what psychotherapy and mental reactions to a traumatic experience have in common when both—the former by healing, the latter by doing damage—are capable of bringing about changes in the internal object world of a person's mental life.

The answer is: regression. Apparently it crops up (in cases of natural disaster or misfortunes not man-made, just as with violent attacks by fellow human beings) as a consequence of experiencing complete powerlessness, helplessness, or being at the mercy of others, when all opportunities have failed for mastering the situation as an adult. Whoever experiences being completely at the mercy of others, powerlessly and helplessly so, tends to revert to his childhood, that is, to a time when he could experience support and care from parents and other close friends in situations of helplessness. This is a kind of self-protection that prevents the existential anxieties surfacing in moments like this from intensifying to the point of the unbearable (Ehlert and Lorke 1988).

It has frequently been observed that victims of natural disasters do not suffer as much from psychological consequences as do victims of violence inflicted by fellow humans. One thing that helps explain this is the way regression in a relationship of one human being to another can develop with relative ease. Other factors playing a role are the extreme disparity of power and powerlessness between perpetrator and victim and the victim's condition of being at the mercy of others without psychosomatic bounds. One might say that regression emerges from the perpetrator-victim relationship just as it does with a patient on the psychoanalyst's couch. While psychotherapy works toward healing the psyche, however, torture aims at the victim's destruction. In the latter case, as a result of superior power and isolation, regression takes place much faster.

For most of our patients, the psychological wounds are more serious than the physical injuries. Seldom, if at all, do they heal spontaneously. Instead, they act like a foreign body in the soul, resting in the psyche while largely cut off from consciousness, yet also capable (under everyday conditions, in dreams by day or night) of slipping into consciousness, where this foreign body is un-welcome, and where it creates unbearable anxiety and feelings of shame. A per-son traumatized in this fashion has to expend a major portion of his mental energy, including his zest for life and his creative powers, keeping this internal foreign body away from his conscious self-image.

On the basis of this brief summary, what can we say about the aim of psycho-therapy for extremely traumatized persons? With our patients we experience how the power-powerlessness disparity experienced between perpetrator and victim turns up again in the weakness of the good, stable internal objects of early childhood experience compared with the new internal images originating in trauma. Therefore, independent of individual therapeutic arrangements al-ready existing, the first step in the therapeutic approach should be to strengthen the good (meaning emotionally supportive) parts of internal objects. Right from the start, this means an attempt to eliminate mistrust and offer the patient an intimate relationship, like one experienced in an earlier time; then, in a second step, it means drawing on these positive resources from the good parts of internal objects by using techniques like storytelling, pictorial representation while the body is relaxed, painting, body movement, and role-playing. The first goal is to strengthen the self, the patient's self-confidence. From there the path leads in exactly the same direction that the patient's psyche is constantly trying to follow in its efforts at repeated (though unsuccessful) attempts at self-healing by day and by night, namely toward reawakening traumatic experiences, only this time under the accompaniment, direction, and protection of the therapeu-tic guide. This gives the patient an opportunity to live up to and fully live out all previously suppressed feelings and emotions of anxiety, powerlessness, despair, and rage, or (as they put it in gestalt therapy) to complete the big, open, overwhelming gestalt of the trauma, so that those who have survived torture physically can also become (and remain) psychological survivors and not victims.

That sounds easy. In practice, however, it requires a great deal of patience and perseverance for the patient and the therapist. It means constant move-ments toward, around, but also backward again. Sometimes it also means inter-rupting and resuming therapeutic sessions when the patient, but also the thera-pist, feels capable of moving forward a bit.

The Man from Doboj

A 32-year-old married man from Doboj in Bosnia, the father of two children, has been living as a refugee in Berlin since 1992. He stutters and is under a great deal of mental pressure and tension. In his mind's eye, he is besieged by friends, relatives, and neighbors who were killed when his village was attacked by Serbs. He survived, but he had to witness with his own eyes how his father, other family members, friends, and neighbors were slain. All these people now populate his inner world with pale faces and threateningly malicious expressions. His wife and children frequently experience him as absent-minded. When he is spoken to while in this state of mind, he lashes out, forgetful of himself and his surroundings. His children experience him as someone who is partly unavailable, partly unpredictable and violent. Just like the Serbs. "Papa, please don't hit me like the Serbs," pleads the oldest son under his father's blows.

Month-long treatment with psychopharmacological drugs of all kinds and in every conceivable variation brings no change. So Mr. I. comes to us. After the first interview, he is greatly relieved, because he had previously feared that I was a psychiatrist who would treat him with electric and cold-water shocks.

Initially Mr. I. displayed an unreasonably high and overvalued estimation of me. But shortly after that, as soon as he saw his hopes betrayed for a quick cure by my "magical" powers, he began to put me under heavy pressure. He impatiently said that since I already knew what it was like for him, what was left for him to tell me? What good was this eternal talking? And if I didn't prescribe something for him or undertake some other medical treatment, he'd leave again. In his imagination, he viewed me as all-powerful. All my objections, in which I tried explaining to him how I could realistically help him, he just cast to the winds.

Even the time frame for therapy became the subject of repeated and energetic arguments. I tried to explain to him how experience indicated we would need a lot of time to cope with the things that had happened to him. Psychological changes are time-consuming, like the growth of a plant. As a doctor engaged in psychotherapy, I saw it as my job to see that there was enough soil, water, and warmth for the plant to grow. Images, allegories, and metaphors were things that Mr. I. had always understood quite well. Images were themselves making him suffer. Yet through images, he could also make himself understood and understand himself. But now Mr. I. shook his head, wanting to see me as a surgeon removing a foreign object or an abscess from his head in a quick operation. In his eyes I now appeared as a great magician, but one who wanted for inexplicable reasons to withhold his magic arts.

Actually, this disagreement preprogrammed the break in our therapeutic relationship within the first few hours. But suddenly something different, something completely unforeseen, intruded. The next hour he arrived all agitated and frightened. He said it would be impossible for him to return to Bosnia with his family, even if the war should end there, for the Bosnian government would call to account as deserters all those Bosnians currently in exile. He and his family would then be murdered by his fellow countrymen. And now a social worker in his Berlin dormitory had informed him that the residential permit for himself and his family would expire shortly, and he would soon have to go back to Bosnia.

It was a very turbulent session, during which he and I jointly scrutinized his thoughts and fears for signs of reality content. I said that, of course, with everything going on over there right now, we couldn't just dismiss offhand what refugees returning later might have to endure at the hands of their fellow countrymen who had stayed during the war. But, on top of this alarming idea, additional suspicions had crammed themselves into his head, culminating in the notion that his helpers in the refugee home were instigating his family's return to Bosnia. I tried to counter this with rational arguments. I was not very successful, however, and I saw how much he was clinging to his convictions. But what I also saw, and registered with some relief, was this: because of how he now perceived the others as extremely "evil" and as persecutors, I was released from my previous transference as a magician who was withholding his magic out of "evil" intentions. Instead, I had again become his "good" savior, who could protect him from the "evil" intentions of the others. It was clear how anxious and threatening fantasies were becoming so vivid for him and how they were able to take the place of reality. This kind of thing is only bearable when an extremely "evil" world can be confronted by an extremely "good" one. In his eyes, I had once again arrived at the latter place. This provided another opportunity to keep the therapy going.

Subsequently, for a while, this therapy began to move along quite well. With

the aid of relaxation and breathing exercises done in a reclining position—
which awakened and animated in him bodily sensations, images, thoughts,
memories, and feelings, all of which had nothing to do with the irreconcilable
tension between the extremes of good/evil, perpetrator/victim, and power/
powerlessness, but which instead lay within the benevolent spectrum of those
richly contrasting shadings in between—Mr. I. gradually succeeded in not
seeing me as a good or evil superman, but instead accepting me in his thoughts
and imagination as a friend and traveling companion. Once, on one of these
imaginary journeys, he took me to his hometown, where on a Sunday after-
noon in peaceful times his entire circle of relatives and friends, children as well
as adults, used to sit together in harmony and enjoy themselves swimming,
grilling, and playing. I let myself be treated to highly detailed portraits of these
beautiful scenes. It was an extremely valuable and precious reminder of what
had been an intact world of traditional community life and customs with his
friends, but also a world with moral strictures whose value and meaningfulness
is now painfully revealed in the so thoroughly decayed and destructive present
following the atrocious afflictions of the civil war.

Alarming images of the dead later reappeared to dominate him and take up
hours of our time, however. Then Mr. I. would feel like someone hunted and
chased by the ancient Greek gods of vengeance. In moments like these—when
I felt vulnerable to seeing all the little building blocks of progress becoming
totally destroyed, of getting caught up in the wheels of his clichés, and of coming under renewed pressure from him to prescribe a medication or take other
medical measures—I, too, was subject to feelings of powerlessness and helplessness and believed I had completely failed.

"I understand you very well, Mr. I.," I replied one time when he was putting
me under pressure again. "As a result of this pressure I'm feeling at the moment,
and of my feelings that sometimes I'm just as helpless and powerless as you, I
can all too easily put myself in your place. It's not just a matter of *what* is said,
but of *how* it's said. And from that place, just like you, I experience feelings of
menace and the pressure of powerlessness from inside. Only, look: I'm still
sitting firmly on my chair here, because from my experience with you I also
know that there have been very lovely and affirmative episodes in our joint
communication, and that there will be more of these."

Interventions like this, which also—and regardless of everything that was yet to come—were particularly meant to show that I would be reliable and continue the therapeutic sessions, sometimes helped keep things going. But there were also arguments between the two of us, in which he stubbornly demanded guarantees from me about his recovery and the therapy's duration. And in spite of our momentary antagonism—I did not even dream of promising him something that I could not know—at times like this there developed between us a combative atmosphere that was positively pleasurable, as if we were both merchants haggling at an Oriental bazaar. And he laughed out loud when I told him this, and it was as if the confrontation had been blown away without leaving a trace. And my nod toward his profession as a cloth merchant in the Balkans contained a hidden allusion for him: not everything about him was destroyed by the Serbs.

And, over and over again, we headed downward toward those images of the dead that besieged the inner world of the patient's imagination. I let myself be treated to detailed and repeated stories about some of these dead people, how they died, what happened before they died. What struck me even then: the figure of the father, who also tarried in this world of the dead, was seldom mentioned and remained a pale shape, in spite of my questioning and my tentative attempts to direct the patient's attention toward him.

In this phase of the therapy my questions were often moving in the same direction: The dead, what did they look like? Were they possibly trying to say something to Mr. I., or was he asking one of them a question, or would he have liked to report something to one of them? Or else: The dead, why are they walking the streets? Don't they normally rest in their graves? What could it be that is stirring them up? In your homeland, what is actually the custom for burying the dead?

Several weeks get taken up with this theme. What seems to be repetitions are actually approximations recurrently getting closer to something. Both of us, Mr. I. and myself, learn how to deal with the images and thereby to withstand the anxiety and the pressure; once a week, at the same hour, on the same weekday, in the same room with the same translator.

Then comes an abrupt change. Suddenly the talk is of other images that violently break into his thoughts and into the world of his imagination. With every woman that he accidentally encounters on the street, there surfaces a wish to have sexual intercourse with her. Day and night the likeness of an accidental

passerby like this drifts past his eyes, a passerby who can satisfy the sexual desires of his imagination. I take notice of this, plainly and self-evidently: of
course it sometimes happens that men have fantasies like these. This is my way
of trying to relieve him of any pressure coming from accompanying feelings of
shame and guilt, although I don't succeed. Instead, that earlier pressure for
action now starts to weigh heavily on me, in that Mr. I. (just as at our first
encounter) is now pushing and begging me to get rid of these visions—from
the outside, like a surgeon removing a foreign body. I am helpless. It is as if we
were again just where we were at the start of therapy. I make no secret of my
helplessness. Then he resumes criticizing me and putting me down. How much
time would I still need to cure him? Don't I know anything? Not even the
fact that Serbia is forcing young Bosnians to have sexual intercourse with their
mothers? In his vigorous attacks on me, he suddenly seems stuck somewhere.
For a brief moment he's not there. I press on this point. Where had he gone
just now? He cannot say. He stutters—as he occasionally did earlier, only now
it is preventing him from speaking at all. When did this stuttering first appear?
I ask him. And I learn: in the cellar of his father's house, when the Serbs murdered his father. How surprised I was! Of course, that's what it was that everything revolved around. And my surprise became even greater when I established
that all the facts of this ghastly event, including the coincidence of its timing
with his stuttering, had already been apparent to me at the time that I took the
patient's history, but that I had "forgotten" these details again in the course of
nine months. At the very beginning, as it turned out, I had correctly appraised
this core experience and its significance for Mr. I. But until now I had joined
Mr. I. in screening it out and avoiding it. It was not proper "forgetting" on my
part, because I knew the facts. It was the event's profound significance for
Mr. I. that I had "forgotten."

A session later he portrayed one more time the indescribable chaos on the
streets at the time of the raid—how all the residents ran around confusedly in
panic for their lives, this way, that way; gunshots and artillery fire; how the
wind was howling loudly; detonations and burning houses. How friends and
acquaintances ran down the streets, seeking safety for themselves and others,
or in order to help others, or even to arm and defend themselves. They were
all found again, piled up in a mountain of corpses in the middle of the market
square. Mr. I. becomes fiercely agitated. Now it is his thoughts that are starting

to run and taking leaps, tearing off, abruptly changing direction like gusts of wind. Names with which he designates the perpetrators start to drop; Mr. I. yells at the translator that he must be this Mr. B. who killed his father; then he turns to me in the same way, seeming to mistake me also for this B.

"Stop!" I tell him as I try to bring him back. "We're in the therapy room here, not on the street in Doboj back then at the time of the raid." I play back for him what I just observed. Just as he and the residents of his village were running around in panic and confusion back then, now, when he talks about it, his thoughts are similarly in flight, tumbling head over heels. And now I join him in undertaking a little breathing and movement exercise while standing, so as to bring his thoughts back onto solid ground; fortunately, this works.

In the next hour I cautiously broached the subject of the event in the cellar of his father's house, and I suggested that we could very carefully approach this together, or, if this was not yet possible for him, then at least our joint pathway in this direction had been marked out, namely by returning to the situation where his father was murdered before his eyes. At this point Mr. I. let out a scream that set my teeth on edge, profoundly frightening and upsetting me. It was the first time that I had experienced him so deeply and emotionally. At the end of this session he was in a downright contemplative and gentle mood, asking me if another member of his family might come here to the Treatment Center and maybe even come to me for treatment. Pleasantly surprised, I took his request as a sign of regained trust.

Still, three sessions later, Mr. I. wants to leave. He heaps accusations on me of the same kind as at the beginning of therapy. He still suffers from the same ailments as a year ago when he arrived. My psychotherapy wasn't helping; instead, it was just making his condition worse. And I was to blame if he took to beating his children more often. No, he didn't need any psychotherapy, but rather purely medical diagnosis and help. With pills and shots. Or, as he had heard, with a special x-ray that could picture his brain on a screen, pinpoint the fire in there that was creating these images, so that it could then be shot away like machine-gun fire with an injection.

My attempts to clarify in retrospect what had happened and where we now stood bears no fruit. Mr. I. is very agitated, infuriated at me, and angry. He only regains peace of mind when I explain that I am in accord with his departure. But inwardly he also seems to be relieved and to breathe more easily when

I tell him that, in case he wants to continue the therapy, he knows where to find me.

Maybe, as we often experience with other patients, Mr. I. simply had the need to take a break on his own accord, because the therapy was getting too dense and too close, and he needed time to move ahead. Or he feared a mental breakdown and couldn't count on my personality to possess the strength needed for picking him up and piecing him together. Maybe, under the impact of his ever-lurking and pestering expectation that I should finally cure him, I was too rigid and tempted to proceed too quickly. Maybe he will come by again. But maybe what he experienced was simply too hard and overpowering for him to work it through. Will he come again, will he stay away? I don't know. Still, it was sixty hours of therapy with him.

This example should make clear the kind of grave psychological aftereffects with which a psychological trauma can be associated, especially in a civil war of this magnitude, where all the social rules of morality, tradition, and religion are suspended and there is nothing left over in the way of a collective superego, nothing left of dictates or prohibitions, no guiding principles regulating social life. All that is gone, leaving behind individuals who are completely distraught and disoriented. On this terrain a grave psychological trauma occurs, which also demolishes the values and dictates of the individual superego of each person within his family. The impossible really takes place. The father is murdered. What was self-protectively banished and enclosed behind the individual horizon of consciousness in mythological symbols suddenly becomes real. Real, existential anxiety about one's own destruction flows together with real anxiety about one's own instinctual wishes from childhood, consisting of the turn toward the mother and the wish to see the father disappear. The result is a feeling of guilt about the father's death which is connected to a strong anxiety defense in the form of regression into early, pre-Oedipal stages of development.

Marco Pascha: What Is This Work Doing to Us?

In Turkey anecdotes make the rounds about Marco Pascha, a "lunatics' doctor" and manager of a clinic for "lunatics." Just like his profession, the personality of this prominent historical figure from turn-of-the-century Istanbul apparently stirred the souls of his contemporaries so much that, even today, stories of

Marco Pascha live on in the minds of subsequent generations and have become immortalized in literature. So it is, too, with Marco Pascha's final story, about his unfortunate demise on the occasion of a company outing, a boat tour taken by the doctor with his patients. Marco Pascha fell into the water, it is told, and the patients plunged in after him to help him. They all drowned, like the doctor. For they, like Marco Pascha, did not know how to swim.

In this somewhat malicious, mocking story, a profound truth is hidden. In contrast to Marco Pascha's patients, who jumped in after their doctor to their deaths out of blind trust, a person is usually more critical before he enters into psychotherapeutic treatment. His muted, often unconscious questioning at the outset of a therapeutic process is typically, How deep is the reach of the personality, life experience, and knowledge of the other person, and how far is he ready to go in accompanying me without becoming uncertain himself and getting trapped in the whirlpool? Can he swim? Will he also be able to keep me afloat over deeper waters, when there are stronger waves, eddies, and dangerous currents—and will he also want to make this effort?

Patients unconsciously test their therapists about the extent to which they can rely on them. And the patient's readiness to get involved is linked with the degree to which their doctor and therapist is ready (and was willing earlier) to peer down into the personal abyss of his own unconscious. This is a truism and ground rule of psychotherapy in general, but it is especially valid for people who have experienced an extreme existential trauma. To relive the unbearable and unspeakable is hard on the person affected by the trauma; and, indeed, it is also hard on those of us who want to offer therapeutic help. After two years of psychoanalytic and medical work at the Treatment Center for Torture Victims, I believe that the depth of contact with patients increases with their readiness to form a long-lasting, positive transference toward me. On my side of it, I also believe that I am only at the starting point with my patients, measured against the incomprehensibility of the events they carry with them.

The therapist has many unconscious opportunities to maneuver his way out of contact with his patient whenever it gets to be too much for him. And, of necessity, this is quite often the case. Concretely, what having the "right" contact with a patient means is maintaining a proper distance from him. Too much closeness, just like too much distance, can mean that I, as a therapist, seek to avoid the patient or the touchy chapters in his life story. And the feelings, thoughts, and fantasies that transpire in me during contact with the patient, my so-called countertransference, can serve as an important measuring instrument telling me—assuming that I'm taking notice of them—where I find myself with the patient at any moment.

One of my first patients at the Treatment Center for Torture Victims was a 15-year-old boy from Bangladesh. What he told me right at the start of the very first session was a uniquely gruesome story. Without any sign of emotional involvement whatsoever, like a child telling his parents about a recent school outing, he reported in minute detail the circumstances of the murder of his father, then an influential politician and party leader, by a group of thirty men from a rival party. And about how, weeks later in a second attack, his mother was raped before his eyes by his father's murderers, and how he was then taken hostage so as to induce the mother to revoke the complaint she had lodged with the police. During this kidnapping he broke his left forearm when he was shoved onto the floor. As a result of not getting medical attention, major complications developed; first a severe local inflammation, then later a generalized bacterial infection, leading to a local hospital stay lasting several months after his release. His left hand and forearm, which missed being amputated by a hairsbreadth, still had severe contractions and were disfigured. His mother spent what property was not swallowed up by expropriation or hospital bills to protect her son from further attacks by sending him to Germany.

At the time he came to see me, he was living in dilapidated quarters for young people in a section of Berlin where foreigners are frequently subjected to attacks by young Germans. My first impulse was to lend him moral support by giving him a better social environment. So I located a place for him in a church facility where he could have his own room and ties to a family. German language lessons, more schooling, maybe the chance to graduate from secondary school and go to a university—all that was set up for him. In addition, an operation was arranged to address the problems with his hand and arm.

And now what did he do? He refused. Knowing full well the value of my efforts on his behalf and the comfort of the quarters I had found for him, he nonetheless did not want to stay there. Instead, he preferred to go back to his refugee home, where he could get his welfare payment once a month and then earn additional money selling flowers and other things, which the church facility prevented him from doing. He wanted to earn quick money and save to support himself and his mother. In addition, he had debts amounting to 800 marks, which he had decided to incur with fellow countrymen in order to pay his outstanding long-distance phone bill for calls to his mother in Dhakar. In order for me to get his approval and get him off the street and away from the nightlife, I was almost tempted to provide him with money from a fund in our treatment facility.

Now it is entirely obvious how involved I had become with this patient. What I regarded as the right thing was not what he wanted. He was thinking of a stay in Germany lasting at most two years, during which he wanted to quickly earn money, so that he could soon return home to his mother with a small fortune by his country's standards. In spite of all the likely dangers, he was homesick, pure and simple. And I? I overlooked this and became identified instead with his mother, who had given him this assignment when he left Dhakar: go to Europe, go to school, study at a university, and when you have made an academic career and become a rich and influential man like your father, then come home and seek revenge for his death.

And just as he, in order to keep on living, needed to banish from his consciousness those feelings linked with his traumatic experiences (instead roaming around the city restlessly by day and night), so, too, was I preoccupied (by energetically organizing a social network and planning a future for him) with avoiding and holding back my emerging feelings of helplessness and powerlessness, of sadness and rage. I do not mean to imply that social support is a mistake in principle; it is important and necessary so long as it does not cross the line where, instead of fulfilling basic needs, it treats the patient like a child and serves to disregard emotional areas in therapy.

It is worth noting how this example demonstrates a link between keeping too great and too narrow a distance. The distance I kept vis-à-vis my patient was too great, inasmuch as I identified more with his mother than with him and his situation, but the distance also became too narrow when my unrelenting activity on behalf of his welfare made me do the same thing that he was doing while overplaying and avoiding my own feelings.

Additional indicators pointing toward too great a distance between doctor and patient in therapeutic contact could be boredom and listlessness on my part; tardiness; forgetting or not keeping appointments. Or I am inattentive during a treatment session; my imagination wanders somewhere else, and I find myself looking out the window. Or I feel anger, maybe even disdain for the patient, or a feeling of mistrust or even animosity. Or I avoid certain topics or am content to give quick answers. It is clear that these kinds of countertransference on the part of a therapist do not facilitate progress in a psychotherapeutic relationship.

When therapy stagnates in cases like this, or when it is threatened with a cutoff, the therapist himself is initially threatened in the case where there is too narrow a distance between the therapist and an extremely traumatized patient. In cases like this the doctor himself (just like his patient) can suffer from psychological and even psychosomatic symptoms. He can lose his inner equilibrium through insomnia, nightmares, inner turmoil, tension, and a heightened internal level of agitation, not to mention psychosomatic ailments, so that, along with his patient, he is in danger of sinking into anxiety, ideas or delusions of reference, helplessness, and feelings of powerlessness.

Feelings like these, these kinds of inner attitudes and opinions, are known to everyone who has come into contact with extremely traumatized people. It is entirely self-evident that feelings like this should surface, and it is a sign that a relationship actually exists. But it is important for me to become conscious of this, either through my own efforts at clarifying what happened in sessions during the course of treatment or else by equivalent assistance from case supervision. Using case supervision—that is, describing cases either to colleagues (intercollegial supervision) or to a supervisor (classical supervision)—I can get feedback from others about whether I am too distant from the patient or too close to him. I can also get advice about how to correct my course in order to escape the likelihood that the therapy will stagnate or that I will become too deeply enmeshed in those personal risks to the therapist described above. It is for this reason that I emphasized, above, what an important measuring instrument or compass countertransference can be, so long as it is not ignored and the psychiatrist knows how to use it meaningfully.

Looking at the Bosnian case study mentioned above, anyone can picture the maelstrom of countertransference emotions in which I tossed to and fro. First there was the temptation to represent me as the great magician, savior, and omnipotent power—a temptation to which, in the eyes of a critical observer, I may have succumbed, inasmuch as I actually took on this treatment believing I could do something. This was followed by the sudden devaluation of my person and my work, together with the feelings of inadequacy and power-lessness that were showing up in me. This, in turn, was succeeded by phases in which a more stable, trusting, and peaceful relationship was established, so that the sessions started to resemble little sailboats escaping from squalls, reaching still waters, and finally gaining traveling speed by slowly filling out their sails. And then, right after that, there was another change in the weather, to stormy seas, in which the patient indirectly made it clear to me how, in his opinion, my therapeutic interventions were putting him in danger—for example, by the way he showed me the black-and-blue marks all over his body and explained how he was hit by a bicycle because, while out on the street, he was thinking absent-mindedly about our last sessions, became agitated, and stopped paying attention. Or again, when he made a point of describing his periodic condi-tions of complete absent-mindedness, in which he believed that he could throw himself off a train, or when he told me about his impulsive attacks, in which he would threaten family members.

Here it became evident how, in his transference to me, he viewed me as the perpetrator, for in his eyes I was to blame for the bad things that happened to him and for the bad things he did. In crises like these I had to see to it that I did not get caught up in his acting out, that my anger or want of empathy for his psychological situation did not lead me to try extricating myself from him, or, conversely, let overnurturing actions and interventions seduce or absorb me into his circle of helpers—or maybe both (extrication and intervention)—by committing him to a psychiatric hospital. Rather, the one thing that seemed decisive to me throughout all these crises was that I simply must remain seated, that I must not run away, that I repeatedly had to guarantee continuity in the treatment, and that I must not let myself get too seriously shaken out of the equilibrium of my own feeling of self-worth and inner composure. For that was exactly what had happened to him. His deeply traumatic experience during the Serbs' attack had ripped this once healthy man's self and feeling of self-worth (both psychologically and physically) from its moorings. This self can only regain its anchor using a helper whose connection to the ground is (to some extent) firm and secure.

For all of us who are active in this helping field, the biggest danger (in my estimation) is more likely to be keeping too narrow a distance rather than in maintaining too great a distance: in overidentifying with the victims. And, as with our patients, our feeling of self-worth can also be damaged. We can just as easily succumb to anxieties, and in extreme cases even to paranoid ideas or ideas of reference. Or, if we can no longer stand how the patient, even in transference, depicts us as being on the "evil" side of the perpetrators, we may be tempted to join him in militant action against an "evil" outside world, in fighting officials for a resident permit or for social welfare support, for example, all of which takes energy. One typical result: an accelerated burnout syndrome on the part of the helper, who cannot maintain the proper boundaries and distance from the client's distress and from his psychic and social pressures.

As the case study of the man from Doboj illustrates, even the therapist in his relationship to the patient can be at the mercy of extremely contrasting feelings. Depending on how firmly or how loosely his own feeling of self-worth resides in him, the therapist either is or is not attuned to the situation. In the midst of everything that is going on, it is naturally desirable for the physician and therapist to be in possession of sufficient inner stability so that he can maintain his inner, realistic, experience-based centeredness as a model for the patient's orientation and growth. Conversely, the more unstable the treatment provider's feeling of self-worth, the more he rides along in the same mental roller coaster as the patient, alternating, for example, between unrealistic and overvalued notions of his own therapeutic opportunities and the depressing sense of powerlessness coming from a suspicion that he cannot do anything for the patient.

As long as the mental roller coaster is not too rocky, a precondition for empathetic, therapeutic contact is that the treatment provider go along for the ride. But the therapist should be conscious of it as part of his countertransference. Where this doesn't happen, he runs the risk of acting out these feelings vis-à-vis his patients or the colleagues on his team (Lansen 1993).

A therapist who is forced to feel that he is a failure with his patient at a given moment consequently experiences what the language of physics calls a "negative charge." What does he do with it? Is he conscious of it, or not? Of course, he can give it back to his patient by angrily rejecting him. But then he simultaneously deprives the patient of the chance to transfer some of the patient's own overwhelming feelings of powerlessness to the therapist. Yet if the therapist keeps this negative charge to himself, locking it up inside, there is a long-term danger that he himself will become depressed and even suicidal. Or let us assume that he, too, cannot make this negative charge conscious, since it might then do too much damage to his unstable self-esteem and therapeutic self-image. In this case the only option remaining to him is to rid himself of the negative charge by peacefully and quietly deprecating a colleague's work, thus becoming the presumptive carrier of a positive charge again. And what of the colleague? He, in turn, can pass this on to another colleague. In this way quiet, invisible currents of negative psychological charges build up among the colleagues on the team. These can lead to sideswipes in daily relations. These digs at each other can take the form of actions, or of pointed, razor-sharp utterances and casual remarks that (compared to what goes on in other medical, psychotherapeutic, and psychosocial institutions, where they don't have to deal with the victims of violence and abuse) contain a conspicuously high frequency of mutual put-downs, expressions of contempt, and sometimes even incriminations.

In extreme cases, when the quiet stream of those carrying psychological charges inside a team of colleagues is aimed in one particular direction, it can even reach the point of polarization, rather like the way charges build up in a condenser until a spark flashover is galvanized, and the team collapses.

As a result of collective countertransference, an entire institution is capable of forming a common conviction that it is the only establishment dealing "correctly" with extremely traumatized people. In cases like this, interestingly, a dogmatically rigid attitude toward therapy develops concerning contact with people whose fate it was to have encountered dogmas and the representatives of dogmas, then to have clashed with them, and who now are suffering from the results of such an encounter.

What happens in a case like this? Any individual or institution claiming this kind of monopoly on representing the victims is displaying, at least in this dogmatically rigid attitude, the same characteristic as the perpetrators, the patient's persecutors. The therapeutic relationship with people injured by torture draws out aspects of the therapist that resemble those of the perpetrators. If they remain unconscious for him, he runs the danger of acting in a way that moves in this very direction (Lansen 1993; Bustos 1990; Wilson and Lindy 1994).

Conclusion

The above account was not limited to treatments that were successful; it also dealt with episodes that did not run so smoothly, where crags and traps emerged for the therapist. But it is from these perils that we can learn the most. My intention was to make clear how much energy and care the relationship with a patient demands when it comes to dealing with patients, colleagues, and even oneself. For me, over and over again, the psychotherapeutic treatment of severely traumatized people is like experiencing a little miracle. It is the miracle of how people, in spite of the destructiveness and inhumanity they experience, can always find their way back to their roots and to the sources of their inner growth; of how, over the course of several months, gestures of body and speech become more secure and more decisive; how facial expressions become softer and more open; how pain and the protection from pain through muscle tension gradually abates; how mistrust and hopelessness give way to new hope, and healthy parts of the personality from the time preceding the affliction reemerge. But it is important that we give the patients and ourselves enough time, patience, and a great deal of attention, *especially for the small changes.* It is extraordinarily important to register the patients' changes along a fine, delicate scale, where the order of magnitude is in millimeters. Patients must be encouraged to keep going, to get stronger. It is critical that they not be seduced by their excessive expectations or by their own impatience to make progress all too quickly, and that they not be trying to judge that progress with a yardstick.

CHAPTER TWO

Psychic Trauma through Torture— Healing through Psychotherapy?

Norbert Gurris

For the victims, torture is unpredictable in a way that is unlike anything they have ever known before, and at the same time it is unavoidable and usually uncontrollable. For these reasons, torture is also something that cannot be mastered. The almost always unanticipated breakdown of the self, of the self's values, leads to the experience of one's own total failure, to self-blame, and therefore to overwhelming feelings of shame. The betrayal (often unavoidable under torture) of friends, relatives, and comrades with shared convictions could not have been foreseen.

Often, the conscious mind covers this up later on, with the result that feelings of shame and guilt become more intense but also more diffuse, expressing themselves in agonizing psychosomatic symptoms. In many cases a traumatic tie to the torturers takes place, in that these people become subliminally protected and spared after the fact; sometimes it even gets to the point where victims identify with their tormentors. Many victims do not experience simple, goal-directed rage and aggressive feelings toward their torturers; instead, they tend to lash out against themselves. This can also express itself in destruction directed against a guiltless environment.

One patient says: "At first I thought they were going to beat me to death. I was prepared for that, and if only they had just done it after all. But the worst part was the pauses; I never knew exactly whether and when they would torment me again. Instead of this, the torturers slowly drew me in with their remarks about my sex, with bad jokes. Even more terrible than the pain was being alone after the torture; that drove me crazy. I felt like an animal, a dog that is kicked yet becomes ever more dependent on the goodwill of its sadistic master."

What Happens under Torture?

Linguistically and emotionally, the question can only be grasped in an approximate way. Even for the torture victim, in retrospect, the *reality* of torture usually evades comprehension and reflection in thought, understanding, and evaluation, since the person's core, the personality, has been fundamentally shaken and injured. Through torture, the unity of body and soul (psychosomatic unity) within the person and his organism is significantly and profoundly disturbed.

What comes under attack are the functions of the autonomic nervous system, that is, that system in the organism that ingeniously organizes teamwork among all the different biological functions. Those functional cycles that human beings usually experience as automatic—like cooperation among organs, nerve impulses, release of hormones, and information transmission, all in order to guarantee a flowing equilibrium in everyday life—are not just fundamental preconditions for living. Rather, they safeguard a kind of original psychobiological protection, complete with fuses and alarm systems against dangers and threats, and they activate reflexes of adjustment, struggle, defense, and flight. Usually it is only in situations of crisis and shock that people ask, Why is my heart really beating so reliably every day, every minute, each second? Why is my nutritional intake transformed into energy or digested? Why do all my organs and my nervous system perform this work for me each day, uninterruptedly and tirelessly, without even receiving any thanks from me? In the Western world, followers of Milton Erickson's hypnotherapy stressed the importance of this psychobiological "unconscious" in psychotherapy. Erickson's followers took those "wise and protective" powers and resources, which fundamentally have "good intentions," and drew them into psychotherapy as a source of healing. This psychobiological wisdom and this competence were acquired over many centuries in the history of human development. Even if these processes tend to seem enigmatic in everyday life, in that all they do is "function," they nonetheless become seriously and visibly activated when a human being faces existential threats. Thus, during torture, the cerebrum (much younger in terms of evolutionary development) may already have taken part-time leave from its work and its skills. Pain, anxiety about death, and the loss of self-values will then no longer allow coordinated perception, thinking, evaluating, and methodical action.

Yet the organism that remains alive has emergency responses at its disposal. For a while, complex courses of action can be organized automatically, and it is also possible to create responses like protection, flight, or even paralysis, responses that the cerebrum, with its inherited values and moral system, would no longer understand or approve. It no longer fits into our familiar maps of thought and evaluation for a grown human being to become completely helpless, to cry or beg for mercy, to void the bowels and pass urine in the panic of uncontrolled anxiety, to wish simply to be killed at last instead of having to vegetate, and to have even this last bit of autonomy refused. Under these circumstances, naked biological survival can lead the tortured person to betray anyone and everything. So after torture the victim finds that he is still somehow alive physically but has been psychologically destroyed.

For the treatment of torture victims, this aspect of trauma is of fundamental importance: that over the long haul the "wise unconscious," this life-supporting force, has been persistently and repeatedly attacked and wounded just at the time that conscious control had already been lost and when feelings and emotions were barely even noticeable. With respect to those emergency responses (like begging, pleading, crying, or betraying) that still provide adequate protection under extreme conditions, the people who are affected condemn themselves after the fact; they pronounce themselves guilty and punish themselves accordingly. From the outside, the tortured person will then often appear as someone who no longer dares to activate rage and hatred against himself, who punishes himself by damaging himself, who no longer feels his own body, who rejects it or perceives it as a foreign body. It is *as if the person's own expulsion were taking place inside him.*

The body, in contrast, seems to want to reflect the agony it is living through, its every wound and devastation. And the body seems to want this all the more intensely when the old self acts more judgmentally, more absent-mindedly, and more divisively in the way it perceives, thinks, and evaluates. So the body displays pain in every conceivable manifestation. These manifest pains have a far more symbolic form than can be discerned by looking at them as symptoms of readily comprehensible, underlying organic disturbances. They are often diffuse and present everywhere in the body. But they also appear as a cry for help and as a signal from the unconscious to the conscious mind following torture: *Accept the wounds, support and respect the good unconscious forces that strive to maintain life, integrate the experiences of torture as a reality into the old patterns of the self. In case of an emergency, change your life script accordingly.*

So long as these signals cannot be registered and honored by the conscious mind, painful emotions will stabilize themselves according to the rules of the vicious circle: these painful emotions will be maintained and intensified by muscular tensions, by perceiving the pain as a burdensome foreign body. Agony and alienation of the cerebral person from the visceral person, the internal conflict of the victim, seem to continue tragically and have a perfidious effect by appearing as the torturers' long-term success. One patient experienced and described his pains and misapprehensions as a voracious monster, another as the devil's claw, a third as a choking, climbing plant made out of metal. The patient's predominant desires are often to free himself from the pains in a magical way, either by using every medication available, or via the therapist's imagined omnipotence, or at worst through suicide. Therapists therefore often find themselves feeling helpless, as if their patients were throwing themselves at their feet accusingly.

But, from the perspective of psychotherapy, psychosomatic pains also have a function that is initially meaningful and easy to understand: they prevent the conscious mental and linguistic integration of torture's reality. In other words, they enable and stabilize avoidance behavior, one of the major features of behavior patterns that people display following extreme traumatization. Whoever feels pain cannot think and reason clearly and therefore cannot think about what is horrible. The more that the affected person concentrates on painful emotions, and the more he displays the *behavior* of pain (Flor 1991) (as this behavior takes shape across time) with a corresponding *expectation* of pain and with muscular tension, then the more effectively avoidance can function. Pain and avoidance are therefore a rescue effort and should never be seen as simulation or lack of motivation for a treatment that divulges the source of the pain.

During torture, conditioning (meaning learning in the broadest sense) takes place at the physical and therefore also at the psychological level of the unconscious: emergency responses and even changes in the organism are created and continue even after the trauma, in that they repeat themselves, either in their original or in a similar form. The experiences of torture appear like a deeply etched pattern, as if the organism had learned extreme reactions to extreme stimuli. Even after the torture has ended, these reactions continue to be reproduced, although they are apparently disconnected from the original threat. Learning and behavior models tend toward a simple explanation of how avoidance behaviors, and therefore authentic symptoms of posttraumatic stress disorder (PTSD), can emerge from the situation of torture.

Situations like persecution, abuse, rape, and other acts of torture can be seen as complex stimulus patterns that are extremely aversive, that is, especially painful and threatening, not predictable, and therefore particularly uncontrollable and unavoidable. The natural responses are pain and fear, accompanied by extreme nervous excitement. People who have not been tortured might remember situations in their lives, like separation or the loss of a person through death or repercussions from a serious accident, in which they experienced constant nervous overexcitement with sleeplessness, nightmares, and anxiety and panic reactions over a considerable stretch of time. Torture, which attacks and wounds the self, often leads to a permanent condition of very intense excitement and hypervigilance.

In the entire situation of torture, in other words, all possible stimuli that are available become stimuli of memory, which get bound up with responses of pain and fear. It could be the voice of the torturer; the room's color or interior design; the nature of the instruments of torture; the smells, sounds, or kind of lighting during the traumatic situation. Thoughts and emotions that transpire in these situations turn into internal triggers that can elicit anxiety reactions later on, when the torture is over. This learned (conditioned) pattern persists even when the probability of torture threatening the victim no longer exists, even after the flight into exile has led to asylum status and the guarantee of some security in life.

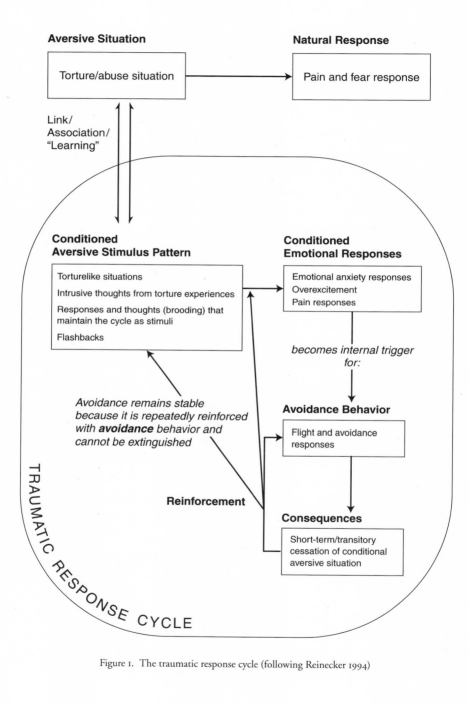

Figure 1. The traumatic response cycle (following Reinecker 1994)

In this way any and all kinds of environmental stimuli that are normally insignificant can become "charged" in a traumatized person and trigger reactions just like those that happened under torture.

A patient from Iran told me how he used to notice the smell of sweat when he was back home. That smell practically assaulted him in a way that reminded him of the military jail, and it was so intense that he simultaneously associated the memory with the smell of blood, filth, and vomit, with the screams of people being tortured, and with his own pain under torture. Suddenly the whole terrifying scene he had experienced reemerged. A sudden panicky anxiety welled up in him. A growing, intense agitation—with a racing heartbeat, an outbreak of sweat, shortness of breath, and sensations making him feel as if his head would suddenly burst and his limbs rip apart—brought on this panicky flight. He ran out of the room into the open, and then he wandered around aimlessly in the city. This condition lasted for hours, until the agitation abated.

A Bosnian patient was no longer able to travel on the bus or subway because the clicking noises reminded her of the cocked guns with which she had been threatened all day long by the Chetniks during their raping spree.

As a result of this change in how the environment is perceived (an environment where anything and everything can trigger a learned anxiety reaction), comprehensive avoidance strategies are formed. Often, the people affected avoid commonplace daily activities, like using public transportation and meeting other people. Some will not even venture out in public, so they isolate themselves. Some also develop compulsive behaviors, for example, by always and repeatedly having to check whether they have closed the door, or they develop cleaning compulsions, by attempting in a graphic and ritualistic manner to cleanse themselves of guilt, stains on their honor, or shame. Another form of avoidance behavior can be expressed in unconscious hyperactivity or in excessive politicization, which allows one's own experience of torture to be split off and sometimes even denied or reinterpreted. Frequently, the avoidance behavior is interrupted by phases in which the torture victims throw themselves into traumatic confrontations—unconditionally, vehemently. They impetuously expose themselves to painful and dangerous situations again and again. Thus, we hear Bosnian men tell us in group therapy how they repeatedly find stimulation at their clubs by showing gruesome private videos that document atrocities in their homeland. It seems as if the psyche is desperately seeking solutions by inundating itself this way, as if, in a fit of impotent rage, one re-opens a wound in order to numb an underlying pain by using a self-created pain.

The tragic thing about all these forms of avoidance behavior is that it is precisely this kind of behavior that repeatedly intensifies the originally learned anxiety reaction. The kind of avoidance that leads to short-term relief thereby repeatedly prevents anxiety reactions from dissolving. Thus, avoidance com-pletes a vicious circle that becomes more stable with each passing year. For this reason, posttraumatic symptoms and reactions of strain can be maintained across an entire lifetime. Even today, for example, we hear about Holocaust survivors who continue to suffer in old age from symptoms they once believed to have gotten under control. In fact, symptoms can regress into phases of life shaped even by positive experiences like work, marriage, and raising children. But the entire array of symptoms erupts again, with all its original vehemence, when the children leave home, or when people are released from the world of work and into retirement, or when a life situation has been dramatically altered.

An Iranian patient who was tortured almost twenty years before under the shah's regime developed violent reactions when the Wall came down in Berlin. This person had been able to stabilize his Marxist-oriented identity in the GDR. The externally induced breakdown of this identity acted like the burst-ing of a dam that had held back his experiences of torture. Suddenly he was again experiencing situations of torture he had believed were long forgotten, in nightmares that were as sharp as photographs, accompanied by anxiety and panic, as if he were just now going to be tortured again.

Some people undertake efforts at healing themselves that resemble avoid-ance behaviors; they get stuck in philosophies, in complicated attempts at ex-plaining something that is barely explicable intellectually, or else they turn to helping other victims without having processed their own trauma.

Just *thoughts* about parts of the torture situation, which often arrive unbid-den, can trigger a wholesale traumatic response: reactions of anxiety and flight emerge, with intense physical arousal and sensations of pain. This brings about efforts at avoidance in thought and memory; most victims expend considerable energy trying not to remember, not to think about what happened to them.

But this, too, does not succeed, because fragments and scraps of terrible memories reemerge arbitrarily and invasively, in a flood from the unconscious. These phenomena are called *flashbacks*, the sudden appearance of terrible images from situations of torture. In contrast to nightmares, flashbacks make their appearance during waking states. They are accompanied by nervous overexcitement, anxiety, and panic; in other words, by conditions that appeared during the actual torture sessions.

This entrapment in the past also prevents new situations and events from being evaluated appropriately; no meaningful conclusions resulting in a realistic assessment of danger and security can possibly emerge. The person's fundamental biological security is thereby shaken, his perception altered, and his capacity to evaluate and assess fundamentally disturbed.

At the cognitive level (thinking and evaluating), fundamental assumptions about the world and the self acquired earlier in life are shattered. These kinds of assumptions are, following Janoff-Bulman (1992):

—The world is sufficiently well-ordered and meaningful;
—The world is fundamentally just;
—The individual's personal security is guaranteed;
—Each individual can protect himself or herself when threatened;
—Human beings are fundamentally helpful and good;
—A person can make decisions and influence or control situations on the basis of free choice;
—Events and behaviors are calculable and predictable within a framework of learning;
—One's relationship to oneself is calculable and familiar;
—Relations to other human beings are calculable;
—There are ways out of dangerous situations.

These fundamental assumptions are shaped in different ways depending on the culture and political situation. But they are human assumptions having, at bottom, universal validity. When long-range traumatization occurs in threatened and persecuted communities, however, these fundamental assumptions can be profoundly shaken, even among children. The same is more or less true for the children and grandchildren of those tortured. But these assumptions really get shattered, as Janoff-Bulman indicates, under the kind of torture suffered by oneself, during the assault on the identity of the individual.

Under torture, trust in oneself and in other people is so systematically violated that many patients say:

"What kind of human being am I for this to have happened to me?"

"My body is ugly and soiled. I don't want my body anymore."

"My whole life is destroyed. I can't tell a single person what I experienced."

*"My soul is sick, my head is crazy, and I'm living like a bird with broken wings,
like a withered tree that's lost its leaves."*

Tortured people no longer trust their senses: other people are experienced
as threatening, even when they behave in a friendly and supportive way. Vis-à-
vis friends, and even spouses and children, it can reach the point of inappropriate aggression, of incomprehensible behavior, of disturbances in contact and
communication. Often we see an oppressive speechlessness between those who
have been tortured and the members of their family. It usually is not possible
for victims to relate what they really experienced. But excessive cravings for
understanding, caretaking, and protection can emerge subliminally in these
victims. Feelings of inferiority, helplessness, of losing their role, can evoke insol-
uble conflicts in familial relationships. In addition, relatives and friends, in light
of the unfathomable terrors of torture, sometimes avoid and turn away from
the victims in subtle ways, since an encounter would also trigger anxiety, defensiveness, and avoidance in them (the relatives and friends).

Sometimes, those who have been tortured also partly reexperience torture
by projecting their experiences and perceptions, which allows them to live out
feelings that were blocked and buried during their own real torture experience.

Not infrequently, we learn that both spouses had been tortured. For one
couple, it became especially obvious that torture's long-term impact had destroyed their relationship in a tragic and tormented fashion. The two engaged
in mutual projections about power and helplessness, in a bizarre "game" where
they competed with each other about whose experience had been the worst. It
reached the point where one attributed torture methods to the other, where
they made mutually unrealizable demands for understanding and care on each
other, and where they lost the ability to love, although they both yearned
for it. After nearly twenty years of this desperate struggle, the marriage was
dissolved.

Ways for Psychotherapists to Proceed with Tortured Persons

The variety of human existence, in all its cultural and social contexts, requires therapists to be engaged in rethinking old treatment philosophies and developing new ones. Flexibility and adjustment to different levels of human experience and behavior are required.

The rigid theoretical models of traditional therapeutic schools and ideologies are no longer suited to the challenges we face in treating extremely traumatized torture victims. Instead, philosophies of treatment must be developed that enable patients and therapists *to get moving.* Paralysis, horror, and the vicious circle of the victims' psychotraumatic burdens require movement and flexibility; these are qualities for which the therapist is a model and a hope for salvation. The shift from one level to another can happen by drawing on the playfulness and creativity that is available in the methods and content of several, even quite different, therapeutic concepts. With a variety of methods, levels, and creative possibilities to draw upon, even the so-called therapeutic setting stops being a rigid corset. The setting designates the overall configuration of the therapy. It extends from the shape and arrangement of the room, through the fixtures (chairs, seats, mattresses, blankets, the carpet, objects whose character is challenging, symbolic objects, the psychodrama stage) all the way to questions like: How do the therapist and patient encounter each other? Are there perhaps even two or more therapists at a single session, and are they working with a group, with a couple, or with the patient's entire family? Is there a translator present?

The classical setting in therapy, where a therapist sits across from the patient maintaining eye contact, can function in a way that diminishes and that harbors a danger of retraumatizing torture victims. We must remember that the person sitting across from the patient represents authority, that of the government-licensed therapist, who is posing very personal and intimate questions. Or else the therapist shrouds himself in silence, stares at the client (either occasionally or constantly), and seems to be waiting for something. For people who have been tortured and abused, this situation can quickly trigger very unpleasant feelings, and they react to those providing treatment with intense anxiety, with mistrust and aggression, as if the treatment providers were torturers or rapists. This can happen whenever the patient transfers negative features of the perpetrator's image that are clearly recognizable onto the therapist. The therapist is able to cut the Gordian knot whenever he (in a manner that the patient can clearly understand) thwarts the patient's negative assumptions and (working against the patient's expectations) does not behave like a perpetrator or like *the* perpetrator (Fischer and Gurris 1996). Perpetrator transferences among our patients often consist of behavioral routines that cannot be observed from the outside, that lie behind a polite, sometimes submissive facade, and that may initially remain hidden from the therapist. Stable avoidance behavior, anxiety, and mistrust can lead to a situation where the victims often cannot speak. For therapists, too, the horror of trauma as it is concretely expressed is virtually unbelievable, thus making empathy difficult. So anxiety and avoidance reactions can just as easily be triggered among therapists, and these reactions can, in turn, lead patients to assume that they cannot entrust their fate to the therapist, or that their therapist is just confirming their own negative self-image of self-rejection and of ascribing blame and failure to oneself.

We also have to engage in a delicate balancing act with respect to the danger of overidentifying morally or even politically with the patient and, thereby, of acting in a way that transgresses boundaries. To overreact in the opposite direction, we can also be tempted to hide our own dismay behind professional masks. Therefore we have to deal very carefully and authentically with the boundaries of people who have been tortured, as we must with our own limits. When, even with the best of helpful intentions, we do not succeed at this, the therapeutic process can easily turn into its opposite, and the traumatization will further stabilize as a result. Helpers, as we have now painfully learned from experience in many of the world's treatment facilities, are vulnerable not only to the dangers of burnout but also to so-called vicarious traumatization (Lansen 1992). If the work lacks appropriate reflection and supervision, a treatment center can turn into a version of a torture center: paranoid thoughts, perpetrators' and victims' accusations, ostracization and isolation, can spread among the helpers in a psychiatric team, and the team members can get so caught up in this that they become crippled and traumatized themselves by these phenomena. An additional danger for therapists is this illusion: with the proliferation of omnipotent fantasies and desires, the danger grows that therapeutic helplessness (itself quite understandable)—but also overidentification with the victims and disillusionment on the part of the helpers—will not be confronted. The illusion of being able to do competent multicultural work can also take a toll on the honesty and authenticity of the therapists. One's own cultural background can too easily be devalued or even denied. But honesty, self-confidence, and self-knowledge—normally aspects of one's own culture—are professional prerequisites for the ability to practice psychotherapy with torture victims.

This means that Western therapists who practice in the country where their tortured patients have found asylum will essentially have to master and apply their acquired craft using different therapeutic methods. Therapists can only encounter aspects of the other culture in a learning posture. The little bit that therapists have understood is something they must then translate back again into their own cultural and methodological context. So, for example, hypnotherapeutic concepts do allow internal images, metaphors, stories, and fairy tales from the other culture to be used on behalf of patients. Here the therapist is merely the agent applying material that the patients themselves produce.

For people who had to flee into exile but also want to establish a foothold where they are, finding their way in the new environment is as vital as preserving and treasuring their cultural identity. So, to the patients, therapists also become representatives of their new country, and the patients properly expect these representatives to provide them with perspective and information on it. Therefore, one therapeutic task is to educate the patients about this alien culture in a manner that is enlightening, sensitive, and neither injurious nor condescending.

Often this question is posed to us: Can therapists avoid these pitfalls? The answer to this question has many aspects. Here are some of them:

When therapists do not succumb to the error of having to empathize with and understand *everything* that patients experience, when they recognize their limits and are honest with themselves, then it is possible for them—with empathetic engagement, but also with a professional sense of security—to join the patient in approaching the complex of torture and, acting as an agent, to help the patient integrate this complex.

Therapists do not have to feel they must bear the burden themselves. Instead, when it comes to comprehending the reality of torture, they can only get as far as they themselves are capable of proceeding. On this matter we owe it to our patients to give them clear signals and information. If this feedback does not materialize, there is a danger that the patient will start to worry about the therapist and develop feelings of guilt about having contaminated him with the patient's "filth." Therapists happen to be models, too, and therefore they are responsible for the conditions of "not putting up with" and "not having to bear the burden." The message to the patients is: torture is not something that any human being can or need put up with!

Therapists are human beings first and foremost. Working with torture victims is not something that can be accomplished at a constant level of energy and intensity. There are days when therapists are vulnerable and less able to approach the abyss. Major changes in the therapist's sensitivity also need to be reported back to patients in a simple and open manner, free of hidden complaining. This, too, is model behavior with a message: I want to stay healthy, to do myself some good; I want to create energy that I can share, and I don't want to violate my own boundaries for the purported well-being of someone else. Burned-out therapists are an imposition on patients.

Integrative Psychotherapy with Tortured People

In shaping therapy, it often proves meaningful to shift from an initial phase of behavior therapy into a phase that is psychodramatic or gestalt, while simultaneously making use of hypnotherapeutic or family therapy techniques, or creating a nonverbal design on a mural, or sitting on the floor and putting the inexpressible on paper with a crayon. By getting away from sitting on chairs, by turning toward daylight streaming through a window while introducing a breathing exercise or a directed imaginary journey, it is possible to dissolve a rigid body posture and put it in motion.

The goal of therapy is the conscious internalization of the entire traumatic reality into the patient's self-concept, so that at some point he can say: Yes, I really did experience that; it happened to me, but it's history. I am no longer a victim; I'm a survivor instead. This kind of integration requires a variety of methodical therapeutic steps at different levels in one vivid setting. Enlightenment and information are, above all, part of this, as is providing skills in mastery (for the body, too) and a search for a new perspective on the meaning of life.

Psychotherapy in Action—an Example

Mr. A. had been a veterinarian in Bosnia. Before the war he used to travel tirelessly from one village to another in his region, where he knew all the local people within a circumference of about sixty kilometers. He loved his profession above everything else. Mr. A. is appalled at how he, a man who was always completely healthy before his internment in the camp, now feels sick and "probably crazy in the head." Mr. A., the doctor, does not understand his pains. He has severe headaches, backaches, and pains in his legs. His heart is going crazy. He sweats, and he keeps having to jump up suddenly and run out of the room. He can no longer sleep and has terrible thoughts. When he does sleep, nightmares haunt him. Then blood rushes to his face, and he constantly seems agitated, as if everything were suddenly about to explode inside him; he is restless and uneasy.

Mr. A. tries to be politely interested, but his tartly bitter, cynical remarks, with their undertone of contempt, and the play in his facial gestures all reveal how profoundly he has lost trust in the world and in human beings. He tries, laboriously, to display gallows humor, just in order to maintain any kind of persona. Simply sitting in his chair becomes a torment to him. He seems to experience the first hourly session as a battle. So, for example, he says: "Why are we sitting around here and talking, instead of sweeping aside my pains? It would be better if you x-rayed my head, or tried an electroencelphalogram, or did a CT scan. Where can we find those good German pills? You guys are rich and live in peace. What do you know about what I've experienced?"

Treatment of Symptoms

Mr. A. cannot find any peace. His permanent condition of excitement and painful tension torments him day and night. I use a simple sketch to enlighten him about the relationship of excitement to tension and pain, as a vicious circle. It is also clear to Mr. A. that the traumatic shock of what he has experienced has psychologically and even biologically engraved changes in his organism, so that hypervigilance and overexcitement are prompted by no particular occasion. When I show him the schematic drawing of the cerebrum and spine with simple stimulus-response models, Mr. A. grins. As a veterinarian he was not aware that it was possible to portray this so simply.

With his permission, we practice different breathing and relaxation routines. As a therapist, I adjust to the patient's rhythm, and I also use myself as a model demonstrating different exercises. After each individual exercise the patient gives me feedback on his state of health, and especially about any feelings of pain. It now surprises Mr. A. to learn that he can still experience distinctions in his perception of pain. I fortify this sensitivity to distinctions and encourage him to carry out the exercises several times a day at home or during a stroll.

With Mr. A. it is already becoming possible to provide the "inner eye" of his imagination with a graphic illustration of his body's internal organs. This kind of imagination strengthens relaxation. For example, *"As you follow your breathing in and breathing out, you can imagine how this expands through the entire body, like a warm light or a healing power. Maybe you can also imagine how, with each exhalation, the muscles of your stomach walls and intestines relax, while your heart is able to beat quietly and evenly to the rhythm of your breathing, which comes and goes like ocean waves, comes and goes. Maybe you can imagine the inner spaces of your body, the rib cage with the lungs on either side and the heart, that is able to beat quietly and evenly, the stomach area, like a big, warm cave, the pelvic area, big and warm, like a safe, protective cave that can get wide and wider."*

Relaxing journeys of the imagination like this, traveling through the body, are the first countermeasures (counterconditioning) against experiences of torture that are stored in the body, which express themselves in excitement, tension, and pain (anxiety). The patient experiences interruptions in his states of unrest. Simultaneously he wins back a small amount of control over his body, together with the feeling that he need not always be at the mercy of these conditions.

Retrieving Life before the Trauma

Many tortured people are so imprisoned by the trauma of their torture that they experience their entire life as worthless and as something overshadowed by the torture. When we ask about memories of the time before the torture trauma, and when our patients then complain that there no longer are any good memories, we sometimes have to say, "If it were like that, you wouldn't be sitting alive in front of us today." We then provide information about the effectiveness of a person's pretraumatic resources, about how these resources help those who have been tortured to maintain their hold on life, in spite of their injuries, and about how these resources cannot be destroyed but instead only get covered up by horrible experiences. Then I issue an invitation to join me in taking an introductory journey heading in the direction of those submerged resources, and I encourage the patient to discover the "wise unconscious." I start out by recalling the difference between the waking state and sleep, the brief but intense moments in which many imaginary notions can flash before the inner eye. Just imagining this condition creates a desired mild trance, which can be intensified even more by some ground rules about relaxing.

I observe how Mr. A. is already in a light trancelike state. After a brief flutter of the eyelids, his eyes are half shut. The mouth is also half open, and his hands lie on his stomach, which rises and falls evenly. I invite Mr. A. to direct his inner eye toward the time before 1992, to turn on his inner "searchlight" and search for scenes or images. I ask what season of the year it is in his imagination, how and where he is standing or walking or sitting or lying down. I ask him to describe the surroundings and to pick out a scene he finds pleasant. In the image forming for Mr. A., he can see himself in a car traveling through the Bosnian countryside from patient to patient. In the villages he sees the people who know him, who summoned him and who like him. He envisions the animals he treats, imagines himself engaged in conversations, quoting sayings, and making witticisms in close contact with the village residents. As he imagines this, his facial muscles relax, and his expression softens. His body sinks a bit farther back into the chair. I now anchor and fortify this image by having him imagine this scene's smells, and I also let him wander among different smells. This is followed by imagining different familiar sounds from this scene, and finally by colors, light and dark tones, as well as sensations in the body and skin. Tying these positive resource images to qualities of sense perception stabilizes the effectiveness of positive internal images.

The link to smells is especially effective. In human development, smells have a special meaning for their early and reliable sense quality. Even impressions with prelinguistic meaning can be readily activated by smells. Mr. A. now also "knows" situations based on these kinds of sense impressions, without having to put them into words. Toward the end of his imaginary journey, I ask him once again to link the scene with feelings. He mentions feelings of pride, satisfaction, recognition, and fun (which makes him laugh), and it occurs to him how, after working with the animals, he used to sit together over a schnapps at a pub with village residents. This scene, too, is something I let Mr. A. relish fully one more time, so long as he is in this trancelike state. Finally I offer him this strengthening suggestion:

"Whenever, over the next few hours or days, you find it does you good to have this happen, your unconscious can haul this scene before your inner eye again, and you can smell those familiar and pleasant smells again, hear the normal sounds, and see the familiar colors again, when you imagine that day, how you made your rounds as a veterinarian traveling in the countryside. Maybe you can feel again how proud, how free, and how satisfying it can make you to imagine this, and you will know that nobody can take this inner image away from you and destroy it, regardless of where you are in this world. Look around for just another moment, now, and take your leave of this scene in the knowledge that you can summon it up anytime over the next few hours or days. Come back, now, in this room, to a time that's pleasant for you. Now take two or three deep breaths, clench both your fists tight; crane your neck, stretch, loll about. When you notice that you want to yawn, just let it happen. Your eyes can open again."

In the trance, Mr. A. reacts to this notion with surprise: "I didn't know I still had this in me!" For a while, Mr. A. had forgotten his physical pains. He is still impressed by the positive impact of this imagined image. There is no onset of any feeling of loss or sadness; instead, he spontaneously utters, "I'd be happy to help out with a veterinarian for a while, in or around Berlin, without pay. That would do me good."

Other patients, however, are easily overwhelmed by a feeling of loss or sadness when introduced to positive images from the period before their trauma: they mourn the lost homeland and murdered family members and friends; they lament their alienation in exile, the loss of political ideals, and the destruction brought on by torture.

I inform the patients beforehand that positive images can easily become disturbed when feelings like this crop up, or by images of terror. I explain that these are similar to invasive flashbacks, and that we must first get this unintended occurrence under control by encapsulating it like an ulcer. The goal is to prevent these terrible feelings and this major sadness from gaining admittance unannounced. These feelings, in their totality, are worthwhile enough to be invited by us into our "protected therapeutic house" at the right time, and at a time when they are wanted. Therefore they must not be allowed to tramp around in our everyday life like stray metastases, and they most certainly cannot be permitted to break into our storehouse of positive resource images. In order to protect these images, we learn to "frame" them. It helps to set signals using a "mental pause," by arbitrarily changing the body's posture or by changing breathing while concentrating on regions of the body below the head that are beginning to relax. A simple metaphor is helpful here: one pushes a button as if by remote control in order to change channels from the terrible program to the desired program. Or, to pick another metaphor, it is a matter of cutting off transmission to the torturer.

These skills help Mr. A. deal with the flashbacks that often overpower him outside the therapy sessions. I inform him that this way of cordoning off invasions of terror is only a helpful technique at the outset for creating some temporary relief. I explain our thesis about how the terrors of torture are frozen in body and soul, that they cannot be forgotten or sent packing somewhere outside. In the long run, they also cannot be simply tuned out. Even if we can and must encapsulate the trauma, it is going to remain a pressure cooker with explosive, destructive energy. Mr. A. can now agree to this perspective. A Bosnian saying occurs to him: *"Better nosebleeds than brain hemorrhages."* His suspicious defense at the outset of therapy has given way to an attitude that is now curious and acquiescing. His sarcastic gallows humor melts more and more into exonerating witticisms, which the therapist supports as a vital resource. Now it is time to take the next step.

Confronting Traumatic Experiences

I offer Mr. A. the suggestion that while we sit together in this secure and familiar therapy room, he invite me to share in his terrible experiences. I remind him how he had believed, at the outset, that he could relate all the horrors to me within ten minutes. I make it clear to him that we have hours and days of time for this. I give him the assurance that we can also repeat this in three months or a year.

I inform Mr. A. about the procedure. *"When we take a look now at the ulcer called 'camp,' you can have me join you as we step into these terrible images. We will do this step by step. You have the opportunity to stop the procedure at any time. I will ask you to try putting each one of these steps and images (including details) into words. Some of the words and sentences I'm going to repeat, and sometimes I am going to ask you: 'What happens now?' I'm asking you to put the words and sentences in the present tense. We will repeat this in several stages. In between these stages we'll relax again, just the way you now know, or we'll take a little fantasy journey to a 'Place of Peace and Energy.'* (For Mr. A. this was an image from his childhood: after an exhausting soccer game, he would rest under a tree in a meadow, all alone.) *The first time, you are going to find it hard to form words and sentences. You will also find unpleasant feelings coming up, like your flashback attacks: it could be that you will start to sweat profusely, that your heart will race, that you will experience rage and anxiety. But all this is present inside of you, it is the ulcer's content, and we will see to it that it doesn't poison you. You will start to speak more fluently (as early as the second or third time), and details will suddenly occur to you that you no longer knew. After each stage we will also 'measure' whether your pains have changed. Now and then these will be getting more intense; mostly, however, the pains will diminish the more stages you go through. You can be sure that I as your therapist will be feeling stable and can hear what you experienced. I will go as far along with you as I can. Therefore you won't have to worry about me."*

I now ask the patient to stand up with me and wander around the room with me for a few minutes. As a therapist I locate myself about half a step behind him and to his side. From this position I can duplicate his thoughts and feelings. The movement in the room supports a preference for roaming thoughts.

Mr. A. asks: "In other words, I should talk about the camp. When I arrived here, I had imagined this would be easier."

"Pay attention to your inner voice. Can you hear an inner voice? Breathe in lightly two or three times, hear your way into yourself."

"Yes, two voices."

"Give both your voices a place, maybe one voice on your right and one voice on your left, or maybe anywhere in the room. Will that work?"

Mr. A. selects two inner voices, one on the left and the other on the right. He starts out on the left. I let his head incline downward and slightly toward the left in order to facilitate his speaking. He begins: "It really is like an ulcer. At last I want to talk about it, maybe this will work here. I can't do it at home. Even in the club, with my friends, it doesn't work. I'll get it done here, but . . ."

I had placed myself to Mr. A.'s left, the side that now "has the voice." After his "but" I say: *"Stop! Let this voice sound one more time in your ear. The voice says: 'I will finally try to talk about the camp; I want to unburden myself, here in this room.'"*

"Yes."

"So now let's listen to the other voice." Now, from behind, I lightly incline his head toward the right and downward. I ask the translator to place herself in a mirror image to me, behind the patient, and from this position to translate the right side's voice directly:

"It's always the same. I'm afraid to think about it; when I think about it, I immediately get agitated." Mr. A.'s body begins to sway slightly, and I see how blood is rushing to his head.

I am now behind the translator, and I say: *"I'm afraid of getting all agitated. I need protection."*

"Yes, but actually . . ."

"Stop! Lend this voice one additional moment of attention—listen closely to it! . . . Thank this voice for wanting to provide protection." I now step in front of the patient and ask: *"Do we want to listen to and look at both these voices one more time?"* Mr. A. is still somewhat dazed, and he asks: "What was that?"

I guide him onto a little elevated stool. *"So, now you can look at this from above."* I ask the translator to take a seat next to me on the floor. We are now representing the left and the right voices. I ask the translator to take the part of the right voice and to mirror the dialogue with me, the left voice, in front of the patient. The translator now has an additional assignment, to translate her side of the dialogue and mine in turn.

As a result of his position on the heightened level, Mr. A. is now unburdened, and he grins through the entire event. Even before the performance has completely ended, he interrupts us laughingly and jumps down from the stool: "Oh, you two really are a good pair; let's just let the two voices work together. One of them dares to talk, while the other pays attention."

We reassume our original positions across from each other in the room, with the translator retreating slightly into the background. I emphasize the significance of the caretaking "watch out" voice and suggest that this voice can give clear signals during the ensuing confrontation with the camp. I ask Mr. A. how we can do this.

"I'll raise my right arm, and then we'll take a break."

"And then what?"

"Again, one of your relaxation journeys, or (laughing) we could go out and have a smoke."

"Any idea which one of the relaxation journeys you'd like to take, then?"

"Yes, the one with the meadow and the tree, and ideally as I lie down and have a smoke."

Mr. A. has now become more relaxed. The most important thing: we did not break through any so-called resistances (anxieties), and we did not trick him into the procedure. We also did not sit for hours working off these resistances verbally or by facial and bodily gestures.

The decisive thing is that the patient gain the security he needs to decide each step of the procedure for himself. We did not simply persuade him verbally to come to an agreement; instead we worked out this compliance mutually, and we used the movement and the freedom in the room for this. This way his body also went into action, sharing in the conflict and the dialogue.

I inform him about the next step: *"I will sit down on the sofa next to you. After a moment of relaxation I will ask you to imagine the day you were brought into the camp. We'll both imagine ourselves sitting next to each other at the movies, with a screen on the wall across from us, right over there. You can then try to imagine what happened at the camp, just as if it were now happening in front of us like a movie. You know that at any time you can stop the film, or play it back, or let it run in slow motion or fast forward, or, most importantly, you can turn it off completely, just by raising your right arm."* Mr. A. smiles and extends his arm toward the translator: "That's your side!"

I change places and sit down next to the patient. Changing the seating level is very important. The confrontation with trauma cannot take place if therapist and patient are sitting across from each other eye to eye because the level of imagination would be disturbed by the person of the therapist. This way, during this phase, we consciously get around the "transference resistance" of which psychoanalysts speak. It is not appropriate in this first phase of trauma confrontation for the patient to transfer part of his terror onto the therapist. Now the therapist is still clearly assuming the role of witness and supportive human being.

I now sit next to Mr. A. on the sofa and introduce a brief exercise in bodily relaxation. Then I ask Mr. A. to join me in imagining the movie screen.

"Imagine, on the screen, the day on which you were hauled away by the Chetniks. You told me it was the second of July 1992. Imagine this day as if it were today, the second of July. It's summer, and is it raining, where we are now, is the sun shining, or is it overcast? Maybe you can also close your eyes, or you can leave them open while you let your mouth, your lips, form words; you can start now."

"Yes, it was on the second of July in the morning. I'm sitting at home and just about ready to go. I hear the sounds of an engine from a truck outside. And then male voices, somebody shouting something. I hear women screaming and men cursing. I want to head toward the window, but two Chetniks have already come in and are holding their machine guns to my head. They yell at me: 'What are you doing sitting around here? We want to invite you to take a lovely excursion, or do you want to turn down our invitation?' I ask: 'What's this supposed to mean? What do you want from me?' As an answer, one of the gun butts hits me on the head. I fall down on the floor and get kicked."

"The Chetniks kick you? What part of your body do they kick? Where do you feel the pain? I am now going to put my left hand between your shoulder blades so that I have better contact with your voice."

Mr. A. groans, and I ask him one more time: *"Where on your body were you kicked?"*

An involuntary movement seizes his body, and he makes a demonstrative gesture showing me the areas of his body that had been kicked. He points to the pit of his stomach, his head, and his abdomen. The motor movements he makes to accomplish this do him good, releasing him from his rigidity. I mirror this and then modulate his breathing: *"Take two light breaths and let your exhalation flow back deeply into your stomach. Put your hands on your stomach and feel the rhythm of your breathing. Maybe your bottom can sink back a bit deeper into the sofa. What's happening now?"*

"I'm feeling that my head is bleeding."

"How can you feel that?"

"It's running down my head, all warm. But I can stand up; they're pushing me out the door. There are lots of other men there, a lot of them bleeding, some lying on the ground, women and children screaming. Among the Chet-niks standing around there I can see my school buddy Ervin (name altered). He sees me, too, and lights a cigarette. I call out: 'Hello, Ervin, got a new job?' He turns around and leaves."

"Stay with this encounter for a moment. You see your school buddy on the tortur-ers' side?"

Mr. A. shakes his head and breathes harder: "That's pretty crazy, isn't it?"

"Yeah, that's insane! When you now imagine your former friend in this scene, do you have an impulse about what you could say to him or do to him?"

"Don't know—well, I'd have a lot to tell him after all." Then in an embit-tered and cynical tone: "I will certainly pay him a visit some day to have coffee, and then I'd really have something to tell him, or maybe I'd just want to look at him, who knows?"

"Good—let's save that for later. Let's go back into that scene; what's happening now?"

The encounter with his school friend is one of the key experiences whereby the pains emanating from mistreatment and the acts of torture are magnified by incomprehension and meaninglessness. Here is where the person's former self-image and his familiar understanding of his surroundings begin to break down. In subsequent therapy sessions where we used this technique of imagi-nary presentations, dialogues with this former friend were conducted once again, where the therapeutic goal was to track the patient's desperate search for any kind of meaning, and if possible to work on developing new meanings. Just the therapist's effort to undertake this joint Socratic dialogue with the pa-tient can bring a modicum of comfort into the attempt at understanding. Sel-dom is it possible for the inner psychic peace of bygone times to be restored. For many patients it is horrifying how deeply feelings of rage, hate, and even revenge have nested themselves inside their personalities, feelings they did not realize they had before. It did patient A. good to be able to relate these feelings to the therapist. With the therapist's backing, he decided in a later session that he would testify before the War Crimes Tribunal in Den Haag.

In the meantime, the trauma confrontations are continued. The patient re-ports exhaustively about his roundabout trip on top of the truck's platform, heading ultimately toward the Serbian camp. Renewed feelings of anxiety, uncertainty, and especially concern for his family are reawakened in the patient. At this time he still does not know where his family is.

The following is another excerpt from the scenes in the camp:

Mr. A. begins: "I am brought into a room in which I'm left alone. The door is closed. From the adjoining rooms I hear men screaming. I see the room's walls; they are sprayed with blood."

"You feel the contact with my hand between your shoulders? Is it possible to stay with this image for a moment? You hear *the screams, you* see *the blood on the walls. You're thinking . . . ?"*

"Now it's all over for me; they're going to kill me. Hopefully it'll happen quickly. The worst is that I can no longer say anything to my wife and my children."

"You can see yourself there, alone in the room and afraid of dying?"

"Yes, this fear of death, it comes up later one more time when they have led me to the place of execution. At least two times I figured it was all over. And then there was that day, in another camp to which they had taken me, when they told me they had already killed my wife and my children. That was the worst day. Later it turned out they had been lying, in order to provoke me."

"What was it you would have wanted to tell your wife and your children while you were alone in this room with your fear of death?"

"Try to get out; give up the house; save your lives; live on for my sake. Goodbye until we meet again in another world."

"Those are consoling thoughts in those seconds when you are experiencing the fear of death?"

"Yes, those are the most important feelings, that somehow you can take your leave with dignity and that you know that the others are safe."

"Take a look at both these feelings for just another moment—the fear of death, they're going to kill me, it's all over, and also at where you sense these feelings in your body (in this imaginative presentation, Mr. A. is physically almost rigid), *and now send the feeling of consolation, the feeling about your family's safety, that they can live on, into your body. Will that work?"*

Mr. A. is breathing deeply: "Yes, the thought does me good; at least everything makes sense this way." His body has again relaxed from its rigidity.

"Go for a brief moment to this fear of death, how you're expecting that it's all

over. This anxiety that is spreading all over your body. Every living creature has this anxiety in moments like this. Imagine that there is an expression of all these wise unconscious forces inside of you, which you want to protect. When you imagine this anxiety as the last attempt of your unconscious to protect you, you can perhaps imagine how you would want to show this anxiety your gratitude. Perhaps you can understand that this anxiety will keep coming back later on, how it really has no choice but to come back in order to protect you, because in this experience you're sharing with me, you really are standing on the brink. Can you pay attention to this anxiety later on, because it's really something that wants to do good?"

"Yes, I never saw it that way. Until now I always wanted the anxiety to go away, because I thought it would eat me up."

Here, for a moment, that transmission is established that leads to the symptoms of posttraumatic stress disorder. The symptoms make sense. Changing the meaning of invasive anxiety attacks into protective forces flowing logically from what was experienced can liberate the patient from a perspective in which he experiences himself as disturbed. He can see his symptoms as a meaningful psychobiological reaction to what was experienced. This also reduces his avoidance behavior: he can readmit his anxiety about death, his absolute helplessness in the face of threat. This way he can also talk about it and take up the search for meaning with the help of therapy.

During this session we go over all the horrible experiences from the camp in this manner. Some detailed scenes ensue about how he was mistreated and tortured. It is especially onerous for Mr. A. to relate how he was also sexually tortured, by having objects put up his anus, and how mercenaries urinated on his naked body. He was only able to speak about it in the first place when the therapist told him, "We know that lots of men in the camps are also sexually humiliated in every conceivable way." It did Mr. A. good to shift levels with the therapist and work out ideas about the torturers' intentions. A little understanding of meaning resulted from the attempt to take on the perspective of the torturers: How can one destroy a human being most effectively? What is worse and has a more lasting impact than beatings? How does one create embarrassment and guilt feelings to last a lifetime?

One day Mr. A. learned, based on information from the camp, that his two sons had been abducted into another camp where women were being raped en masse. He witnessed the gruesome murder of his brother-in-law, the acts of torment to which his sons and so many other camp inmates were subjected, and the hangings or the torturing to death of his fellow sufferers. So Mr. A. also had guilt feelings just for having survived, guilt feelings that are familiar to us from survivors of the Holocaust.

In this way we spent several sessions and many hours together with the *reality* of his trauma, a reality that nothing can expunge from this world. The patient needed therapy from the people at the Treatment Center who were ready to go down this road with him one more time. With Mr. A. we repeatedly went down this road until it almost became a ritual. Whereas previously his psyche had required the utmost energy to get rid of and to bury this reality somehow, he could now take the horror he experienced and see it as belonging to him, to his self, and to accept it. Painful conditions hardly ever cropped up anymore, and the constant overexcitement diminished significantly. Within the psychic energy that was now set free, there was again a bit of space for uninhibited and hearty humor, and even for a future. Sometimes we even laughed heartily and loud during sessions. This, too, is part of therapy that seeks survival as meaning. A few weeks ago Mr. A. found a veterinarian in Berlin who let him sit in on his practice.

In the next installment of therapy, we invited his wife and his children to joint family therapy sessions. The family was traumatized as a whole, as a system. It was not enough to treat each member of the family individually, even if each one had been tortured most brutally of all. The trauma had to be integrated into the comprehension and understanding of the entire family, so that speechlessness and delegating things in ways that induce illness would be overcome and prevented, so that the unspoken did not seize the family like a virus and wreak more havoc there.

In one of the last sessions, Mr. A. said: "When I first arrived here, I was a different person than I am now. Here I have learned how to look at traces of my life and hold onto them. I especially feel a desire now to resume my work. The worst thing for me now is the waiting, that I can't work here. I would like to go back to Bosnia as soon as possible, to do my work more meaningfully and consciously. I also see my future with new eyes. I believe I have become a little wiser. I'd like to ask you to write up how my therapy went from your perspective. I would like to hold onto this writing for safekeeping, like a diploma."

And yet: We are still not sure, we don't have a feeling that he was "cured" in the usual sense. And even if the impression was sometimes created that Mr. A. had inwardly defeated his torturers, I was sometimes overcome by a feeling of unsettling concern when he occasionally sat there, all quiet and mellow, wrapped in silence, as if he had closed himself off somewhere.

AUTHOR'S NOTE: I would like to express my gratitude to my friend and "trauma-colleague" Janet Varner Gunn, who accompanied me through several drafts of this essay. Author of a survival narrative, *Second Life: A West Bank Memoir* (Minnesota, 1995), she is now writing a book on Anne Frank's diary and other trauma narratives.

CHAPTER THREE

The Vestige of Pain

Psychosomatic Disorders among Survivors of Torture

Mechthild Wenk-Ansohn

"When I close my eyes, I see terrible pictures in front of me—soldiers breaking into our house, wrecking everything, children screaming, they approach me . . ."

The patient sits across from me and has lost eye contact with me. She has wide eyes, anxiously peering into the distance. Then she lowers her head for several seconds. When she looks up at me again, an expression of sadness darts across her face for a moment, and then she tries to smile. "I am trying to stop my thoughts, to think about something else, trying not to see what comes before my eyes, but I'm not having any luck. I have headaches day and night. Can't you x-ray my head and see where these terrible pains are coming from? They hit me on the head. Maybe here is where the source of what ails me will turn up." At these words she strains her brow; it is getting obvious how she tenses the muscles in her head in order to stop her thoughts, and how she tries to shut her eyes to the images that are surfacing. But she isn't having any luck. By escaping to Germany she was able to rescue herself, but in her thoughts she has brought her tormentors along, so deeply have the threatening, hurtful, degrading situations buried themselves in her memory.

On the x-ray picture we would not see anything that would explain the pains. Maybe we would see the remnants of an older wound to the brain tissue in a CT scan—but even these changes do not explain aches and pains in most cases. With medications we can alleviate the pains for a time but not dissolve them. Pains expressed in the body often come from the psyche and give expression to the unbearable: something a human being wants to forget but cannot forget; feelings that are threatening.

I make her an offer: "We can take time out together. If you would like, you can tell me something every week about what is bothering you, about what is so painful in your life that you can't forget it. I'd like to get to know you, not just what you've suffered, but also how you lived beforehand and what, earlier on, was important and fortifying in your life."

When patients come to us, bodily disorders are often the occasion for seeking help. We find scars and restrictions on mobility as the result of wounds and difficulty walking owing to pains in the feet after repeated beatings on the soles (*falanga*). The latter may often be alleviated by physical therapy exercises and orthopedic supports, but not cured. Or else the patients come with damage to their teeth, with eardrum or eye injuries. Often the vestiges of torture are not visible on the body, and yet almost all patients talk about persistent pains. In only a few cases do we find physical causes explaining these pains. The trauma has left a deep trace in the psyche. *Pain is embodied memory.*

In one of the following sessions, the patient speaks again about her headaches. "They're always there—they never let go of me, always the same." I ask her about the "how" of the pain, that is, about its manner and intensity, and also about how it was on different days last week. I request that she use colored pencils on paper to express symbolically what happens as the pain proceeds.

It isn't easy for her, because she is illiterate, and it's unusual for her to hold a pencil in her hand. But then she starts to have fun trying out the different colors, and she picks red for pain. It strikes both of us how, on different days, the color red turns out to have different intensities in the drawing. She is surprised to learn that the pain was not always as constant as she initially remembered it.

I point to an especially strong red and inquire what was so special on this particular day. This leads her to remember: "The evening before, my aunt called me up from my ancestral village. They had picked up my uncle. He has five children, and my aunt is pregnant. In the night I woke up, and my husband was also awake. I screamed, he says."

"Do you remember whether you dreamed?"

"Yes. I was at home." She cries. After a while she tells about how she lost a child in the sixth month after a military raid on her house and beatings to her belly. "After a week, I had to have the dead child removed in the hospital—the womb and fallopian tubes, too. Now I'm only half a woman."

The 35-year-old Kurdish patient from Turkey (called Patient A in the text that follows) is the mother of three children. Together with her family, she left the country after she and her husband had been tortured repeatedly. Her physical examination showed vestiges of torture that, so far, she can only talk about by intimation. With her family, too, she doesn't speak about what happened to her. Two of her children are also under medical treatment because of psychosomatic ailments. Physically, she also suffers from back and lower body pains. The psychic symptoms include sleep disorders with nightmares in which she relives the situations of persecution and torture over and over again; during the day, she also is invaded by images that she cannot defend herself against. She experiences depression, anxiety, inner turmoil, and difficulty concentrating.

Next to one's own experiences, a big role is also played by concern and mourning for close friends and family members; over the last two years, ten of Patient A's family (including children) have either died violently (and sometimes been located cut up in pieces) or else been counted as missing persons (if they are not in jail).

Toward the end of the session we take a new look at her painted depiction of the headache's progress over the last few weeks. I ask her how it came to be that the pains relented somewhat again. "Sometimes I don't feel the pains as much, when I'm playing with my children, when I'm distracted. But on that Monday I got very ill and threw up. Yes, that's how it is sometimes—when I throw up, I feel better."

I tell her about an expression we have in German—"finding something nauseating"—and ask whether there's a similar expression in Kurdish. She says yes. "It really does make you nauseated what they did to me; they were like animals. Right afterward, I was often extremely angry. But that's so long ago, and now I can only cry when I think about it all."

Her remark leads me to assume that her rage against her tormentors is no longer accessible to her, or that at least she can't find an opportunity to express it. I ask her whether she can now experience rage in everyday situations and show it. "No, I am really always friendly. But sometimes, with my children, I quickly just lose it completely. Then I am sometimes so unfair that I can't even control myself—and then it makes me feel ashamed."

Her feeling of shame is a theme repeatedly articulated in the first sessions. She feels ashamed in front of me. She feels ashamed in front of the attorney and the officials at the hearing (unfortunately, so far, male examiners are often the ones who interrogate women). To all of them, she had to reveal as much as possible of what it was she suffered through. Even in front of her husband she feels shame and cannot speak with him about her traumatic experiences: "What kind of a person must I be to have to have this happen to me? And do I even have the right to take refuge and look out for myself here, while friends and relatives in my home country continue to suffer?"

The patient's headache is the physical symptom of a complex internal event. It has the function of absorbing the deepest feelings of violation and shame, feelings compatible neither with her earlier self- and world-image nor with the challenges of her current situation in exile.

Figure 2 attempts to elucidate the connection between trauma and symptom formation, to arrange observations and thoughts in order to arrive at a deeper understanding.

Preexisting Personality

We encounter a person who has experienced a traumatic situation at a certain time in his life, or we may even encounter one who has lived through lengthy and persistent phases of trauma. Before the trauma, he had a personality structure that had developed through the confrontation of his own powers, wishes, and impulses with the possibilities and limits of reality as well as with the perils of everyday life. He had lived in a familial and social context, a culture with rules, prohibitions, and taboos. He had developed modes of behavior and defenses against anxiety suited to everyday situations of stress.

Prior to the situations of persecution and terror they experienced, most of our patients had no significant disorders; neither they nor their relatives re-

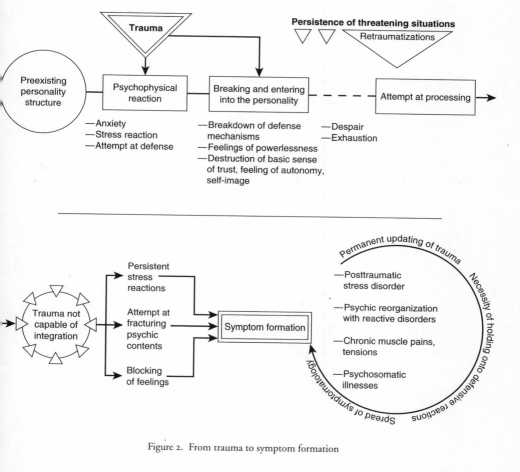

Figure 2. From trauma to symptom formation

ported any pretraumatic symptoms. But a few grew up in families and surroundings characterized by persecution and violence. Sometimes, the father had already been jailed for a lengthy term in their childhood. Because anxiety was a permanent part of their childhood, we have to reckon with the preexistence of a greater vulnerability.

During one therapy session, a 16-year-old girl (Patient B), also a Kurd from Turkey, painted her mother as she used to stand in front of her house while weaving: a spindle-thin body with a gigantic head and big, dark eyes. "My mother, she always looked so sad and was always so thin. I always prayed that my mother would not be so sad anymore and would gain a little weight. When we sat down to eat at home, fear always sat down with us. Sometimes we could hardly swallow a single bite: we were always listening to noises outside, to see if they were coming to attack us. When my father got out of jail after five years, he was a cripple and could hardly walk. At that time they said to him, "Now we'll get your children."

The patient herself was 13 years old when she was picked up for the first time and tortured over several days. The torture struck her at a time when she was still a child. She also did not understand why she was being tortured. This patient's basic sense of trust is deeply shattered. Panic attacks accompany her in daytime, nightmares after dark.

When, during relaxation exercises, she manages to lie down briefly on the padding, when the tension abates and her breathing gets deeper, the slightest irritation is enough to make her sit straight up again, with her eyes wide open and her heart pounding. Over and over again, we work on ground contact, that is, on the perception of underlying support; on gradually gaining more confidence to depend on the ground for lying, sitting, or standing. The constant tension gives the patient pains in the head and in the back. She wants to get rid of these pains. Yet, for her, tension in the form of a continual attentive posture means security and a state of preparedness, so that renewed aggression does not strike her unexpectedly and overwhelmingly. Only slowly will she rid herself of this tension. When it becomes possible to let rage and indignation into the therapy sessions, there are moments in which the patient seems more relaxed. These are brief moments in which she relives the onset of her own strength and self-worth. They show her that, all the destruction notwithstanding, there are still sources of authentic strength accessible inside her. "Aha—I can feel this way too, so I'm also really strong."

Psychophysical Reactions to an Everyday Situation of Stress

We are all familiar with stress reactions, for example, when we are driving a car and another car suddenly turns the corner into our path. In situations like that, bodily action is the immediate result: we hold our breath for a moment, the body tenses, and the heart races even before we consciously perceive the other car and realize that there might be a crash. A quick braking or evasive maneuver and—luckily nothing happens. We keep on driving. Maybe a hot, stabbing feeling in the stomach persists, for a while the rapid heartbeat remains, breathing is now accelerated, and we feel a slight trembling in our limbs. We are wide-awake, drive more slowly, and the image and shock accompany us a while longer. That evening, when we relax, the image might surface again. We are very relieved that nothing happened.

Heightened muscle tension in a situation of stress, just like involuntary reactions, is a type of bodily preparation for defense and flight.

In a severely life-threatening situation, for example, in an accident or catastrophe shattering the framework of all previous experience, often no braking or evasive maneuver is possible. After experiences like this, characterized by a thoroughgoing helplessness, involuntary stress reactions and tension can keep on going.

This is especially true for people subjected to torture. They cannot defend themselves in the situation, are shackled, held down; the superior power of the others is unambiguous. Resistance may induce one's own death. Thus, bodily reactions stay stuck in the preparatory phase.

Breaking and Entering the Personality

A human being under torture finds himself in a situation where the whole of his body and soul are deeply wounded. He is wounded physically; unbearable pain is inflicted on him; he is degraded, humiliated; his feelings of shame are slighted, and he finds himself alone and powerless in the face of overpowering forces treating him with inconceivable inhumanity. Anxiety and terror spread inside him, and in this extreme situation previously learned coping strategies offer no protection. The person is struck in his innermost core. Basic trust and feelings of autonomy are swept away, self- and world-images shaken or destroyed. Feelings of powerlessness and a deep mistrust are what remain, often accompanied by feelings of shame and guilt as well. Guilt feelings are not necessarily bound up with something specific like the inability to resist any longer or with the possible betrayal of others; instead, what often results is a general kind of self-accusation: "What kind of person am I, that this could happen to me? I'm no longer worth anything." In particular, the kind of sexual torture often used plays an enormous role in destroying self-esteem.

More strongly than in the case of a one-time traumatic situation, the *persis-*

tence of a threatening situation under conditions of incarceration and torture—along with repeated subjection to extreme psychic and physical violence while completely powerless—gradually leads (as is the aim of systematic torture) to exhaustion and despair. At the physical level, the struggle against inner submission is also linked to heightened muscular tension. Presumably, in this context, it can result in special tension in the region of the lumbar vertebral column. There, especially, the conflict between the desire to submit and the desire to remain upright finds bodily expression at a muscular level (Kütemeyer 1979). A great many of our patients complain about chronic pain with high muscle tension in this region.

Attempt at Processing—Symptom Formation

To people everywhere, being tortured is a decisive event in their life history. It is as if the lifeline is interrupted, while one's relationship to oneself, to others, and to the world has been sharply altered. The person laboriously attempts to find a new equilibrium, a way of surviving. Since the trauma is so hard to integrate into one's former self-image, a processing procedure like this is often not possible without the formation of symptoms. The nature of the symptoms can be both psychic and physical, and the symptoms can emerge immediately after the trauma or months, even years later, when the unstable equilibrium becomes threatened by change or retraumatization.

Think back to the patient described at the outset (Patient A): She has fled, but in her thoughts she has brought her tormentors along. Even if the threatening situation is over, psychic and bodily reactions persist among many people who have been tortured, even when they are thousands of miles away from the site of traumatization. It is as if they are still in the situation, or as if the situation could still be an immediate threat.

Traumatizing events linger like fresh wounds in the memory, where they are constantly reproduced. They surface as nightmares after dark and as thoughts and images during the day. They are sometimes triggered spontaneously or may arise in the train of some everyday event that recalls the trauma: the sound of heavy footsteps on the floor of the asylum hostel, a special smell, an appointment with the public authorities or at the doctor's that brings the interrogation back to mind. Traumatized persons anxiously scan the environment for threats (Gersons 1995) and attempt to avoid such situations. They linger in a state of inner tension and excitation, or in a state of paralysis. Phases of inner excitation can alternate with phases of paralysis; both are an expression of the basic mood of anxiety. Anxiety is often coupled with the feeling that there is no way out, that all is hopeless.

The concept of posttraumatic stress disorder (PTSD), as defined in *The Diagnostic and Statistical Manual of Mental Disorders* (*DSM-IV*) (APA 1994), captures a portion of the many-sided psychic consequences of trauma. Post-traumatic stress disorder has a variety of physical equivalents. These include persistent elevated alertness (hypervigilance), with associated changes in breathing, heart rate, gastrointestinal function, and urogenital function, on the one hand, and persistent muscular tension, on the other. Muscular tension leads to pain in the region of muscle groups and nerve supply areas—for example, in the region of the laryngeal spinal column and of the head or the region of the lumbar vertebral column. Pain leads reflexively to countertension and this, in turn, to renewed pain, so that these events continue in a kind of vicious circle. Psychogenic pains can, however, also arise without muscular tension; it is as though they are stored at a central location in the brain. They can be triggered by associated stimuli, memories, experiences, or actions.

Bodily disorders in organ systems and in the skeletal system are therefore partly determined by persistent reaction to stress. Their source may also lie in failed attempts at processing traumatic experiences, and they are a kind of attempt at processing conflicts not otherwise soluble for the person at this moment of consciousness and in this real situation. Within the realm of organ systems, "instead-of" reactions develop. Bodily reactions take place, behind which split-off psychic contents hide themselves or try to find an outlet in this manner.

The emotional life of human beings is fundamentally bound up with bodily reactions in the neuromuscular system and the realm of involuntary functions. Every one of us surely is familiar with physical sensations in moments of sadness, before tears well up and bring relief. Bodily reactions like these also take place when emotions remain unconscious or ill humor persists.

In this way, persistent disorders in psychic equilibrium can impair the run-

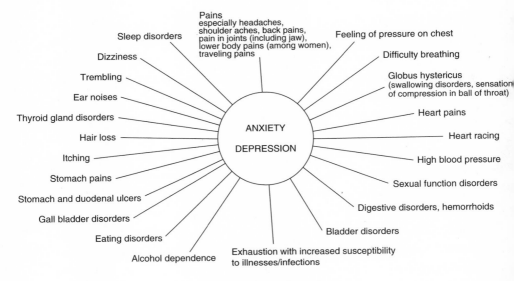

Figure 3. Frequent psychosomatic reactions to trauma

ning equilibrium (homeostasis) of the internal organs. Neurological and humoral processes (mediated by hormones, tissue hormones, chemical messengers in the blood, and other bodily fluids) that take part in the transmission of psychic processes within the body then lead to changes in tissues and organs. On the physical level, over time, persistent posttraumatic stress reactions and lack of sleep lead to a weakening of the immune system, so that the organism becomes more vulnerable. The constant release of epinephrine brought about by a permanent state of physiological alertness can lead to a weakening of recovery processes in the organ systems, so that these become more susceptible to disorders.

In figure 3, the psychosomatic disorders we most frequently encounter among our patients are summarized. They are mostly the physical equivalent of anxiety and depression, and they often include feelings of impermissible rage. Aggression, self-defense, and hate would be adequate reactions against the tormentors. The tormentors, however, are not within reach, and the feelings are too overwhelming. They are ultimately directed back toward the victim's self.

Aggravation of Symptoms by Constant Updating of the Trauma

In a setting where the traumatic situation is reawakened in the form of nightmares and internal images, the result is a permanent updating and expansion of anxieties (see fig. 2). Retraumatizations—for example, owing to xenophobic assaults on foreigners, humiliations in the context of their situation as asylum applicants, or news from the press and by telephone about the ongoing war in the homeland, as well as concern about those who remained behind—add to patients' inability to achieve inner peace while constantly demanding the maintenance of defensive postures. The interplay between posttraumatic stress disorder and retraumatizations such as these is thus a vicious circle, aggravating and extending symptoms. The treatment of traumatized refugees is made more difficult because they most often find themselves in a condition of persistent traumatization.

In the course of therapy, the young Kurdish patient mentioned above (Patient B) was able to unburden and stabilize herself somewhat. Following a police inspection in her hostel—which was not even meant for her, but during which a policeman broke into her apartment—there was a renewed exacerbation of her ailments. In her dreams, figures now surfaced mixing the shape of the torturers with the features of German police. She lost all hope of being secure here. The insecurity and mistrust extended over several sessions to include those of us providing treatment as well. Weeks later the patient, noticeably pale, showed up for treatment again; she had also lost a lot of weight. She had received a report that the fields in her native village had been burned down and the entire harvest destroyed, and that her parents had been threatened several times. She described her condition this way: "I sit at the table and tell myself: you have to eat. But I can't get a single bite down. Always I see the burning fields in front of me. It's as if my heart were burning"—at this point she clutches the region of her heart—"and sometimes I have that feeling, again, that I can't get any air." Then she paints a picture showing the burning fields and her parents' house. I asked her about the little black figures in the house and on the roof. "Those are soldiers that have broken into my home."

The house may also be understood as a picture of the whole of her body and soul. The soldiers and torturers have gained entry into this house; she has lost her boundaries, and she no longer determines what goes on in her abode. It appears as though she has internalized her tormentors and lost her autonomy.

Retracing the Vestiges

It becomes evident how complex and multilayered the meaning of symptoms displayed by survivors of torture can be. The symptoms are what is visible on the outside, while their roots reach deep into the psyche. There is certainly no one whom such extreme experiences would leave unmarked. In therapy we retrace these vestiges in order to recognize the meaning and dynamic of the person's symptoms in a joint effort between patient and therapist. It is a matter of returning those parts of the psyche into conscious perception which were expressed in bodily symptoms or in psychic symptomatology, to find new opportunities for solutions. In therapy, relief gained by articulating the previously unspoken is often an essential step. To understand that the symptom is a completely normal reaction to a wholly abnormal experience can be a second helpful step. The person thereby remains less of a victim of his pain and of his unacceptable life history. He feels accepted as a human being who has understandable reactions shared by many other human beings. The precondition for lasting change, however, is to admit and express the feelings that were threatening up to now. The conflict bound up with the symptom then has the opportunity of finding other pathways to a solution than expression in the body or through psychic symptomatology. Preconditions to work one's way through traumatic experiences are the construction of a relationship of trust between the person providing treatment and the patient, and the joint detection and promotion of inner resources that the patient had developed before traumatization but that were shattered. During this construction, the patient must also find support in a more stable social situation, for this is the fundamental precondition for healing.

When we observe how torture means to destroy the subject, to disintegrate the personality, it becomes clear how difficult it is to find a path toward healing. Forgetting is not possible, although it might be possible to form a kind of scar, making what was experienced less painful. The scar tissue will probably remain sensitive, and small wounds can lead to renewed breaking and entering. It is a matter of finding new paths toward equilibrium, allowing for greater freedom of action, for the assumption of relationships with fellow human beings, and for a turn toward the future. It may be possible, after working through the torture survivor's past, to build a future and to live with less pain. The earlier the opportunity to process the traumatic experiences presents itself, the better the prospects of finding a pathway toward a new equilibrium.

CHAPTER FOUR

"In My Fingertips I Don't Have a Soul Anymore"

Body Psychotherapy with Survivors of Torture— Insights into Work with Concentrative Movement Therapy

Sylvia Karcher

Coming to terms with the recent history of the National Socialist crimes my own people committed is an essential aspect of my personal background when it comes to working therapeutically with people who have been persecuted, locked up, tortured, and nearly killed because of their political, religious, or cultural identity. The Third Reich and the systematic extermination of human beings linked with it are my parents' history. I do not have to assume responsibility for what happened and what people failed to do. But, as a member of the second generation, I do feel an obligation to be especially attentive to human life and to preserve its dignity and inviolability.

Our therapeutic work with extremely traumatized persons is based on physicians' and psychotherapists' experiences with survivors of the Holocaust in the Netherlands, Poland, Israel, Norway, the United States, and Germany. They have described in detail the delayed consequences, mental and physical, for concentration camp survivors, especially their heightened mental vulnerability, as well as the impact of traumatization within the parents' generation on the next generation and, frequently, on the one after that. We can confirm their experiences based on our work with survivors of torture and their traumatized children.

The Effects of Trauma

"In my fingertips I don't have a soul anymore" is how a Kurdish patient in our treatment center described his numb fingers. He had been tortured with electroshock applied to the ends of his fingers. In the world of his imagination, body and soul are one. The body is ensouled down to the fingertips.

In its simplicity and clarity, this patient's statement contains the entire drama and destruction that torture is capable of causing in the life of a human being: *the loss of unity in body and soul.* This is what physiotherapy and body psychotherapy as represented by the Concentrative Movement Therapy work with.

The body as the place where the soul resides is significantly injured and violated by torture. The body's boundaries, which are simultaneously the boundaries of the ego, are no longer respected. Torturers forced their way into the innermost recesses of the human being, not just at a symbolic level, but in a completely real sense, too, for example, by inserting objects into bodily orifices.

The tortured person becomes the victim of an overwhelming power that threatens his life, the life that is in the hands of the torturer. The person abandoned in this way falls into a condition of absolute dependence, comparable to the situation of an infant, which is what he was at the beginning of this life. In contrast to that earlier condition, however—where, as a rule, he was loved, cared for, held, and carried, and where, as a result, he was able to develop a sense of security, trust, and positive feelings about the body—now there is no one there who responds. Now physical touching means suffering injuries, and in this desperate situation he is not picked up and taken into protective arms. The destruction threatening him creates an existential anxiety, and eventually he exhibits severe regressive symptoms. The person affected loses his feeling of self-worth and no longer feels at home inside himself. He experiences the destruction of body and soul, and thus of his identity.

These destructive feelings and traumatic experiences remain engraved in body and soul as a dammed-up horror. They leave behind traces and are stored in bodily memory. It is against this background that the symptoms of patients have to be understood and treated.

Psychological and Physical Symptoms

Torture always happens at both the psychological and the physical level, which is why psychological and somatic complaints can hardly be separated from each other. This also corresponds to our integrated image of the human being and the way we understand therapy.

As a consequence of physical torture methods—beatings, forcing the body into painful postures, hanging by the arms and legs, electroshock torture, and rape—*pain* is the main focus. Of the patients seeking out our treatment center, eighty-seven percent complain about symptoms of pain that are localized in the muscular, skeletal, and joint system. Even pain in the inner organs often accompanies disorders in the motor apparatus.

Headaches can result from the impact of blows to the head and the cervical spinal column (e.g., whiplash trauma or cranial trauma). Most often, however, our patients have tension headaches resulting from bracing in the musculature of the neck. These headaches could also have taken on a life of their own, leading to dysfunctions in the cervical joints. The trigger could be sleep disorders or nightmares as well as situations of pressure and stress, such as threats of deportation. It is *as if the anxiety were breathing down the patient's neck.*

Pains also show up frequently in the region of the lumbar spinal column. Here, too, it can reach the point of malfunctions in the spinal column that cause pain and lead to serious muscular tensions. But all of the aforementioned painful conditions are usually less a result of the blows' direct impact than they are psychosomatically determined.

Pain in the calves and feet, burning sensations in the soles of the feet, and problems walking are the result of *falanga* (blows to the soles of the feet). The tissues of the calves and especially of the soles of the feet are destroyed by intense swelling in the acute phases following torture.

Additional symptoms are restricted movement caused by severe pain, disorders in motor function, circulatory disorders, and feelings of numbness. Tension in the joints of the jaw, shoulders, upper arms, and back is conspicuously frequent. Displaying tension is often the only opportunity traumatized people have for expressing rage instead of keeping it inside. It also provides protection against beatings. Even after the torture has ended, this tension continues, as if the torture were still going on.

In the case of involuntary nervous symptoms, trembling, sweating, restlessness, racing hearts, and hyperventilation are the most frequent. In addition, there are feelings of pressure in the stomach and chest, sleep disorders, anxiety, and depression with such leading symptoms as passivity, apathy, and flattened affect.

Disorders in Bodily Experience and Perception

Next to the more physically identifiable kinds of symptoms, one especially encounters disorders in bodily experience and bodily perception.

Disorders in bodily experience. Patients no longer feel at home in their body. They reject it; they don't like themselves anymore. They feel unattractive, often experiencing themselves only through pain, restlessness, and trembling. They see their scars and other traces of their wounds, feel deformed, and sense that they have lost mobility and energy. We observe their depressed mood and physical posture, their quiet voice, their insecurity about the way they present themselves to other people.

Loss of bodily perception. One of the disorders in bodily feeling is that survivors of torture can no longer sense certain parts of their body, such as their hands, feet, or even their entire body. They then become almost rigid or frozen, and they no longer have any feelings about the boundaries of their body. Helen Epstein (1990) speaks of blocking out feelings: of having survived death, only to have become one of the living dead.

Feelings of fragmentation in bodily experience. Traumatic experiences can cause the survivor to feel that parts of the body are split off. Connections between the head, arms and legs, and the rest of the body are no longer perceived. There is no emotional connection; therefore bodily feeling is fragmented.

Body image disorder. "The body image should be understood as an internal model that each person has of his body and that counts as a matrix for his bodily experience, for the ways he imagines his body, and for the way he deals

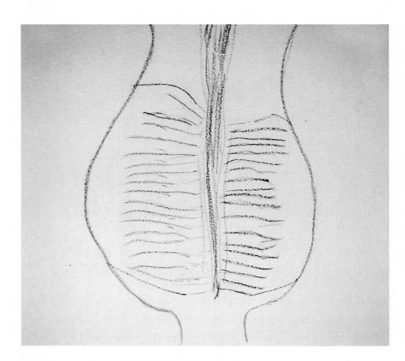

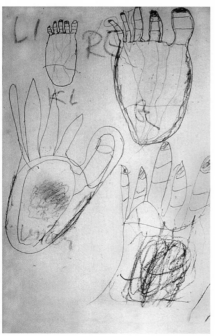

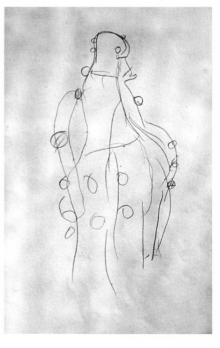

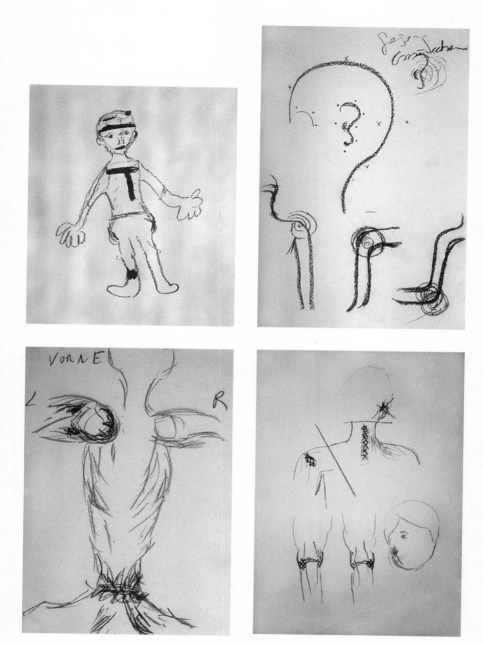

Figures 4–10. Body images

with his body actively" (Besuden 1984, 2; for a comprehensive treatment of this subject, also Budjuhn 1992).

Bodily experience, imagining the body, and dealing with one's body are interrelated. They are in constant motion and act retroactively on the body image, especially when the body has become a carrier of symptoms, as has happened with our patients.

Most of these patients have symptoms of dissociation, which can range from disorders in feeling and perception all the way to experiences of depersonalization. These conflicts and disorders can be rendered dramatically visible by creating body pictures. This can be done with body drawings or by representing the body with objects like ropes, marbles, stones, balls, wooden sticks, and so on. In this way the experience of one's own body gets expressed as well as one's emotional relationship to it, and the conflicts that led to an impairment of bodily experience become visible.

Therapeutic Goals

Judith L. Herman writes that "a definitive dissolution of trauma is just as impossible as a total cure. The victim is going to feel the aftereffects of the traumatic event for a lifetime" (Herman 1994, 303). In spite of this assertion, or perhaps because of it, what are the therapeutic goals of physiotherapy and body psychotherapy?

At first, priority is given to painful conditions in the motor apparatus. For this reason, the initial goals of treatment are alleviating pain, achieving the greatest possible freedom from pain, and restoring motion functions that had been restricted or disturbed.

However, since pain has a multifaceted meaning within the disordered equilibrium of the traumatized person's body and soul, applying measures to alleviate pain will usually not suffice. The pain shows up again, sometimes at another place within the body.

Pain is the expression and image of a psychosomatic unity in disarray, and our assignment is to comprehend this connection, which means that not only do we have to see that the pain is more than a symptom of a physical illness, but we have to understand its meaning in cooperation with the patient. This therapeutic understanding leads to the following comprehensive treatment goals:

— Perceiving the body in a differentiated way again. This means no longer just loading it with imaginary notions and fantasies but comprehending and getting to know oneself as a physical reality. For example, anchored in the imagination of many patients is a picture of their feet swelling up exactly as they do after falanga. What frequently accompanies these bodily misconceptions is a rejection of the feet, and they keep being rejected, even today, since they are unwelcome witnesses keeping alive acts of mistreatment from back then. In therapy, hands-on work with the feet can allow memories of torture to be named, and it can also allow real and eventually new experiences to be created, so that the feet are no longer swollen, the scars are healed, and joints can move again. A new posture can result from this: "My feet are worthwhile enough to be touched and handled."

— Devoting oneself again lovingly to one's own body, including its painful spots.

— Letting the body be felt in all its liveliness, via breathing, voice, movement, energy, and creativity, so that it can be experienced positively again.

— Testing and broadening room for maneuver in movement and action.

— Finding access to "dead" zones of the body where feeling has left, to immobility and rigidity and to the traumatic experiences closely associated with these.

— Letting the body's physical boundaries be experienced, perceiving spatial boundaries, observing limitations on time.

— Working on the disordered body image by taking up intensive contact with one's own body (e.g., by touching, pressing, kneading with one's own hands or with the therapist's hands).

— Performing resource work. This can be memory work, for example, guided fantasy trips to "places of energy" in life that have remained intact, or else focusing on a place in the body that is functioning normally.

Even if it is not possible for the trauma to be dissolved and for healing to be complete, a long-term therapeutic process can at least result in getting the traumatic experiences to be increasingly integrated into the personality; in this way, mental and physical pain can also be deprived of its exclusivity. As a therapist I see my job as being someone who accompanies the patients and helps them rediscover (and then, also, to endure and to bring out) their liveliness, which is often completely buried or frozen.

Physiotherapy

To take an exact history and to set up a treatment plan—especially in order to become clear about pain, restrictions on mobility, and paralysis—knowledge from the fields of neurology, orthopedics, internal medicine, surgery, and gynecology is required. There must also be muscle testing and examinations of mental function.

All the relevant treatment methods used in physiotherapy have stood the test, at least to the extent that they are not applied in a rigid and one-sided way but are instead handled dynamically and with due attention to the patient's cultural background. By way of introduction, it is often easier to pick up on a method that is familiar to the patient from his own culture, such as yoga, for example. Among the proven physiotherapeutic treatment methods are manual therapy; treatment following Berta Bobath, a physiotherapist from Great Britain; functional movement theory, proprioceptive neuromuscular fascilitation; relaxation methods; breathing therapy; acupressure; massage; foot reflex zone massage; applications of heat and cold.

Basic methods of alleviating pain include using hot packs, massage, acupressure for relaxation or other relaxation techniques, breathing therapy, and shiatsu. Procuring devices like arch supports or special resting cushions and obtaining prosthetic care are also part of the physiotherapist's job description.

In addition to those therapeutic methods, which are predominantly functional, some proven techniques are body-related methods representing an integrative approach and spotlighting perceptions of the body. Here, too, it is not a question of exclusivity but of connecting different possibilities in a meaningful way. The integrative methods include breathing therapy following Middendorf, Feldenkrais, shiatsu, and yoga.

Concentrative Movement Therapy (CMT)

CMT is a body-related psychotherapy. It proceeds from the assumption that both mental experience and events experienced physically are stored in body memory. They are articulated in bodily experience and in the expression of the body as posture, in movement, and in behavior. They determine a person's relationship to himself and to his environment. They result in an embodied life history. These psychosomatic connections can be experienced by concentrating, that is, attentive devotion to one's own body. This kind of perceiving and moving is used as a foundation for experience and action. On the basis of cognitive models from developmental psychology, depth psychology, and learning theory, firsthand sense experience is linked to psychoanalytically oriented processing.

In the therapeutic situation, the patient is offered a space for play, activity, and experience that allows him to experience his capacity to relate to himself, to his body, and to his feelings. How to deal with the space and with time is important. Materials are used—such as balls, ropes, rods, stones, blankets, and sandbags—whose real nature (form, weight, size) allows for concrete experiences and whose symbolic content can impart a special meaning. It also becomes possible to establish experiential or behavioral room for maneuver in the patient's dealings with other people (whether in a group or in individual work with the therapist as partner).

In CMT, the patient is invited to observe or interact with the body. There is no "right" or "wrong," there are only different possible solutions. The experience with movement is important, in order to find out what is authentic, to accept it, or even (depending on the patient's own possibilities and limits) to change it. The capacity to choose and to decide can be restored and then developed further, as a prerequisite for autonomous action.

In taking notice of his own, authentic personality and its associated emotions, the patient may be able to visualize the contents of his current situation in life. But in time he may also reach the point where long-forgotten, often unconscious processes are brought up to date, processes that can sometimes reach back deep into the patient's prelinguistic past. In the protected therapeu-

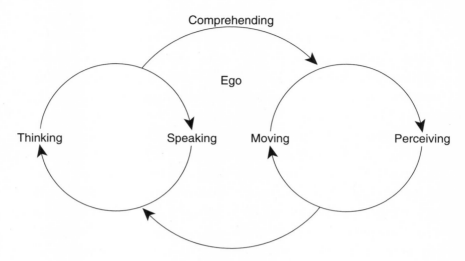

Figure 11. Regulatory cycle

tic space, the forgotten and the repressed, both pleasant and traumatic, can be reexperienced in the flesh.

The nonverbal parts of CMT are always processed in therapeutic conversation. This is when concrete bodily experiences and the perceptions and feelings associated with them need to be articulated and thus brought to the level of consciousness. It then becomes possible to place them in their proper biographical context, reflect on their meaning, and deepen them through association.

Through role-playing it is possible for the insights that have been gained to be comprehended so as to guide the patient toward new behavioral possibilities. Viktor V. Weizsäcker has given us an impressive portrait of this with his gestalt or regulatory cycle. Both "gestalts," the nonverbal one of moving and perceiving and the verbal one of speaking and thinking, are part of a larger gestalt cycle, that of comprehending. This perspective makes it possible to start out at any point along this regulatory cycle (Stolze 1989).

Concentrative Movement Therapy is especially well suited to working with extremely traumatized people, because they have experienced their traumas in a situation where they were thrown back to the level of speechlessness. What they experienced could not be expressed in language, and it also gained no hearing. It remained enclosed within the body, where it was cut off, because the dread that was experienced overtaxed all the normal defense mechanisms and left no room for maneuver. Using CMT we can reach patients at this level of speechlessness, because concentration on sensorimotor processes occurs within the nonverbal arena of perception. Feelings of anxiety, guilt, shame, and rage are blocked and cannot be expressed. These feelings are physically transformed into psychosomatic complaints, which is how they find expression. Thus CMT, which activates experience and action at the level of the body, is capable of reconnecting pain with the emotions originally associated with it. The gradual dissolution of blocks finally permits feelings to be processed and integrated into bodily experience.

CMT is, like every other psychotherapeutic procedure, something that happens in relationships. If we proceed from the assumption that healing essentially transpires in dialogic contact, then one prerequisite for therapeutic work is the establishment of a sound relationship between patient and therapist, in which it is possible for an encounter to take place.

Martin Buber, the Jewish philosopher of religion, gave persuasive expression to the concept of encounter. In his system of thought, he assigns central importance to a concept of encounter called the "dialogic principle" (Buber 1984). The basic experiences of encounter (*Begegnung*) and misencounter (*Vergegnung*)* are his points of departure. Encounter is something that encompasses two persons, not just as they meet each other but also as they experience each other, grasp each other, each with his whole being. He describes a mutuality that encompasses becoming aware of and affirming the other person in all his or her diversity and dignity. Speaking and hearing, being silent and responding, shape human togetherness. By misencounter Buber means the absence of a real relationship. Encounter, in short, happens in dialogue. It can have a healthy and therefore a healing effect, and it takes place during the growth of a trusting relationship.

In the encounter we find the place where we can confer respect and attention on the tortured person, where we can offer to go along with him as he tells his tale of suffering, trusting in our capacity to endure this with him and, in so doing, to let him see and feel us as human beings and as allies.

Recollecting the experience of helplessness and abandonment under torture

---

* The word *Vergegnung*, translated here as "misencounter," was apparently coined by Buber.—Trans.

awakens the longing for a savior. When we therapists are assigned this role, it usually comes to us with a major allowance of trust. Idealized expectations are pinned on us, which we cannot fulfill. Unconsciously, the patient senses this, and he wavers between being affectionately inclined toward us and attributing omnipotence to us, on the one hand, while showing mistrust and backing off from us, on the other. Here are two examples:

When one of our Bosnian patients embraces and kisses me after the first hourly session, which obviously did her some good, this triggers in me, quite apart from the effect of being surprised and caught off-guard, a feeling that she wants to commit herself to me, but above all that I am now forever bound to be just as good and successful as I was in this first session.

A patient from Kurdistan arrives at therapy with great expectations. Anxieties and panic attacks are tormenting him, as is a trembling that almost incessantly passes through his body. He hopes that I can make it "go away." Subsequently, every session was to have its share of disappointments. I could remove neither his anxiety nor the trembling. Only temporarily would it be possible for him to come to rest. Then he was capable of lying down, entrusting himself to the earth's solid hold, relaxing to the music of a flute, and often even falling asleep for a short time. But immediately thereafter he would ask me suspiciously why and how the things I was doing were supposed to take effect against his anxiety. He continues to have this problem. Every time he would put me to this vote of confidence. Ultimately I could not fulfill his idealized expectations. After one of these sessions he became quite enraged and accusatory. In a helpless and desperate rage he shouted at me: "Look here, see how I'm trembling. You're not helping me at all." Thereafter, for quite some time, he did not come to therapy.

Often I get the impression that my patients are subjecting my competence and capacity for coping with strain to an unconscious test. Then I seek relief through debriefing with my colleagues and through case supervision.

First Contacts

Sometimes, when I have my first contact with a patient, I let him show me on a map where his home is located. Then I ask what it looks like there and what kinds of things are grown there, and I have the patient tell me about the rivers, lakes, and mountains and describe a favorite place from childhood or from later in life.

So that I am better able to imagine all this, one patient paints me a picture of the mountains from his homeland, which are covered all over with swabs of color depicting flowers. The smell of these flowers is what he misses most of all, he says. I can understand him quite well, and I tell him about the narcissus meadow near my childhood home in Austria, in the Salzkammergut. I believe this mutual storytelling about our flower meadows has allowed a bit of trust to emerge.

As our conversation proceeds, I talk about the treatment I have in mind, which I explain with some precision. Frequently this results in an initial long discussion with questions. I take an interest in what kinds of experiences the patient has had in his lifetime, that is, with body movement or with physical immobility in his native country. With regard to the latter, what frequently occurs to the patient is something that happened during his time in prison. Or else I ask what illnesses the patient knows from his own life, and how his family dealt with them. This is often followed by a description of current pain symptoms. Sometimes, at the start of a therapy session, the focus is on the patient's current situation in life: the unbearably cramped living conditions; altercations in the refugee housing that make it impossible to get any sleep; the impending hearing; his great fear of the authorities or of deportation; reports of battles from the homeland, where family members still live and are involved. But problems with partners and difficulties with children also flow into the patient's current emotional inventory, intensifying the pains, beating the patient down, making him anxious, helpless, and apathetic.

The following example shows just how much of an immediate impact mental anguish can have in the form of physically felt pain:

One of our Bosnian patients had made it through two awful years in a Serbian camp. After she had witnessed the massacre of her parents, she fled to Germany. She is filled with anxiety and sadness, feels very sick, senses heavy pressure on her chest, and has intense pain in her right arm, extending from the shoulder down to her fingertips. When the protected zones in her homeland around Srebenica and Zepa collapse, the pain in her right shoulder becomes palpably stronger: "I am suffering with my people," are her words; "I am carrying the burden of my people on my shoulders." Each new battle, in which her brother, who remains behind, could very well be involved, causes her to have additional pain. If she is living safely here in Germany, she can't be allowed to feel well for as long as her people are suffering so. Actually, she says, I would rather be there, joining in the struggle. She is sad, and I feel powerless and helpless. I sense my own rage at this terrible war. I can reveal my feelings, and because of the way I place my feelings at her disposal, she is finally able to cry. Her rage over the loss of her parents, sister, friends, and homeland continues to lodge, all tied up as aggressive impulses, in her right shoulder, where it still is not allowed to be released. That would be too threatening, even now. At the moment all I can do is endure her sadness along with her and become someone sharing in what she knows. Since she still comes regularly to each treatment session (even though she finds everything hopeless and meaningless), I ask her if there was anything that did her good at that last session. Suddenly her attitude becomes very concrete, and she says: "The little, careful movements that you made with my right shoulder. For a little while they helped me in a good way."

For a moment there was a hint of how it could be without pain, without an inner struggle, when peace prevails again. In her body, too.

Loss and the Work of Grieving

Our patients have suffered endless losses, and they need help with grieving. Members of their families have been killed in camps, jails, or battles. By fleeing into exile, most of them have lost their village or town, their home, hearth, and work. The familiar sounds of their native language, their homeland's smells and noises, which provided safety and security, have faded. The grieving rituals that are found in every culture, and that contribute toward overcoming loss, are usually absent; either that, or a hasty escape made it impossible to carry them out.

It is repeatedly driven home to us just how important it is to grieve for losses suffered whenever we see our patients stuck in stagnation and depression, not feeling anything any longer and describing themselves as if they had been buried alive. The losses they have experienced make them speechless and immobile. Often they are closely linked to physical pains, in the back or distributed across the entire body. The psychotherapist Marie Langer speaks of "frozen grief" as the "psychic condition in which someone finds himself who has suffered a hard loss but was forced by circumstances to forgo even lamenting it. The grief is then sometimes pushed aside, where it slowly poisons both person and family" (Langer, cited in Bittenbinder 1992, 3).

The following example describes how grieving that is not carried out gets expressed in nightmares.

Mr. B., from an Eastern European country, has hemiplegia with a speech disorder as a result of beatings on the head in jail, which triggered internal bleeding. Physiotherapy takes up a significant portion of his treatment. But there are also many sessions where he arrives at therapy totally confused, incapable of getting involved in the exercises we are offering to treat the damaged right side of his body. He complains about sleep disorders and a recurring nightmare. He tells this haltingly, painstakingly searching for the words. It makes him angry that he cannot properly relate his nightmare. This changes abruptly when I finally suggest that he paint this dream. There now emerges a very precise picture of what is hounding him each night: against a midnight blue background near the window in the refugee home, he can see the head and torso of his dead friend. This friend, like him, is Jewish and was his best friend. They were together in jail. However, while Mr. B. had already found safety in exile, his friend remained in jail. Soon after the friend was finally released, he died in a mysterious auto accident. Mr. B. never had the opportunity to take leave of him and bury him. He hadn't mourned him; there was some unfinished business left over, and he wasn't even able to talk over his guilt feelings with his friend. The friend didn't leave him in peace. With the picture he had painted, Mr. B. now had a visible counterpart. Would he still like to tell him something, still ask him something?

It is a moving farewell, with lots of "Why" questions. Saying Kaddish, the Jewish mourning prayer, finally helps him to release his friend, so that the nightmares affecting the friend can cease.

The extent to which suppressed grief can solidify as pain in the body was something that became clear to me and my colleagues in a group we jointly conducted with Kurdish men. Earlier, because of their persistent pain symptoms, we had treated the patients mostly with physiotherapy and movement therapy on an individual basis, without much success. So with these men we decided to start a pain group. At the start of the first session we spread out a map of Kurdistan and let everyone mark the places they came from with brightly colored stones. And there, in front of the map, sat all these impressive men, all of whom had been forced to leave their homeland under sometimes harrowing circumstances, and the tears were flowing down their cheeks. They helped each other find all these places. A few discovered that they came from neighboring villages. A collective grieving became possible. Some had kept their pain at the loss of their homeland locked up inside them for years. Now, for the time being, it became a group of mourners, and the link between their loss and their pain suddenly became quite clear to all of us. "My pain is Kurdistan," is how one patient formulated his feeling during this session.

Body Dialogue

As soon as I consciously touch a person with my hands, I get quite close—literally, skin-close—to entering into a body dialogue with him.

The positive experiences we have in life of tenderness and pleasant touching, just like the negative ones of beatings and other abuse, have left behind memory traces in our body.

Our patients have experienced massive violations of boundaries that, in the truest sense of the word, have gotten under their skin. As a body psychotherapist, I experience a great deal of closeness to patients while I work directly on the boundaries of their bodies. Touching with my hands triggers positive and negative experiences. So the quality and the intensity of the first contact are of fundamental importance for the further course of treatment.

A first requirement, however, is the patient's consent to being touched, along with clarification about how many protective layers he needs between his body and my hands (like clothes or a blanket). It's all about careful contact through touching, lingering, and holding. Sometimes more pressure provides security, sometimes a tender touch is all that's required. This has to be found out by asking. What's important is the assurance: I'm there, you can feel me, and I comprehend something about you. The result can be a dialogic body contact, between the patient's breathing and the therapist's responsive hands, for example, or through an emerging pattern of tension or relaxation. In spite of the patient's permission to touch him, the surface of his body and musculature can clearly send out signals of defensiveness by tensing up. Mostly, however, the warmth and care of the therapist's hands are experienced as pleasant.

Examples of Treatment

The following examples of treatment relate exclusively to individual work with Concentrative Movement Therapy. It would go beyond the framework of this chapter to offer a more precise account of physiotherapeutic treatment related to the special problems of torture survivors, so I refer the interested reader to the book *Physiotherapy for Torture Survivors* (Prip and Holten 1995).

Concentrative Movement Therapy offers experiences that are oriented toward the patient's emotional state of health, as well as toward the ongoing therapeutic process. Here is an example:

One of our patients was attacked by a group of youths one morning while he was delivering newspapers. The papers were knocked out of his hand, and he was pushed against the wall while these words were uttered, "Down there's where you belong." He relates this occurrence rather unemotionally and then immediately says, "I lose my composure so easily." This topic determines the rest of the session.

I invite him to assume a body posture with which he is familiar and that makes him feel safe. He kneels and sits back on his feet, puts his hands on his knees, and describes this posture as one he knows from political discussions held at home. Then he assumes a traditional praying posture and explains some customs from his country. Suddenly he lies down on his stomach, stretches his arms forward, and says: "And this is how they dragged me away. Across the ground, over sharp stones."

By resuming the physical position in which he had been dragged away, this patient is reviving painful memories. Previously, he had never been able to talk about it, and now he is physically feeling how much this humiliating physical posture, this posture of being at someone else's mercy, has injured his dignity and how—together with the memory of being attacked while delivering the newspapers—it has also triggered the feeling, "I lose my composure so easily."

Toward the end of the session, in order to stabilize him for the trip back to the place where he lives, I work with him on his upright posture, on bringing clarity to his bone structure (which I show him by using light pressure from my hands) and also on his stability and energy.

Another approach used in Concentrative Movement Therapy is basal body work using basic experiences from human life: one's own space or place and one's experiences in lying down, sitting, standing, and walking. These invitations to therapy are not culture-bound. They represent a feasible foundation, and through their ego-stabilizing effect they are capable of providing our patients with the kind of security and matter-of-fact quality that has frequently been lost to them.

To have a place of one's own in life is something very fundamental for us human beings. To be at the right or wrong place, to have picked this place or have it assigned to oneself—this has an impact on our feeling of self-worth and well-being, and on our room for maneuver.

For our patients, this topic is often bound up with many difficulties.

"Take a blanket for yourself, look for a place in this room, and then spread out your blanket there." Frequently, when we issue this invitation, what occurs to the patients is their real-life situation: the place assigned to them in the refugee house, where they often have to share a narrow room with several people. What belongs to them is just a bed, 0.90 × 2 meters.

Sometimes patients are unable to find a place after they hear us ask them to pick one. They ask me where they should put down their blanket, and I encourage them to test things out. *"You can pick a place by the window, near the door, in the middle of the room, in a corner, or maybe a completely different spot will occur to you. Try out different places and then decide which one is right for today."*

Regaining autonomy is what it is all about. In the protected therapeutic space, it is possible to try out alternatives and rediscover what's good. The patients develop ideas and perspectives about their own spaces, whose content they can then shape. By playful experimentation, imagination and creativity can be stimulated.

By asking "What kind of place did I choose?," memory work can be evoked. For example, Mr. S., a patient from Ethiopia who had spent twelve years in jail, picked a small rectangular spot in the darkest corner of the room. The same size as a cell, as he later told me. I prompt, *"What body posture would I like to assume at my place? Do I want to be lying down, sitting, standing?"* Mr. S. is crouching in a shrinking posture on the blanket, his hands coiled around his knees, his gaze fixed on the door. The memories have caught up with him, and in a quiet voice he takes me along for a visit to his experiences in the cell. The horrors he experienced there can be seen in his body posture. They are literally seated in his bones, even though his time in jail lies several years back. For the first time in a long while he can give in to his old anxieties that he will be destroyed and talk about them. Slowly, the tensions in his body can dissolve. Later it becomes possible for me to suggest that he take me up on an extended offer, an invitation to connect his memory of the jail cell to his present situation.

"Is there something that you would like to change right here, at this place?" Mr. S. stands but doesn't move from his spot. To me, he looks if he were surrounded. I notice very tiny movements of his feet, which I grasp: *"Are there impulses in your body making you want to move? Try seeing what it's like to follow them."* Cautiously, Mr. S. shifts his feet across the blanket and slowly starts to walk, within the confines of his blanket. He notices that there's not much room to walk. *"What can I do so that I have as much room as I need at the moment?"* Mr. S. remains within the confines of his blanket as he walks to and fro.

During the verbal processing, it becomes clear to him how much he had incorporated his tiny prison room. He experienced it bodily in walking to and fro. He can understand and transfer its meaning onto his current life: at the moment it's not possible for him to get involved with anything new or unknown. He still needs the protective space of his own boundaries; it would be too soon to step out of them.

As treatment proceeds, during the next therapy session, body work in a lying position might be indicated for Mr. S., where the theme is how to be aware of the body's inner spaces.

I often observe not only how our patients fail to take up enough external space for themselves but also how they feel internally constricted and how they are barely able to spread themselves out physically. The protective posture assumed under torture—which is visible in shoulders that are drawn forward, a head that is drawn in, and a body posture that is bent over—has usually become physically ossified. Breathing movements, too, are barely perceptible. It appears as if these people hardly dare to take in air properly.

One possibility for experiencing the body's inner spaces is to take a guided body trip, in which breath becomes the signpost. The journey can be undertaken either seated or while lying on the floor. A floor offers the body an optimal space for support; its solidity, as a rule, provides reinforcement and security.

I address the floor as a buttressing ground, along which it is possible to feel the body's resting points and even to feel one's own weight. Different body postures can be assumed. So I encourage patients to make themselves as small or as large as possible, at any given moment, in a position on the stomach, back, or side. I inquire: *"What's pleasant? What kind of body posture do I already know on my own? What seems strange to me?"* Enlarging oneself, extending oneself, and taking up space with arms and feet is something unfamiliar to our patients. Becoming small provides more protection and is less obtrusive.

Following this introductory preparation I encourage patients to lie on their backs, and I draw attention to the breath: *"Notice your breath, how it flows through the nose, spreads out in the cavity of your mouth and throat, flows back into the chest cavity, and escapes again."* The breathing movement can be detected by laying hands (one's own or the therapist's) on the rib cage or belly. The body's inner spaces can be experienced by the breath as it expands and contracts. To feel breath this consciously can make it possible to experience a sense of one's own liveliness.

I further encourage patients to imagine that their breath can spread out farther: into the joints of their shoulders, across the upper and lower arms and all the way down to their fingertips. In their imagination, their breath should be floating through the entire body, from the stomach cavity into the pelvic cavity, into the thighs, the hollows of the knees, down to the tips of their toes.

I wrap up the body work by inviting my patients to sprawl, expand, and stretch. Sprawling and expanding can trigger yawning impulses; it becomes possible for tension surrounding the joints in the jaw to loosen up, and the cavities of the mouth and throat can open up.

"Stay a while in a position you find pleasant now. While you're lying there now, try to sense what the feeling of your body is, how you're breathing." Patients then often experience themselves as wider or even warmer and have the feeling that they have more room to breathe. "I've become much bigger now inside," said one patient shortly after this exercise. Externally, too, most patients will have spread out more.

Boundaries determine our room for maneuver and our radius of action. To be internally constricted means to be incapable of developing in one's environment and to be incapable of seizing space. The experience of opening up inside through breathing and of sensing all the contexts related to this in the body has a benevolent and satisfying quality, because it enables an experience of wholeness.

The transition from lying, through sitting, to standing can be followed consciously each step along the way, something even an infant has to try out until he's capable of standing. Standing up requires abandoning the broad supportive space provided by a floor. In standing, only the tiny spaces on the soles of the feet are connected to the floor.

"How do I experience the floor? Is it hard? soft? cold? warm?" "How much of a load are my feet capable of bearing?" "How steady do I seem?" "How am I standing there?" "How broad or small is my stance, how firm or mobile?"

Frequently there are answers to these questions like: "My feet are hurting me; I can't stand." "My knees tremble when I stand." "I lose my balance when I stand." "I can't hold myself up on my legs."

Statements like this have as much to do with the mental pain preventing a firm, secure stance as with insecurity and the absence of a firm hold. Among our patients, pain in the feet is usually the result of blows to the soles of the feet. Before work is done on getting the patient to develop a conscious stance, therefore, it is necessary to undertake a physiotherapeutic treatment that has a supportive and stabilizing impact on the feet and where supportive measures are undertaken for damaged arches. So that the patients can recover greater access to their damaged feet, I invite them at the outset to take one of their feet into their hands and make it the special object of their concern. This allows them to discover softness, roughness, the parts of the foot that are angular and sensitive, as well as swellings and all the in-between spaces. This foot can now be perceived in a new light. Contrasting this foot with the one left untouched, the patient can now feel how handling the foot has perhaps rendered it warmer, clearer, more expansive, livelier. After this discovery is made, the other foot can be explored.

Scars, deformities, changes in the skin, and hardened arteries often act as reminders of maltreatment. Sometimes the feet were so badly wounded that patients could only crawl for weeks on end or had to be carried by fellow inmates. What remains is a feeling of feet that are unloved, that would be better off not being felt at all, as well as the experience of not being able to walk properly anymore. Taking feet into one's hands, consciously and perhaps even lovingly, or feeling them through the therapist's hands, can be a first step toward ceasing to reject them and slowly coming to accept them instead, as something belonging to the patient and deserving to be integrated into the life of the body. Afterward it is usually easier to stand on one's feet and experience a stance that is secure.

In body work, standing on one's own feet consciously means, in the first instance, giving special attention to the feet's connection with the ground. Sometimes I invite patients to imagine a big tree with roots that reach deep down into the earth, so that the tree is securely anchored. But standing is not just a static occurrence; instead, maintaining equilibrium is a constant balancing act. One precondition is mobility in individual joints. Thus, when I invite patients to try out their own mobility, it means, "How much room for maneuver do I have in my ankle joints, in my knees, and in my hip joints?" Then I guide patients up farther, toward the pelvis, spinal column, shoulders, and the movements of the head.

In this playful experimentation with loosening and holding on tight to the joints, it is possible to experience both the flowing, permeable interplay of joints and rigidity, immobility, and the emergence of tensions whenever the joints are blocked. This can be an important experience: the ability to exert influence via self-initiated movements, so as to stop being immobile and to use body movements as a way of noticing how what is rigid starts to stir.

The prerequisite for being capable of standing up to other people or other demands is the ability to feel one's own footing. In our body, the structure that gives us security is the hardness and firmness of our skeleton. Consciously taking cognizance of this internal scaffolding is also a part of basal bodily experience. This is made possible by experiencing mobility in the joints or by trying out this exercise: bending over consciously and then, slowly and from bottom to top, straightening up. In this way the back can be experienced for its support-giving function, and the spinal column felt as an internal brace. In our language we express this with sayings like, Human beings have backbone, or Their backbone has been broken.

However, when pain in the back or in the feet is in the foreground, bending over and straightening back up are usually not possible. Then it becomes a matter of testing out how much support the back needs in order to become more pain-free. It becomes a matter of thinking over, together with the patient, where and when he can obtain support in everyday life. One Kurdish father gave a detailed account of how much he needed support for his back. He lived with five of his six children in Berlin; his wife, together with the youngest child, was still back in Turkey, sitting in jail. Taking care of his five children completely overwhelmed him. His back constantly hurt, and he asked about getting a supportive corset. In the follow-up sentence he said, "Because my wife isn't here yet." Here, for the time being, the spotlight was on exonerating himself and his family. The next step, then, was to find out how much support and stability he still had inside himself.

Taking a *first step* from the position of a secure stance means agreeing to participate in the fluctuation of holding and letting go. To initiate this interplay oneself—and therefore to experiment with leaving a secure location and heading on a journey of discovery into the room—is repeatedly a test of courage for our patients. Going into motion—and thereby taking up space step by step—has a direct connection to the patient's everyday world. In the symbolic action of standing and walking, autonomy is tested, as is detachment, ultimately from the therapeutic relationship, too.

Ending Treatment

The question of when to conclude treatment is also a question about when it is possible to leave the sheltered therapeutic space. This theme preoccupies us over and over again, in individual therapy as in teamwork with colleagues, and occasionally in case supervision too.

An impressive answer to this question was recently given us by Mr. S. from Ethiopia. He was one of our first patients in the Treatment Center, and several staff members had a warm relationship with him. We all took a lively interest in the many highs and lows we shared with him across the period of nearly three years during which he was a regular among us. Little by little, things got better for him, mentally as well as physically. He became more independent and established social contacts. But we let him leave only reluctantly. During a period when he had no longer had any physical complaints, I decided, after consultation with my colleagues who were also treating him, gradually to end his physical therapy. The patient responded by incurring a knee injury. He had an operation on the meniscus and had to keep visiting me for several weeks of postoperative treatment. Limping on two crutches, he demonstrated how he was still not able to walk. For him, as for me, the weeks that followed were very intensive, and they were important when it came to feeling out and working through what it means to stand and walk independently. To be sure, all that had already been tried, but apparently it wasn't enough. In the meantime—with the beginnings of emotional distance already foreshadowing his impending departure and often with considerable humor—he had gotten into a good position to reflect on the extension of therapy he had chosen for himself. One day he showed up, brandishing his crutch in front of him like a marionette, put the crutch in the corner, and said that now he could walk on his own, without crutches. Both sides, now, were ready to let go. From time to time, he still comes to the center for a visit and a recharge.

CHAPTER FIVE

The Frozen Lake

Gestalt Therapy Dreamwork with Torture Victims

Sibylle Rothkegel

When I told my colleagues at the Treatment Center about my special interest in gestalt therapy dreamwork, and when I asked them to pay attention to our patients' dreams and then collect them for me, an interesting thing happened: at first my colleagues offered me a profusion of dreams that they had themselves dreamed during the period when they were working with their tortured patients. On the surface, these dreams were usually about conflicts in the team, and so their themes (violation of boundaries, discrimination, debasement, power and powerlessness, persecution, danger, violence, and death) bore a close resemblance to our patients' dreams. This clearly shows how the physical and mental injuries our patients have suffered can crop up as feelings and images among us, and how they can have a destructive impact on us if we don't watch out for them. We can also regard our dreams as attentive advisers urging us to take care and watch out for ourselves. "Sleep watching" is what "dreaming" means in Persian when it is translated literally. The Persians believe that the soul goes traveling during dreams. Dreams often lead us into alien or even familiar places and landscapes, to strange, exciting, perhaps even alarming encounters, and sometimes into a fairy-tale-like world replete with images and symbols (Dieckmann 1978).

Throughout human history, dreams have fascinated us because of their puzzling, attractive, or threatening nature. Artists, philosophers, and scholars have attempted to track down their hidden meaning and have variously interpreted their content (depending on the cultural context) as God's revelation, as a foreboding of the future, and as an opportunity for self-knowledge. The history of dream interpretation begins with attempts to understand dreams, not as a psychological phenomenon, but as real experiences of a soul detached from its body or as the voice of ghosts and spirits. In Eastern cultures, the dream was interpreted according to a fixed religious and ethical frame of reference. Early Oriental dream interpretation was based on the premise that the dream represented a message that human beings were receiving from godlike powers who were including these humans in making important decisions. In India and Greece, especially, it was believed that dreams could predict illnesses, that certain symbols referred to certain somatic symptoms. Aristotle emphasized the rational side of dreams. He assumed that we have a more refined ability to perceive subtle bodily processes while sleeping, and that we are preoccupied with plans and rules of proper conduct more clearly recognized in dreams than during the day. The Talmud contains an ingeniously elaborated theory of dreams. There were supposed to have been twenty-four professional dream interpreters in Jerusalem at the time of Jesus. Thus, preoccupation with the symbolism or meaning of dreams goes back to ancient times, and it was taken for granted in a wide range of cultures. But dream interpretation has lost its status in the modern West. Here patients from different cultures have much to teach us, and we can use their own beliefs about the essence of dreams to expand on our ideas.

Work with dreams was something Fritz Perls accorded a very special meaning in his concept of therapy. He viewed the dream as an existential message—"from yourself to yourself"—and in it he saw more than an unsettled situation, more than an unfulfilled wish, and more than just a prophecy. He used the concept of "dreamwork," and he understood this term to mean work *with* dreams rather than Freud's definition meaning something accomplished by the dream itself; with his approach ("Every dreamer is everything in his dream") Perls created something obviously practical for dreamwork.

Freud called dreams the *via regia,* the royal road, to the unconscious; Perls, by contrast, emphasized that work with dreams was the *royal road to integration.*

For him, the dream was the most spontaneous expression of the human being, and he viewed all the different parts of a dream as fragments of our personality.

The origin of the word *therapy* is Greek and means "healing" (among other things). For myself, therapy is also about surrounding people with care and thereby supporting them in an effort to become as healed as possible. The word *healed* (*heil*) means "whole," so healing actually means "to make whole." If therapy is linked to wholeness, this does not imply perfection, just completeness. Our longing for wholeness is the need to reassemble something that was split. So therapy aims for an inner unity that remains conscious of the ruptures and conflicts of human existence (Wirtz 1989). Gestalt therapy dreamwork can offer one kind of assistance here, since we can use it to fit together different parts of a dream and therefore discover (or maybe even reclaim) projected portions of the personality. This also means that it is possible for dreamers to discover and experience in the therapeutic process a potential previously available to them, although repressed.

In gestalt therapy work, dreams usually are not interpreted. This strikes me as extremely important in any context involving different cultures and value systems or in treating the severely traumatized. Not only does the difference in access to knowledge and power between therapist and patient recall childhood situations and awaken needs for guidance and protection; it also recalls the experience of total disparity in power and powerlessness experienced during torture. We therapists have to be aware that we are often granted a great deal of power by our patients, since they already feel especially powerless by virtue of their difficult situation as asylum seekers in a foreign country. Torture victims' extreme need for dependence can easily tempt therapists into assuming a commanding role. We can assume that our patients are usually not in a position to reject our interpretations; as a rule, patients will "swallow" them and therefore add additional introjections to the countless ones already there. ("An introjection is a lesson that you swallowed whole without understanding it—for example, because it comes from an authority—and that you now apply as if it were your own" [Perls, Heferline, and Goodman 1951]).

Gestalt therapy is a phenomenological method. One of its basic principles is working in the here and now, which means that disorders in the therapeutic process that show up immediately in the process of contact (contact with the therapist, with the topic currently being handled, with the therapeutic situation, with the room, etc.) are made conscious and visible. The spotlight is always on the patient's holistic experience, by way of emotional actualization. Gestalt therapy has developed different techniques in order to support the experience of feelings like shame, grief, hate, and even joy (but also opinions, attitudes, and convictions).

With dreamwork it is very important to examine carefully and precisely what kind of contact there is between patient and therapist and whether it suffices as a basis for working on a very burdensome trauma. If there are disorders in the patient-therapist relationship, it must be a priority to start working on them right away; only then can the real dreamwork begin.

This is especially important when it comes to working with severely traumatized people, because our patients are usually no longer in any position to feel or even maintain their own boundaries after the severe violations of boundaries they have experienced. Only when a sound relationship with the therapist has been cultivated can work begin on these profound violations. People have to be offered the security of knowing that this process is *theirs,* that *they* can determine when they are ready to accept what they have experienced. In research on treating victims of extreme violence, it is often mentioned—and this squares with my own experience—that victims of violence are usually only able to endure therapy when it proceeds in a stepwise fashion. It is frequently difficult for our patients, some of whom have been at the disposal of others for years, to be responsible for themselves. Their tendency has been to learn to abdicate responsibility, and they try to repeat this pattern in therapy (Wirtz 1989). When a boundary is crossed, it is usually perceived too late; we therapists have to be especially attentive and patient about supporting our patients' efforts at assuming responsibility and authority over themselves. Connection plays a very important part in our work. When the therapist pays attention to the patient, when she repeatedly allows him to test whether he really is ready and able to subject himself to or relive burdensome material, the patient experiences this attention as caring and respect. This way, too, it can prove useful just to leave a tormenting nightmare undisturbed, or to put it away symbolically in a corner somewhere, all wrapped up as a package, or simply to bury it.

The boundaries limiting our patients' mental and physiological capacity to cope need to be respected, because their pain can reach a degree of intensity almost exceeding the limit of what can be endured. For some, feelings of shame can be harder to withstand than rage or grief. I believe this aspect can be easily overlooked. Under certain circumstances, a therapeutic intervention can result in a renewed traumatization (Wirtz 1989). Therapeutic guidance requires us to have a great deal of sensitivity if we are going to be attentive and watch out for that moment when it becomes possible for a patient to integrate unfinished and disturbed gestalts into his life, so that we can then go on to gauge the proper dosage for our subsequent interventions.

The long-range traumatic effects of experiencing violence include recurring nightmares, which can lead to sleeplessness when the patient is afraid of dreaming. Patients frequently report waking up at night screaming, drenched in sweat and heart racing. In their dreams they relive, in a tormented fashion, scenes of torture and persecution that really took place. These dreams often guide patients toward us, and they indicate that the time has come to start treating the effects of these traumatic experiences, since the patient's defense mechanisms have apparently stopped working. At this point I can support patients in their effort to articulate as many details as they can (and in whatever way they can) about their experiences with violence. This can happen by telling stories, but also by acting out, screaming or emitting other sounds, or even painting.

In principle, when a patient has a weakened ego structure, the focus is not on processing his traumatic experiences but on strengthening the ego function. What is at stake is restructuring his backup system (of support) and helping the patient discover supportive functions of his own; put differently, it is primarily a question of how to stabilize. According to Kernberg (1978), the extent to which we delve into the problem depends on the extent to which the patient can bear to examine reality. Many of our patients suffer from symptoms that bear at least a resemblance to the diagnosis of borderline personality disorder. In this case I do not use the method of dream interpretation which I specify later on; rather, I build cognitive and structured elements into the therapy itself and, therefore, into the dreamwork as well. I devote special attention to strengthening the patient's autonomy and to helping him differentiate boundaries between himself and others.

Since dreams are always linked both to an individual life history and to the momentary situation in which the dreamer finds himself, there can be no standard meaning for any special symbol occurring in a dream. A particular object in a dream means something different to everyone and must be seen in the context of both the dream and the dreamer. Furthermore, it is very important to take into account the different cultural backgrounds of patient and therapist.

So, for example, the image of a dog in a dream can have a completely different meaning for a German than for a Middle Eastern person who belongs to the Islamic religious faith. As a child growing up in a rural area, I always wanted a dog but never got one. In my fantasies, I always imagined this dog as a steadfast friend who roamed through fields and meadows with me, with whom I could practice stunts, maybe even appearing in public with him so I could earn money, and who would accompany and protect me in the evening on my way back home through the dark woods. Had I encountered this loyal friend and protector in a dream, for me he would have symbolized (among other things) an unfulfilled wish; yet he would simultaneously have been standing in the way of a longing for autonomy. In Muslim beliefs, however, the dog represents something unclean, which a devout Muslim may not allow into his house. In the Arabic linguistic region, it is a terrible insult to utter the curse, "You dog, son of a bitch!" By working on his dream image about one dog, Mr. B. from Baghdad was able (among other things) to get at his feelings of grief, rootlessness, and debasement as a victim: "I am no longer in my house, and I do not know where my mother is. I must be submissive and conform completely. That is what I had to do in jail, when I was tortured, and here in exile I also feel like a dog that has to conform unconditionally. I feel impure and filthy as a result of what happened to me. Anybody can hit me and throw me out of the house."

As previously mentioned, Perls viewed the different parts of a dream as fragments of our personality: afterward we take the parts of our personality that usually get split off, or the feelings we experienced while dreaming, and project them onto other people, animals, objects, moods, or colors. This is why we work with the method of identification in gestalt therapy. We ask patients to imagine themselves as the objects that show up in their dreams and to describe these as precisely as possible using the ego-form. The aim of this experiment is to observe elements of a dream as aspects of one's own existence, ultimately in order to integrate them slowly, that is, to reconnect them with the patient's own feelings of aggression and the need for power, but also grief and joy. The dream sequence to be selected and presented can be the dreamer's own choice. If certain dream elements end up being ignored, I draw attention to them and attempt to help the patient discover whether some kind of avoidance is going on. Sometimes it helps to simply label them as such. In dealing with extremely burdensome dreams, it is necessary to structure the dreamwork, initially by using the technique of identification to experience and gain access to those dream elements that are less burdensome and that can offer the dreamer support. For example, when it is time to work on his dream, Mr. M. from Uganda—who dreams that he is being chased by soldiers shooting wildly all around him—can initially withdraw into a mud house, so that he can watch this menacing scene from a protected space.

In our second treatment session, Mr. O. from northern Kurdistan—who (like many of his neighbors, friends, and family members from a village in the mountains of his homeland) had been severely tortured by the Turkish military—brought me a recurring dream that was tormenting him greatly: "From my neck on down, I'm frozen in a lake. All around me, there's nothing but ice; only my head juts out." In the hope of finding any element that might prove supportive, I inquired after more details, and Mr. O. was then able to recognize his mountains, far off in the distance and quite pale, in his dream image. He narrated this dream completely listlessly, without any recognizable feeling, so that I began to shiver. At this point in our therapeutic relationship and in our process of establishing a connection, I decided—simply and silently, as in the dream—to cover him with a warm woolen blanket. He looked at me with astonishment, and his eyes filled with tears. This was how the ice in our relationship started to melt a little bit. In different sessions over the course of a year, we gave all the elements of this dream their due regard, and I would like to characterize his treatment's progress as a long, continuous melting of ice, interrupted by periods of recurring frost.

In order to shape dreamwork in a meaningful way, it is necessary to ask about triggering or embedding events, that is, to ask about the patient's overall situation in life. What are the foremost themes? What are the impending events; which ones just happened? What night was it when the dream was dreamed, and what was the feeling upon waking up? Every dream contains many aspects and possibilities for processing. Getting back to Mr. O.: Water is regarded as a universal symbol, because it is common to people everywhere; Carl Jung, whose dream theory is the basis for gestalt dreamwork, characterized it as archetypal. Water sustains our lives, and in the history of life it represents the basis for the evolutionary process. The connection to water is both physical and mental. The ice in Mr. O.'s dream image symbolized a frozen life, frozen feelings—an emotional anesthesia, so that unbearable pain did not have to be noticed, so that grief about the loss of homeland and family members did not have to be felt. Many tears remained unwept. In the dream, the living head jutted out of the ice, and this is a telling picture: it could not relax from its vigilance. In a later session, to which Mr. O. came straight from the welfare office, he made an association (from his position in the frozen lake) with this thought: "I just stand there all paralyzed while I am given the ice-cold treatment by the caseworker, and I can't even express myself. But in my head I know that I have to endure this, and that I can't get away." Another time: "When I came to Germany, the first thing that happened is that I got a shock; everything was so strange and so cold. I couldn't move; I felt all frozen up. Sometimes I didn't meet a single human being; I still can't speak German, and from time to time I feel quite lonely. My homeland seems so far away, so that I can barely see it, like the mountains in my dream." *"At first you spoke about the past. In your dream image it was winter, and everything was frozen. When you now walk into the image, what does it look like? Because the seasons change; when there's ice, I think of thawing."*

Mr. O., who in the meantime had starting living with some of his fellow countrymen, began describing how the ice tightly surrounding him had begun to melt a little, and how he was already able to discover a bird that was supposed to bring him news. At the next appointment, he related the bad news, and the frost set in again: "I feel like a dead man who is still living in his head. I just received a notice from the Federal Office for the Recognition of Foreign Refugees that they intend to reject my application for asylum; that means they don't believe what I said at my hearing. I wish I could be in the lake of my dream; my head should also freeze." With this image he was alluding to thoughts of suicide, which as a pious Muslim he dared not openly articulate.

In the following sessions, in my therapeutic work I also fell back on his religious faith to give him support, until Mr. O. finally received justice from the Administrative Court and was awarded asylum. Since the right to asylum does not give anyone a new homeland but merely represents a juridical right to live in exile, he now must slowly learn to accept that the mountains are going to remain far off in the distance; however, he can always zoom in on this inner image. For him the mountains are the symbol of his roots, of security and power; here the method of identification leads no farther, since it is obvious that the patient is not in any position to identify with the mountains. The special, complex problematic of our patients compels us to resort to a more differentiated procedure. The first thing a patient must be able to do is to grieve for the family members he has lost. But, using the image of the mountains, he is immediately able to visualize his own resources, pale and at a distance, then get ever closer to feeling them, and, in the best-case scenario, maybe even rediscover feelings inside him.

Identification with different elements of a dream is made possible, in variations, by the method of dialogue, such as via a dialogue of the dreamer with persons, elements, sequences, or even the dream as a whole (e.g., when the dream is unintelligible but threatening).

Ms. S. from Teheran dreamed repeatedly about her comrades who died during a wave of executions in Iran during the Khomeini regime. She could not take leave of them in any real sense, since she herself had been under arrest at the time. In our dreamwork, I invited her to undertake a dialogue with these dead friends and political compatriots. By saying her farewells, she increasingly took advantage of the opportunity to say everything that had been denied her in reality. The people who kept appearing in her dreams also symbolized the political party they had belonged to, and as such they provided Ms. S. with the opportunity—gradually, by arguing with her comrades—to take leave of her existence as a "heroine" as well as to discover and develop the more feminine parts of her personality.

I often ask patients to give me a precise account of how they mourn in their homeland. Getting acquainted with mourning ceremonies from other cultures or finding out about them from patients helps the therapist support patients in their effort to close open gestalts. I give this topic a lot of attention and space in therapy sessions, because without the opportunity and capacity to mourn we are blocked—we then remain under imprisonment by the dead, by those who have long since passed on, and cannot take additional steps toward personal development and change. The comrades in the above patient's dream provided an opportunity to undertake the work of grieving, but also to take leave of ideologies, of exacting demands, and of the need to pursue the inner compulsion of fighting for freedom. For Ms. S., the latter had meant having to endure eight years of jail and torture.

But her comrades also represented an image of solidarity and mutuality.

Each dream image contains polarities: life and death are united in Mr. O.'s dream of the frozen lake. The concept of polarities expresses a pair of contradictions, two points that apparently contradict each other but cannot exist alone. There is no death without life. On this point I cite Alan Watts: "In the symbols of Western culture, light struggles with darkness, life with death, good with evil, and so the notion could spread throughout much of the world that affirming one meant denying the other." Chinese thought, by contrast, is rooted in the principle of polarity: plus and minus, north and south are different aspects of one and the same system. The idea of psychic polarity was worked out most clearly by Carl Jung in the constructs of anima and animus: in the female unconscious, there is a male part of the psyche corresponding to the woman's unconscious ego. Here Jung picks up on something that already exists throughout the world in the different symbolic circles that contain the polar principle, something also always associated with male-female: day and night, sun and moon (in different languages and cultures, there are different ways of assigning these to female and male), light and darkness, heaven and earth, yang and yin, Logos and Eros (Oesterreich and Rothkegel, 1990).

Another example may be found in the dreams of Ms. F. from Dresden, in which colors play a major role. As the member of an opposition group, she was spied on by supposed friends and betrayed to the state security service. To this day she is not entirely certain who betrayed her. The first dream that she described to me was one that she had dreamed in black and white. Later, more and more colors kept getting added. At this time, in her real life in the West, she kept running into familiar people who, however, behaved quite differently than they had when they were all together in the former GDR (German Democratic Republic, the East German regime, 1949–1990). This change seemed menacing to her and repeatedly prompted the suspicion that this person or that person might have betrayed her. She dreamed: "I'm moving into hall-like rooms with polished objects; the walking surfaces are slanted, and most striking of all are the colors: red and yellow; both have a cold, hypothermic, chilling effect on me, although I usually find these colors so warming." *"How is it that these colors warm you otherwise?"* "With red I feel life. That probably comes from blood, warm blood, like a life stream. Yellow, for me, is the color of light. When I paint with yellow, I have the feeling that there are no borders, because yellow radiates beyond the contours."

In the cross-cultural interpretation of colors, red is associated with animation and fertility. Australian aborigines bury a red stone in a field intended for cultivation, so as to make it fertile. We find red associated with active, male forces of change, and as the color of love that reconciles male and female contradictions. In a way that is similar to how it symbolizes life, red can also become the color of death—as with the hangmen of the Middle Ages who wore red. Yellow is the color of communication—the color tolerates no boundaries; it can easily get lost in other colors and blend in with them. Goethe remarked on the healing power of this color as a warming element; cross-culturally, it expresses the feminine side. But yellow is also extremely sensitive and has unpleasant effects when sullied. This color is also generally associated with negative energies like stinginess, anger, and jealousy.

For purposes of diagnosing a dream, the colors it contains are full of meaning. They are the carriers and the expression of the emotions that move the dreamer. Their intensity, clarity, or impurity provide clues about the power and nature of the emotion related to what has been dreamed. Between the polar extremes of light and dark (or black and white) lie all the colors of this world. Dreams where black and white appear are expressions of polarities, of contradictions, in which no intermediate overtones appear. Black-white: East-West? White, like black, is a "colorless" hue; both appear devoid of feeling, because feelings tell about themselves in colors.

Dreamers can also be encouraged to cultivate associations with different elements of their dreams, be they persons, objects, or landscapes. In contrast to what happens using an analytic approach, the emotions that arise during the associations receive special attention from the therapist, who encourages the patient to experience them. Mr. R. from Bosnia, who suffers enormously from the loss of autonomy he experiences as a refugee in Germany, has imposed upon himself an ideology of being peaceable all the time; this is his way of shutting out the acts of violence perpetrated against him so gruesomely, and he also uses this introjection to block off access to his own aggressive feelings: "I have children. I have to provide them with a good example, and I want to demonstrate that one should live without aggression." He brings me the following recurring dream:

"I am clenching my jaws so hard that, finally, all my teeth fall out. But I cannot disconnect the jaws. In the morning when I wake up, I really do have intense pains in the lower jaw." Many people who have difficulties dealing with boundaries when they get in touch with us—whether the boundaries are too strong or whether, as in this case, the line of demarcation is too weak—really do exhibit serious tensions in the region of the mouth and jaw. Just as Perls has characterized dreams as existential bulletins passing back and forth between components of the self, so it is fair to view many of our seemingly inexplicable bodily processes as existential messages from abnegated constituents of the self (Kepner 1988). Instead of biting, Mr. R. clenches his teeth. By making associations concerning the function of teeth, and by undertaking an intensified effort to trace feelings in his jaw, he was able to feel his aggression, to express it through loud screaming, and thus to provide himself with some relief.

Mr. R. has been mixing aggressive impulses with violence in his mental experience. In gestalt therapy, instances of aggression are promoted as positive contact functions, not in the sense of violent conflict, but rather in accordance with *aggression*'s Latin etymology as "going toward something." Violence is seen as the result of a disorder in aggressive functions. I treasure the significance of all the little steps in every treatment. Many of our patients are inhibited about aggression. A clear "no," raising one's voice, or even a fully communicative glance—these are already significant indications of positive change.

If the dream ends suddenly or disappointingly, this can mean that something remains unsettled, that an answer is missing, or that the end appears so horrible that the dreamer has to wake up. I usually invite patients to cultivate their own fantasies: How might the dream go on? What would an alternative ending look like? The patient who dreams he is being pursued, and who wakes up just as the policeman is hot on his heels, can cultivate fantasies; he has a free hand to create ideas—for example, in which he suddenly gets help, can look for protection, or even find another fairy-tale-like solution. It is diagnostically interesting, as well as revealing about available resources, to see whether patients will even play along and to see what kind of solution they can develop: Are they capable of getting help from others? Will they develop ideas about how to protect, conceal, or even defend themselves?

Gestalt therapy also uses creative media to work on dreams. The dream, or important elements and sequences in the dream, can be danced, portrayed in pantomime, painted, or even cast in sound. Transforming the dream into another medium can bring about a broader understanding. Through color, sound, mime, and gesture, certain aspects of the dream are able to emerge; others are neglected. The result is a new image into which many aspects—including contradictory tendencies—have been integrated, similar to how symbols are formed in the dream. Usually, and especially for those patients who have literally been left speechless, this opens up new opportunities for self-expression. In this way positive and unused potential becomes reactivated to an unusual extent. Therapeutic work evokes these resources in such a way that, even when traumatic material is being processed, it becomes possible to act imaginatively as a means to experience joyful, life-affirming moments and so call forth the courage to change.

Creative media are especially well suited to dreamwork with children and youth. Children, in general, do not like thinking about their dreams, since often the very dreams they can remember arouse a great deal of anxiety, which haunts them. Now and then, too, their dreams are so confusing and fantastic that they try suppressing them from consciousness. This may be one of the reasons why children often repeat the same dream: they make such an effort to repress the dream that it keeps coming back. Even today, children's dreams have a reputation as unexplored territory. Many child therapists concur that children (prior to puberty) apparently either cannot or will not (as a rule) free-associate. Children dream a lot and are prepared to narrate their dreams, but only in isolated cases do they bring along their own ideas about elements of their dreams that have occurred to them.

Seven-year-old M. from Sarajevo related in a striking monotone how he repeatedly had the same nightmare and was therefore terribly afraid of going to bed: "I'm there in my class, and a big monster comes along and gobbles up all of us." He was not ready to take me up on my suggestions, like painting, play-acting and so forth, and he responded by shrugging his shoulders. Only when I asked the following question was M. able to gain some access to his feelings: *"How does the monster do that?"* "He swallows us down like that." *"Does that mean that he doesn't bite you, so that you're swallowed whole when you arrive in the monster's stomach?"* "Yes!" *"You know, that reminds me of a German fairy tale called 'The Wolf and the Seven Little Goats.'"*

In this cautionary tale, a mother goat and her seven kids live together in a house. One day, the nanny goat has to leave the kids alone because she needs to get food. "Don't open the door while I'm gone," she warns; "especially not when the wolf comes and knocks." Of course, the wolf comes and knocks. But the kids say, "We know you are the wolf because of your deep voice." They refuse to open the door. The sly wolf goes away and eats chalk to soften his voice; then he returns and knocks, saying, "I'm your mother—I've returned with good food for you to eat!" The kids open the door and he devours them all—except for the youngest one, who hid himself in the big grandfather clock. When the mother comes home he tells her what happened and leads her to the wolf's home. The wolf is sleeping, trying to digest the six little kids. Carefully, the mother opens his stomach with scissors. Since he had devoured the kids whole, they all jump out alive and hug their mother. Quietly, they fill his stomach with bricks and sew it back up. When the wolf wakes up, he is very thirsty and goes to the well to have a drink. But when he bends over the well, because of the bricks he loses his balance, falls into the well, and drowns. The nanny goat and her children dance around the well.

"I know that one!" M. says. *"Would you like to tell me that story, the way you know it?"* M. sits upright and talks in a loud voice while his cheeks turn red, as if he had to give a lecture in front of a large audience. It can be quite revealing to see which part of a fairy tale makes a special impression on someone. In my own childhood, for example, I was intensely preoccupied with the part where the wolf eats chalk in order to deceive the little goats. M., who is the youngest of several siblings in his family, becomes quite excited, stressed, and detailed when he portrays the moment when the youngest goat hides in the grandfather clock, so that when its mother arrives they can team up to save the siblings and triumph over evil.

Fairy tales correspond to the archaic layers of the human psyche; among almost all the nations of the earth, many of the images and figures in these narratives are similar. The wolf, as in the example of the desert demon Seth among the Egyptians, functions as the antagonist of ordered life, selfishly lying in wait to threaten all of culture. He is both tempter and destroyer. According to ancient folk wisdom, the wolf also embodies power and expresses the demonic will that uses dialectic in an attempt to distort the true nature of things. Fairy tales always represent paths of development leading out of typically human problems; each development is bound up with fear and overcoming it. The wolf not only distorts genuine values, as happens with the seven goats, to whom he presents himself as the good mother; the wolf also destroys an infantile condition, because he devours the children. In the state of being devoured—as this condition is frequently described in the fairy tales, myths, and cult acts of ancient peoples—everyone inside the body of the beast undergoes a transformation. But in our fairy tale, salvation (i.e., transformation) can only come from outside.

It seemed to me that an important aspect of M.'s dream was the very way he processed his dream experience, the fact that he and the other children were not cut up into pieces but swallowed whole. I offer him some tiny animal figures, and he begins setting them up and rearranging them in order to replay his dream. He is very inventive about configuring the dream's ending. For example, there's a little bird there letting all the others know what's going on, and several figures set about defeating the monster and liberating the school class. What is interesting about M.'s imaginative ending is that the mother and father are not in any position to liberate the children; instead, they have to be supported themselves. This is also true of reality. Usually, our patients' children have an easier and quicker time of it finding their way in the new world they confront, and so the usual division of roles within the family is reversed: children often turn into their parents' guardians, just the way it is portrayed in the fairy tale, where it is the job of the youngest little goat to save the family from the big bad wolf. Now and then they adapt astonishingly quickly to the new culture and operate as interpreters for mother and father in dealing with officials and other authority figures. They are supposed to achieve what isn't possible for their parents by being a thread binding the old culture of their parents to the new culture of exile. Over time, however, these children need to process the fact that their parents, once seen as so very strong, cannot protect them from harm (from war, destruction, flight) and also must assume a helpless role in the new world.

The lively relationship between therapist and patient is described in all the theoretical writings about gestalt therapy's method. Therapeutic work takes place in the here and now. With the therapist, the patient may be able to find a simple, humane, and practical answer to whatever he brings into the therapeutic situation. This applies, of course, to dreamwork too. Everything that shows up in dreams as problem areas, moods, images, and symbols summons up an echo. In the therapist, too, moods, images, fantasies, and recollections of fairy tales and myths are awakened. All this flows into the dreamwork, whether it is only sensed or is known and articulated outright. The interaction between therapist and patient is a holistic act of communication transmitted at both verbal and nonverbal levels. Body language—such as posture, facial expressions, and gestures—speech content, voice timbre, and much more all join together to shape the process of communication while simultaneously displaying its multifarious disorders and interruptions. The therapist himself is part of this process, its medium and instrument, because of the way he becomes aware of his own communicative functions, of how he receives the conscious and unconscious messages his patients are sending out, how he lets them affect him, and how he responds to them.

Most of the people who come to us bring into therapy extremely fine antennae and a pronounced capacity for conscious and nonverbal communication, since for quite some time they have acquired practice in sizing up the intellectual and emotional constitution of the enemies they have faced (Herman 1994). This makes it even more helpful for the therapist to give some clear statements or meaningful feedback, or even request the patients to examine their projections. It can also be important, quite apart from the patient or situation, to have the therapist express his own feelings, so as to help the patient get back in touch with feelings from which he is cut off. For example, at the time I started on the first dreamwork together with Mr. O., I did not tell him that his narrating style made me feel chills. Had I done so then, I might possibly have scared him or seemed to be violating a personal boundary. Since then, though, when it strikes me as helpful, I have told him what kind of reactions he is triggering in me. I remain fundamentally cautious, however, whenever I express thoughts, ideas, or feelings of my own. I repeatedly make it clear that whatever emanates from me is my idea, and I ask the patients, expressly and repeatedly, to examine whether this suits them, whether they can get anything out of this. In this way, I learn a great deal about them and from them. In any event, they can always learn to ponder this, then say yes or no and draw a boundary line.

My preference for dreamwork with our patients received support and stimulation from stories told by Holocaust survivors about how they built their dreams into a kind of protective cabin. Prisoners in concentration camps put all the power of their love, all their yearning for freedom and happiness, into their locked-up, fenced-in dreams. Author Jean Cairoll tells about an inmate in a concentration camp who seemed "positively possessed" whenever he—in spite of all the obstacles—would spend a few moments in the morning to "collect" his comrades' dreams. With the dreams they carried inside themselves, these inmates systematically discovered authentic resources of their own—because of how they used dreams about landscapes to trace authentic roots, envisioned dreams about music, melody, and nourishment as dreams of salvation, and gave special meaning (like protection) to light and colors (e.g., the color blue).

Gestalt therapy asks less about the "why" than it does about the "what for" of a dream. The dream is the most personal source of information inside any- one. Most dreams have a theme running through them and transmitting a mes- sage in the language of images. The dreamer's ego has to decipher the message so that the advice can be realized in life. In this way, dreams as advisers can be an important means of strengthening the ego structure. In looking at a dream this way, what seems especially important is how crises and problems are indi- cated, since they can contribute to dealing with conflicts. The symbolic figures that show up in dreams derive their therapeutic effectiveness from the way that ego consciousness comprehends their meaning and expresses it in some fash- ion. Dreams are not just advisers and signposts pointing toward one's own resources; they also have far-reaching implications for a holistic image of hu- man beings. Dreams continue; dream series form the context, supplied by the dreamer himself, whereby a sequence of one dream after another contributes to illuminating a problem from all sides. In the pictorial language of dreams are delineated all the lines of the developmental process dreamers enter into.

Since I started working at the Treatment Center, it has become clearer to me how much we live within a field of tension bounded by polarities: extremes like aggression, destruction, and debasement, on the one hand, and qualities like love, creativity, and esteem, on the other. All the people who come to us have this in common: they have gone through hell, and they survived and after- ward always managed to summon up the energy to come to us for treatment. They had to lose and leave behind a lot, but inside they harbor wellsprings and images, that is, sources of potential, that we can relate to and that allow us to be moved, so that they can be used to build bridges between human beings from different lands and diverse cultures.

CHAPTER SIX

The Healing Power
of Storytelling

Salah Ahmad

I would like to introduce a method of treatment that operates with stories, myths, tales, and proverbs. This method is not very widespread in Germany. In the theoretical literature, we usually just find studies about work done with metaphors. Going beyond the mere application of metaphors, hypnotherapists following Milton Erickson have made the application of stories, myths, and metaphors a central part of their work. The psychotherapist Nossrat Peseschkian, an Iranian living in Germany, has seized on the healing effect that storytelling can have, and he has linked this to Western schools of psychotherapy.

Stories and proverbs play a major role in some societies. In Middle Eastern countries, tales are often the outcome of specific incidents. They deal with the oppressed, with tyrants, or with forbidden love. Real events get dressed up as fables, and people are represented in the form of animals, who then take over human thoughts and dialogues. In many cultures these tales have an orienting and advisory function. They are formulated so that many people can understand their coded messages. This way one can achieve a therapeutic effect with traditional tales or with religious stories from the Koran or the Bible. Many of our patients have strong religious ties. Like pastors in the church, therapists, with the help of stories, try to show people who have recently been through extremely trying experiences that life still has its pleasant side and that problems need not last forever.

As a therapeutic approach, storytelling has two fundamental aims: to begin with, it can help patients find consolation, hope, meaning, and solutions. Stubborn fixations can gradually become more fluid, and the patient can learn to find alternative perspectives on life. Beyond that, the therapist's tales are supposed to encourage the patient to put his own thoughts, feelings, and experiences into words and to activate his own resources for problem-solving.

The healing process of storytelling is also anchored in the Western world as a constructive-narrative approach. Its roots go back to Kant, Wundt, Adler, Piaget, Frankl, and Watzlawick. According to this line of thinking, people suffer not just from events the way they are but also (in the long run) from their interpretations of these events. The very possibility of changing interpretations and perspectives by means of the narrative process promotes healing by ridding the patient of rigid patterns and fixations. We *are* the stories that we tell (McCann and Pearlman 1991).

According to J. Nebez, a political scientist and specialist on Iran, whatever tales are selected have to fit the patient's problems if they are going to function in a way that mobilizes, lends support, and provides direction. In an indirect way, they should help the patient strengthen his capacity to act. The stories' effectiveness is a product of people's beliefs and their ties to their culture. The therapist must be acquainted with this culture and be able to find analogies for events and feelings. The therapist must use his imagination to invent stories himself. This method can be employed without regard to cultural boundaries, since every culture has its own tales and metaphors. I have, however, found that it can be difficult to work in this way with people who have ideological fixations. Many no longer have any relationship to their culture's basic rituals; others only know therapy as a method for treating "lunatics." These people are blocked at first. Therefore it is necessary to introduce them carefully to the form of therapeutic storytelling.

Mr. N.'s Prehistory

Mr. N. has been in treatment for over eighteen months, and the treatment is now nearing its end. Mr. N. was a student in a North African country. In his homeland he was accused of membership in a banned Islamic organization and was sentenced to three years in jail. He comes from a large family with seven siblings. His father was a civil servant who fell in love with a much younger woman, whom he also married. After that, the patient's mother left her husband. She took her children with her, but she asked her eldest son, our patient, to stay at home with his father and stepmother, since she wanted to retain a certain measure of control. The father's second wife is only seven years older than our patient. Mr. N. was beaten by her every day. She treated him like a housemaid by assigning him all the work done only by girls in his culture. His stepmother threatened him with punishment from his father, so the son kept quiet and told no one what was happening to him. In reality, the father didn't have the slightest inkling of how badly the new wife was mistreating his son. Further, he was not allowed to play with other children or to see his biological mother. So for years he suffered, until he finished school and entered the university. Thirsting for knowledge and hungering for contacts, power, and recognition, he joined an Islamic organization. Soon, owing to his talents, he was elected to a high position. He organized large demonstrations against his country's regime. At one demonstration he was photographed and arrested.

Torture Experience

Mr. N. was tortured sadistically. He was hung, sometimes for hours, and beaten all over. Sometimes he was hung by his feet, or from his bound hands. He was beaten on the soles of his feet, tormented with electroshock, and violated sexually. After his interrogation by torture, he was jailed for three years.

While he was being interrogated, his girlfriend tried to visit him. The girlfriend was arrested and raped before his very eyes by three policemen. These images pursue him to this very day. He cultivated a seemingly insatiable hatred. He hated his father because he had married a second wife, and he hated his mother because she had abandoned him. He hated all women because his stepmother had beaten him every day. He hated his brothers and sisters, because they had left him alone with his stepmother. Lastly, he hated everyone, trusted no one, and cursed everyone. When he showed up for his first appointment, he kept eyeing me suspiciously, and mostly he just kept quiet. Only by the fifth session did he slowly begin to thaw.

He said he could not trust me because I spoke his mother tongue. So for the first eight months I treated him together with a medical colleague, and we spoke German. After his application for asylum had been rejected, we did not hear from him for two weeks. Then he turned up again at the usual appointment time, looking terribly ill and exhausted. He revealed to me that he had made a second suicide attempt. They found him half dead in his room; his body was already getting cold, and no one believed he would survive.

Although they were able to save him, he told me that he no longer had any hope. All his hopes had been pinned on the asylum application. If he were now required to return, he would be executed. He was being sought by both sides: by the regime and by his own organization, which blamed him for betraying colleagues under torture and had attempted to murder him back home. This was one of the reasons why he had fled the country.

Mr. N. had many complaints. He suffered constantly from headaches and back pains, from pains in his legs, and from nightmares and anxiety.

Even though he had turned away from his party, Mr. N. remained deeply religious. After his suicide attempt, I at first told him only religious stories, so as to lend him strength. I quoted a sentence from one of the Prophet Muhammad's friends: "Man is a building built by God. Cursed be he who destroys this building!" People who try to kill themselves violate the commandment against killing; people who have killed themselves will stay in hell for a long time. I recited suras from the Koran.

As a rule, when I am narrating I try not to indicate why I am telling the story. Later on, the patient has time to ponder why I told him that. It does not make sense to give patients advice; through stories, however, they can be indirectly influenced and thus mobilized. Through this method, they might rediscover their capacity to think things over for themselves and come up with solutions. However, to achieve this effect through storytelling is not always possible with every patient. Some patients laugh during the stories and tell me that they are no longer children. But there are others who enjoy these kinds of stories for the first time, who think about them later on, and who are able to see connections to their own history.

Mr. N. continued with his weekly appointments, although at first he was doing quite badly. He was dreaming frequently about his girlfriend who had been raped, and he suffered from feelings of guilt, which he handled by displacing them onto other people. But he started interpreting dreams for himself, and little by little he told his life story. Slowly we won his trust. About his suicide attempt, he said: "I don't want to live anymore. It was bad luck that I didn't die, but I will try again." This made me feel as though I were being put under pressure, even though I knew that the rejection of his asylum application was responsible for his despair.

At this point I explained to him how the asylum procedure worked and what had to be done. Slowly it became clear to him that he could enter an appeal against the decision. Afterward he said, "Do you know that I'm in luck?" I asked: "Good luck or bad? You're always saying that you have bad luck." He replied, "Yes, I always have bad luck, but I've been lucky about one thing, namely, getting to know you."

That made me very happy and gave me the strength to work more intensively with him. I transformed that statement he had made into a friendly little provocation: "I can't believe that you're happy with the treatment you are getting from us; otherwise you wouldn't have tried to kill yourself." He said he had made a mistake, but he wasn't going to repeat it. If he would kill himself, he'd be losing this world. Allah would also never forgive him. I told him: "So long as I'm not sure that you'll be coming back, I can't work with you. You might kill yourself. That makes me feel unsettled and deprives me of the peace of mind I need to work with other patients. I don't know what the solution is." He then wanted to know if I was going to abandon him. It wasn't a question of dismissal, I told him, just a matter of cooperation. That meant that I did not want to worry about whether he would kill himself next week. I wanted his word on it. "Promise that you won't try to kill yourself before you've talked to me. If I can't rely on you, I can't work with you either."

I put pressure on him because I was certain that conversations like this are seen as helpful in the patient's culture. It should be noted that, in Middle Eastern societies, patients treat doctors, preachers, and treatment providers with great respect; they are experienced as figures high up in the hierarchy.

The next time, we talked about his imprisonment. He said it had been hell. Every time he was tortured, he wanted to die, and once he begged out loud for his torturers to kill him because he could not stand the pain any longer. Then he began to cry. He went on to tell about how he had been visited by friends from his organization after being released. Finally, a close friend warned him that he was going to be killed by the organization.

I asked him why he had fled the country. He was astonished and said, "I didn't want to die after I got out of jail." I responded: "I understand that very well, but I see that in the meantime you have made two attempts at suicide. If you've done so much for the sake of life and now just want to throw everything away, what kind of way is that to deal with life?" I was fairly confrontational, and he formulated a reply about how, back then, he had been searching in vain for the bright side of life. My answer was: "You're just starting. If you have patience, maybe you can recognize this." I simply ended the session this way. Two days later he called me up and said he wanted to promise me one more time that he would no longer attempt to kill himself. He would work with me to try solving his problems. He was now ready to live with his grief and to fight against injustice. "But please help me." I was very relieved after this call.

For nearly three weeks following the week he called, Mr. N. was so ill that he began to lament again. He complained: "Haven't I said that God hates me? I'm an unlucky devil. I've not only been expelled by my parents, society, and the world, but also by God. Just look—I take all these different medications, but the illness remains." I worked his complaints into a story:

Once the Prophet Muhammad was ill; for a week he lay in bed and didn't get better. They called for a Muslim hakim, who fabricated some medications out of different plants. He tried to heal the Prophet Muhammad, but the plants weren't helping him. A week later, they called for a Jewish physician. The Prophet now got different plants, new remedies, and he was restored to health. His friends arrived and asked him how something like this could happen, that a person of the Jewish faith could heal when a Muslim could not. The Prophet answered: "You know, if Allah wills that I should stay ill for a week, then that's how long I have to be ill. That's why I stayed ill, and then the time came for the second physician to give me plants and help me."

"This was the answer he gave them. You can believe it or not; it's just a story," I said to Mr. N. He was quite astonished at this story. When he was in jail, he had come to hate Islam, because his organization had operated in the name of Islam. But he understood what I had said. That is how we ended the session.

At the next session Mr. N. felt genuinely better. I gave him a joyous smile, and this strengthened my resolve to work with storytelling.

Mr. N. wanted to keep on living. And he had begun to learn German. At one session he asked me: "What do you think? I keep dreaming about the episodes of torture, but if I knew that I could avenge myself or that someone would assume revenge on my behalf, I wouldn't have such bad dreams anymore. But I'm sure that there isn't a single human being who would champion my cause and punish the people who tortured me."

I found his statement interesting and I responded by saying I didn't believe that his tormentors would simply get away without being punished. He was speechless and apparently did not know what he should say. After a while I said: "You know we always have one hope, even if we lose everyone, and this hope is Allah. We need only believe that Allah exists, an Allah who sees to it that there is justice, for you and all the others who have been tortured." He asked, "When will this happen?" I responded: "Allah has patience, and many say that Allah has a great deal of patience, and that the quickest thing he does takes forty years. There's a lovely story about this, and I'll tell it to you if you like." And so I told him:

Once upon a time there was a stork. He always had a hard time trying to build his nest so that the chicks wouldn't fall out. It sometimes happened, after each brood had been hatched, that he would lose some or all of his chicks. At one point the stork tried to find a solution. After he had been flying for a long time, he looked down and saw a preacher, a mullah, who had placed his hat near a lake and was washing himself in the lake. The stork landed near the hat and cried out aloud, "Mullah, Mullah, can I ask you something?" He responded: "Please, by all means. What do you want to know?" The stork said, "How long does it take until Allah punishes someone who has sinned?" The mullah said: "Ah, Allah is patient. Sometimes he waits forty years until he punishes someone." But before the mullah could complete his second sentence, the stork interrupted him and said, "I need your hat right now, for my chicks, because they keep falling out of their nest. Allah may punish me in forty years." He flew away, taking the hat with him. The mullah cried, "Wait, wait, don't fly away!" But the stork didn't listen and kept flying. He got close to his nest and saw that the nest was in flames and that the chicks had already fallen out. He flew back, saw the mullah sitting, and said: "Mullah, why have you done this to me? You said that Allah waits forty years before he punishes someone. It didn't even take more than a few minutes for me to receive my punishment. Why didn't you tell me this?" The mullah answered: "Stork, you didn't let me finish what I was saying. You flew away. Allah can punish someone just as quickly as he did you."

After his application for asylum had been denied, Mr. N. became more sensitive and anxious, and so he believed every rumor, each piece of information, regardless of whether it was false or true. This intensified his mental problems. In order to help him deal with his gullibility, I told him the following story:

There was a peasant who owned an ox and a donkey. Every day he hauled the ox out of the stables and led him to the field. All day long the poor beast had to haul a heavy plow behind him while the donkey got to stand quietly in his stall all day and eat hay. One day the ox started contemplating how he could lessen his heavy burden. Maybe the donkey could give me some advice, he thought to himself. "Dear donkey, do you want to help me?" The ox told the donkey his story and complained about how he had to work so hard and was always tired. The donkey pitied him and started thinking. Then he said: "When the peasant comes home tonight and gives you hay and millet to feed on, don't eat any of it. Then he'll think that you're sick, and he won't haul you out for plowing." The ox followed this advice. When the peasant saw this, he said sadly: "Oh, my ox is sick. It would be a sin to take him along to plow. I'll leave him in the stall today, and I'll take my donkey instead of the ox." So the donkey now had to haul the plow behind him all day long. By evening he could hardly even breathe, so badly were his bones hurting from this work he wasn't used to. He told himself: "I've hurt myself with my own chatter. I should have considered more carefully how I would advise the ox. Now I have to see to it that I get out of this jam." He thought things over, this way and that, until he finally hit on a solution: "Dear friend, how are you doing?" The ox replied, "Very well, thank you, you gave me good advice." To which the donkey said, "I'm very sorry to have to tell you something sad." "For God's sake," the ox interrupted him, "speak up, what is it?" "Something really awful, my dear," the donkey said hypocritically. "Well, today when I was plowing with our master, an ox merchant came our way, and our master said to him: 'You should know that my yellow ox has been sick since yesterday. If he doesn't get better by tomorrow, I'll let you know for sure. Then you should come by and slaughter him before he dies on me.'" Whereupon the ox began to shiver with fear, and at the thought of death his tongue hung way down out of his mouth. Then he stuttered: "Dear friend, you know that I ask you for advice about everything. Do you know any way out for me?" The donkey shook his head, pricked up his ears, and said: "I think there's only one possibility. Tonight you have to eat your feed again. Then our master will assume you've gotten better, and he won't any longer have a reason to have you slaughtered." The ox said happily, "I thank you from the bottom of my heart for this advice." And when evening came, he devoured his hay down to the last straw. When the peasant saw this, he said: "My ox is healthy again," and he took him out to plow. With this lie, the donkey recovered his comfortable way of life.

People who are invested in solving a specific problem also attempt to get the latest information about it, and so they believe everything they're told. There is a Kurdish proverb about this: "He has no faith in the word of a cleric, but he believes the donkey's cry." This proverb derives from the following story:

Once a man came to a cleric, a mullah, who owned a donkey, and he asked the clergyman to lend him the beast. The mullah put on a sorry face and said, "I'm terribly sorry, but my donkey isn't around." At this very moment the donkey let out an audible cry. The man gave the mullah a look of astonishment and exasperation. The mullah said, "Do you believe a donkey more than you would a clergyman?" Mr. N. just laughed; he took the story very seriously. I didn't say anything more.

Mr. N. frequently suffered from having too little money. He wanted to be able to pay for a language course, and at some point he wished to get a driver's license or just treat himself to something nice. He was not allowed to work, and although we backed his request with several letters of support, the Employment Office refused to grant him a working permit. Many refugees wait for years before a decision is reached on their application for asylum. This can make them ill even in the absence of traumatic experiences. In order to put Mr. N. at rest and put his disappointments in some perspective, I said to him: "If one is kind, if one has a good heart, Allah will also help. He will be supportive, and somehow he'll triumph over adversity." Then I told the following story:

Once upon a time there were two brothers. They lived in a little village and were very poor. Their father left them nothing when he died. The brothers decided to leave their village and try their luck in a big city. One day, bright and early, each brother packed some provisions for travel into a red scarf, tied the scarf together, and hung it on his belt. Then they set out on the road. Around noon they arrived at a spring, where the water was magnificently cool and tasted good. They sat down in the shadow of the plane trees that surrounded the spring and said to each other, "We should rest a while here and eat our lunch in peace." The younger brother, whose name was Badbacht, looked at his older brother, Bachtiar, and said, "Bachtiar, let's

*eat your provisions first, and I'll save mine for dinner." Bachtiar answered amicably,
"Most gladly, dear brother," and he untied his scarf from his belt. Then he carefully
placed the contents on the ground, and they began to satisfy their appetite. Badbacht
quickly gobbled down the largest share, since he was very hungry (so he said). After
they had rested a while longer, they pushed on.*

*Time passed, and they came to a small settlement. Gradually their feet became
heavy, and when they got to a fork in the road where they found a spring under the
shadow of an oak tree, they sat down to recuperate. Bachtiar, who had eaten very
little at noon out of consideration for his brother, now was very hungry. He said to
Badbacht: "Dear brother, I'm very hungry. Let's have a snack now before continuing
on our way, because the next settlement seems to be far away." "Oh, by God, I can't
give you anything from my provisions. It's barely enough for me." Bachtiar realized
how meanspirited his brother was, and he was greatly disappointed. But he only
said to him: "You're not a good brother, Badbacht. I can't live with a bad man like
you. I'll continue on my own. There are two roads ahead of us. Pick one for yourself,
and I'll take the other one."*

*So it came to pass that Bachtiar took one road and Badbacht the other. Bachtiar
had not even reached the next village by the time night closed in. He wandered
about until he finally discovered a windmill. Telling himself he wasn't likely to find
anything better, he decided to spend the night there. So he went inside and lay down
on the ground. A little while later a lion came up to the mill, and sat down in front
of the door, and proudly placed his front paws alongside each other. Then a snarling
tiger showed up, followed by a hyena, a jackal, and a fox. All of them gathered
around the lion and looked at him with awestruck reverence. The lion gazed at the
fox. "You fox, you son of a dog, where have you been? Lately I haven't even caught
sight of you. It's been such a long time since you've told me any news." The fox replied:
"My lord, nothing special has been going on that needed to be brought to your attention. But today there are two things I can report. Here in the mill there is a mouse
who owns twelve pieces of gold. Every day, when the sun goes up, it drags them
outside, plays in the sunlight with them, and delights in how they glitter. When the
sun goes down at night, it collects them all and brings them back into its hole. That's
the first item." The lion smiled contentedly, glanced at the assembled group, and
spoke: "That's nice. Now tell me the second piece of news." "My lord," said the fox,
"something has remained concealed from you: the hill behind the mill contains seven
clay jugs filled to the brim with gold. They're all hidden there." Bachtiar had over-*

heard everything and now was so excited that he could not sleep. He stayed awake the whole night and waited for the dawn with his eyes wide open.

Morning was slow to arrive. Little by little the sun raised its head above the horizon, and its rays bathed the mill in light. Bachtiar, who was still hiding, was filled with doubt about whether the fox had really spoken the truth. With bated breath he cautiously let his eyes roam from one corner to the other and waited anxiously to see what would happen. Suddenly a light shone out of a hole, and the snout of a mouse appeared, then the head. The little animal looked cautiously about until it seemed certain that nobody else was in the room. Then it emerged from the hole carrying a sparkling object in its mouth, which it brought into the sun. It was a piece of gold. Quickly the mouse crawled back into its hole and then brought out a second piece of gold. And then it fetched the next one, and slowly the little mouse had dragged twelve gold pieces outside and lined them up in a pretty little row on the ground. Then it began to play with them. Bachtiar, who had kept himself hidden until now, suddenly jumped toward the mouse, caught it with one hand, and placed the other on the gold pieces. After he had spent a while playing with the mouse and stroking it, he let it go free. It crept back into its hole. Bachtiar gathered up the gold, stuck it in his handbag, and left the mill. Then he walked over to the hill and dug up the soil. Soon he happened upon the clay jars filled with gold. Cautiously he took them out and put them in his handbags for safekeeping.

Bachtiar used his riches to buy land, on which he had a majestic palace built in the midst of princely gardens. The entire palace was adorned with expensive, precious carpets, and he was surrounded by maids and servants. One gained entry to the palace by going through fourteen doors, and next to each door there was a guest room in which stood amphoras filled with cold water. Bachtiar gave the gatekeeper instructions that if he should ever see a traveler gasping for water, the wayfarer should be detained and brought to him. Bachtiar's hospitality enjoyed such a grand reputation that, day in and day out, many travelers stopped by to eat, drink, and forget their fatigue. One day, another traveler happened by who finished the last of his water and then let out a deep sigh. The gatekeeper approached him and asked him courteously to come along and meet the master of the palace. So the traveler was brought to Bachtiar. As they stood facing each other, Bachtiar recognized the traveler instantly: it was Badbacht. Bachtiar rose from his chair, heartily embraced and kissed his brother, and asked him to take a seat. After a few questions concerning his health and well-being, Bachtiar said: "My dear brother, as you see, this palace be-

longs to me. It is a gift from Allah. I have attained my goal, and now that I am very wealthy I am able to help many of the poor (thanks be to God). You, unfortunately, never gained a fortune, but that doesn't matter. We are brothers, and that remains so. This should suffice for both of us, and for others too."

Badbacht had no intention of showing his brother gratitude, saying instead vitriolically: "Tell me, Bachtiar, where did you get all this wealth? I want to go there, too, and have just as much as you." In a very friendly manner, Bachtiar explained to him that he owed his wealth to a most unusual accident that would certainly not be repeated. But Badbacht absolutely had to know where the money had come from. After Badbacht kept pressing more and more, Bachtiar told the whole story but urged his brother not to do anything unwise. But Badbacht was ready to go. No sooner had Bachtiar finished speaking than Badbacht started to run like the devil. The mill was far away, and so pretty soon his tongue was hanging out of his mouth. When he reached his goal, he rushed into the mill and hid where Bachtiar had lain. He lay there without stirring. Nightfall set in; the lion came and sat down. Little by little the others arrived: the tiger, wolf, hyena, jackal, and fox. For a while the lion silently eyed the fox, then said: "You, fox, why has it been so long since you've told me anything new?" The fox replied: "What should I tell my master? Last time I brought you two important pieces of news, but a man who had been hiding inside listened in on everything. He waited until morning dawned, took all the pieces of gold away from the mouse, then went to the hill and took out all the jars of gold. This made him so wealthy that he was able to build a giant palace. Now he lives there in splendor and joy. I think that, before I tell you any news, we should search through the entire mill to see if another man might have hidden himself here again." On hearing this, the lion became enraged and roared, so the first thing they all did *was comb the mill. In a single stroke all the animals rose from their places, and when they got inside they found Badbacht. In a fit of rage they pounced on him and hauled him out. Then they tore him apart and gobbled him up.*

Mr. N. was able to laugh. He really liked the story.

Proverbs

Whenever Mr. N. felt offended by an official (or in one of his personal contacts), he made a practice of taking a vow. He would resolve not to speak a word for a certain period of time, and during this time he would answer people in a somewhat impatient sign language. Then he would complain to me about the negative reactions he received in turn. One day I told him, "Put on the crown of courtesy, and you own the whole world!" In German, we have an expression for this: "With your hat in your hand, you can roam the whole land!" That means that friendliness exerts an influence on most people, who are reluctant to reject a friendly person out of hand. Or there is yet another proverb, which says, "Use a lump of sugar to strangle your enemy!" This does not mean that the enemy should be strangled; instead, it means that I can use friendly words and gestures to make a friendly person out of someone who doesn't like me. This is what another proverb says: "With friendly words, even the snake ventures out of his hole."

Here I was trying to use proverbs as a way of indicating to Mr. N. that he can have an impact on other people by the way he behaves. It took a while, and I often had to undertake this effort until it got to the point where he slowly began to become more sensitive to others. At first he only succeeded at this with certain persons, but gradually he was able to improve the way he dealt with other people generally.

After I had learned from Mr. N. about the kind of impact stories can have, I tried to tell a stimulating story for each problem. When he goes home, he continues to make comparisons between these stories and his everyday problems. Often, when he has a problem, he reminds me about the stories. Then he'll say, "You know, this and that happened; but then I remembered the story you once told me." That means that the moral of the story moved him. He has not forgotten my stories; instead, he has made them work for him. He has gained enough courage to study German, look for work, and make some contacts in an alien society, even though he has frequently witnessed setbacks. But the new contacts he is now establishing are also slowly getting better, and that is why I decided to tell him a short story one more time. Apparently, with this story, I reached him again.

Once upon a time there was a woman who had two children. A son and a daughter. Both got married and kept living with their mother. Now, the mother could not stand her son's wife, but she liked her daughter's husband a lot. At night they all slept on the rooftop, the son with his wife on one side of the roof and the daughter and son-in-law on the other. In the middle of the night, the mother was in the habit of getting up and making sure that everyone was tucked in. First she went to where her son was camped out and said, "You have to move apart a little more; it's just too hot." Then she went to her daughter's bed and said, "You have to move closer together; it's just too cold." She said this every night, until one night her son asked her, "Mother, why are there two different climates on this roof?"

I tried to make it clear to Mr. N. that he often seemed to be opting for two different things at the same time. It can't be hot and cold at once. He can't reject people and seek friends. That's the moral of this story.

Over the long run, the cruelties inflicted on people who have been tortured sometimes make it hard to get through to them, because on the inside they are shutting themselves off from the external world. In conversation, they often act cramped, suspicious, and taciturn. The storytelling method is part of an interdisciplinary approach; it helps me attempt to reach patients emotionally and cognitively. Only then, in my experience, are some people able to relax. This is often a way of opening doors to them. The stories I told to Mr. N. gave him food for thought. It was evident how they helped him rediscover his own inner source of strength. I very much enjoyed even the difficult phases of Mr. N.'s treatment and was motivated to carry on. Just like Scheherazade, who secured her survival with a thousand tales, I try to make the stress of exile, flight, and imprisonment into something we can work on. The patients get breathing space.

CHAPTER SEVEN

"Every Perpetrator's Acquittal Costs Me Two Weeks' Sleep"

How Societies and Individuals Cope with Trauma, as Illustrated by the German Democratic Republic

Christian Pross

In the autumn of 1995, during the peace negotiations over the war in the former Yugoslavia, the question heard everywhere was this: How is life supposed to go on after the slaughter is over? The Bosnian foreign minister said there could be no real peace until the war criminals Karadzic and Mladic were handed over to the International Court of Justice in The Hague. Other voices said that an amnesty was the only way to reach reconciliation between the warring parties. How society, the international community, and the individuals affected by dictatorship, war, and genocide cope with all the repercussions determines whether the wounds inflicted will ever heal and whether there will be a lasting, peaceful life together. If what happened in the past is ignored, the old resentments, hatred, and desires for revenge will continue to fester from generation to generation and lead to a renewed outbreak of violence at the earliest opportunity.

In his play *Death and the Maiden* the Chilean author Ariel Dorfman has given us a literary treatment of the high-wire act balancing the longing for revenge against applying the rule of law to cope with the trauma of the Pinochet dictatorship in Chile. A former political prisoner, married to a judge in charge

of a government commission investigating the military junta's crimes, accidentally runs into her old torturer, a prison doctor. Her husband brings this man,
whom he picked up after an auto accident, home and invites him to stay the
night. The wife recognizes her tormentor by his voice. When everyone is asleep,
she seizes him, ties him up, and gets ready to pass sentence on him. The husband comes by and tries telling her she has no right to exercise justice like a
lynch mob. One dare not treat the torturers with the same means they used to
torment their victims. This doctor, too, has a right to constitutional procedure;
only a court of law can decide his guilt or innocence. The play ends with the
wife's desperate plea for satisfaction in light of the horror she experienced. By
the end of the play, it remains an open question whether the doctor and the
torturer are identical. There is no solution. The wife, the former victim, is
right, but so are the husband and judge, who want to reestablish the rule of
law (Dorfman 1992).

Immunity from prosecution for an unjust regime's perpetrators is a patho-
genic, retraumatizing factor for the regime's surviving victims. From concentration camp survivors we know that news about the acquittal of a concentration
camp guard in a German court could trigger severe mental reactions. The Nuremberg trials immediately after World War II, the Eichmann trial in Jerusalem, and the Auschwitz trial in Frankfurt in the sixties had enormous meaning
for the victims of the Holocaust. They created at least a small amount of justice
and satisfaction. Research in Argentina has shown that immunity and the ongoing political influence of the military men responsible for crimes committed
there under the dictatorship have been driving the regime's victims into the
consulting rooms of psychotherapists (Edelman, Kordon, and Lagos 1995).

In light of the inability of the justice system in the Federal Republic of Germany to punish human rights violations in the former German Democratic
Republic (GDR) justly and comprehensively, former civil rights leader Bärbel
Bohley expressed the conflict this way: "We wanted justice, and we got the rule
of law." Obviously, there can be no such thing as absolute justice. The process
of coping with a trauma cannot be free of human tragedies, just as Dorfman
portrays them in his play.

The heroes of a social upheaval have often been tragic figures. After a dictatorship has been toppled, those who ushered in the overthrow of the old order,

after a brief phase of revolutionary euphoria, often find themselves socially isolated again. Since the really active ones were only a minority, only a few positions in the new power apparatus can be occupied by representatives of the resistance. The old regime's functionaries, the experts and civil servants, are essentially indispensable when it comes to maintaining a functioning government and economy. The old-boy networks are usually well organized, have lots of funds at their disposal, are well practiced in playing the keyboard of power, and have good connections.

In Germany after 1945, following a short period of denazification, the end of the Nuremberg war crimes trials and the beginning of the cold war brought a quick return of the former Nazi elite to old offices and titles. Postwar history is littered with scandals and revelations about former Nazi bigwigs in business, politics, and public administration (the case of Globke, the case of Kiesinger, etc.).* In the social climate of the fifties and sixties, the Nazis' victims were burdensome admonishers, a totally isolated minority (Pross 1998). In a country where the Nazi dictatorship was supported by major portions of an approving public, this should come as no surprise.

In the Netherlands, where the majority of the population disdained the German occupation regime and the persecution of the Jews, one might have expected that resistance fighters would have been celebrated as heroes after the liberation, even though only 3 percent of the population had joined the active resistance. After 1945, however, what mattered most to the majority of the Dutch was economic reconstruction of a country that lay in ruins. There was no time to reflect on the past. Claims for compensation by victims of the Nazis were not viewed as a special case, because all of the country's citizens saw themselves as victims of the war. The attitude of the population toward resistance fighters was ambivalent, since they reminded those who had accepted and accommodated themselves to the occupation regime of their own lack of courage.

---

* Hans Globke, a civil servant who had written the major legal commentary on the Nuremberg Laws, which deprived Jews of their civil rights in the thirties, was hired by the Federal Republic's first democratic leader, Konrad Adenauer, to run the Chancellory Office in the fifties. Globke later had a hand in negotiating reparations agreements with Israel and Jewish organizations. Kurt-Georg Kiesinger (a member of Adenauer's Christian Democratic Party but, unlike Adenauer, not an opponent of Hitler) had been a member of the Nazi Party. He went on to become chancellor between 1966 and 1969 in a national unity government that included former resistance member Willy Brandt (a Social Democrat) as foreign minister. In a famous incident, the anti-Nazi activist Beate Klarsfeld spat on Kiesinger in public.—Trans.

Those pension claims demanding compensation for medical injuries that came from victims of the Nazis were rejected just as harshly by physicians among the Dutch authorities as they were by German doctors in the framework of West German reparations (Op den Velde, Koerselman, and Aarts, 1994). It seems to be a general phenomenon that nobody likes the victims of a dictatorship, since they keep alive the bad conscience of the silent majority.

In Germany, since the fall of the Wall, a special situation has arisen that is historically unprecedented: a country that liberated itself from the clutches of dictatorship was swallowed by its rich brother. The countervailing power of the citizens' movement, the reign of the Round Table,* lasted barely a year, only for as long as the GDR continued to exist formally. After reunification on October 3, 1990, the entire power apparatus, along with the economy and public administration, fell into West German hands. The citizens' movements, which had brought hundreds of thousands into the streets, either dissolved into the West German parties or collapsed into insignificant splinter groups. In one last successful act, the occupation of the Stasi† headquarters in the Normannenstraße in East Berlin, the citizens' movement accomplished the feat of getting a law passed to create the Gauck Authority.‡ The public and the individual citizen gained a unique historic opportunity to look deeply into the inner machinations of a dictatorship, into the activities of a secret service, where the culprits of the repressive apparatus (both large and small), the army of informants, could be identified. For the victims, the anonymous Kafkaesque apparatus that persecuted and harassed them received a name, a face; they were able to free a portion of their life history from the fog of anxiety and confusion.

Though the bulk of the Nazi perpetrators were able to conceal themselves after 1945 and then become integrated into postwar society (Nazi documents

* This refers not to the legend of King Arthur but to the institution that governed East Germany between the fall of the Wall in November 1989 and the first free elections in March 1990—a "Round Table" in which the Communists and their old satellite parties were forced to share power with the new citizens' groups (like the New Forum) who had brought down the old regime through peaceful protest.—Trans.

† The East German secret police, short for State Security Service (Staatssicherheitsdienst).—Trans.

‡ The Gauck Authority (Gauck-Behörde), named for the Lutheran pastor and East German dissident appointed to head it, maintains the records of the former East German secret police and makes them available, under certain conditions, to individuals who want to see the files that were kept on them by Stasi operatives and collaborators.—Trans.

only became accessible to the public decades later), a cover-up has been much harder for ex-Communists to maintain after 1989. Even though the social climate has long since changed in the direction of repression and denial, the Gauck Authority and the Stasi Files Law are still around as survivors of the *Wende.** Although influential political forces would love nothing better than to have the Gauck Authority disappear, those who continue to unearth files from the archives of the Gauck Authority see to it that fresh revelations about the past keep appearing.

Mr. N.—From Hero of the Wende *to Permanent Victim?*

A case study of one patient from the GDR makes it clear how social and individual processes for coping with trauma are interlocked.

Mr. N. was raised in a humanistic bourgeois family. At the beginning of the sixties, before the Wall was built, he had a run-in with the state as a 16-year-old high school student. He had taken part in a discussion circle about reunification and had traveled regularly to West Germany, where he met with young people living there. He was arrested and, owing to his contacts with the "revanchist" West and to "counterrevolutionary intrigues," was sentenced to three and a half years in jail, of which he had to serve two and a half. He would later learn from his Stasi file that a teacher had denounced him to the Stasi. At the beginning of his detention pending trial, he was placed in solitary confinement for several months, in a cell without daylight. The inmates drank their bathwater every morning, out of sheer thirst. He was sexually abused by one of the female guards; for thirty-four years he could not tell a soul about this humiliating experience, which filled him with disgust and shame. After half a year he fell ill from a severe lung infection accompanied by asthma attacks, and he was transferred to a prison infirmary. There were hardly any medications there; however, his condition improved because the air and food changed for the better.

As a young man who was still growing up, his idealistic picture of the world would fall apart in jail. By the time he was released, he had become a different person. Upon his departure from prison, a Stasi officer told him that he could

---

* The democratic change of power in East Germany after 1989.—Trans.

find a job in a factory, since studying at a university was out of the question. They would always know where he was, what he was doing. For now, they told him, he must prove his worth to the working class. Otherwise, he would feel the party's sword, and this sword is razor sharp.

The prediction was confirmed: he could not get his feet on the ground, and he led a wholly marginal existence. When he applied for jobs, he was frequently turned down because of his past as a political prisoner. He got by as a transportation worker. As a result of the sexual abuse in prison, his sexuality was disturbed, he suffered from feelings of inferiority, and encounters with women were filled with feelings of disgust. It would take years before he could have a relationship with a partner. Later he would discover a niche in the cultural field, where those in charge did not wear a party badge, and where a looser atmosphere prevailed compared to other places.

His experiences in jail would accompany him across the years. When dealing with officials, he would suddenly get anxiety attacks, his heart racing and his body bathed in sweat. He felt branded; he thought everyone could see that he was a jailbird. When a bell would ring he would have a panic attack, because it reminded him of the telephone that would ring in the guards' office, announcing an interrogation. On the anniversaries of his arrest and release from jail, these memories would come on especially strong.

The year of the *Wende*, 1989, would bring the happiest time of his life. He was swimming, way up on top of the wave of protest that would bring about the end of the dictatorship and tear down the Wall.

He participated in demonstrations, was active in the citizens' committee, and in one regional city, together with other civil rights activists, he founded a documentation center to investigate human rights violations by the GDR regime. He had an office right in the building that used to house the State Security Service. It was an incredible triumph for him, as a former political prisoner, to be sitting at the central switchboard of the apparatus of repression, where for two and a half years he would reside "like a prince." He put on exhibitions, gave guided tours, spoke at school and political events.

Two years after reunification would come the cold shower—the civil rights movement of the former GDR would fall into political oblivion. The documentation center that he had helped build up now had to close for financial reasons. After the period of revolutionary high flying, he now fell into a deep hole. He hid at home, where he declined into brooding and restlessly roaming around at night, unable to sleep. His entire life flashed by in his mind, endlessly, everything seeming to run around in circles. At the slightest provocation he would be overcome by outbreaks of rage, even directed against his relatives. Afterward he would be plagued by feelings of guilt. Recurring nightmares would jolt him out of sleep—nightmares in which he was visited by shadowy figures in gray who rang his doorbell and took him away in handcuffs. One of the figures was his mathematics teacher, who back then had denounced him to the Stasi. He would wince every time the doorbell rang during the day, even when he knew that this would be a visit from a friend he was anticipating. He reports that he had paranoid episodes, where he saw headless men wearing leather jackets and demanding to see his identity papers when he took walks in the woods, and he saw grimacing faces on closet doors.

When he had a look at his file from the Gauck Authority, he discovered that his best friend, with whom he shared everything, had spied on him. Overwhelmed with dizziness, he had to leave the reading room. When he visited the friend, hoping to confront him, all he could do was talk to the man's wife— the friend had cancer and was dying. The wife told Mr. N. that her husband did not show any regret or ask for forgiveness.

He began to feel persecuted by the Stasis again, in part because there was a genuine occasion for this. On the street men had threatened to finish him off if he remained publicly active in the effort to uncover the past. During his period of activism following the *Wende,* he had already been attacked on the street by men who had beaten him to the accompaniment of the cry: "We're the Red Hand, the Stasi lives, we'll come again!" A young man in the "Autonomen"* scene living in an occupied house in his neighborhood had recently shoved a leaflet into his hand celebrating the former Stasi head Erich Mielke as a hero and a freedom fighter. Experiences like this have made him anxious.

---

* The Autonomen are loosely organized groups of radicals, often living in housing they have occupied, whose militance goes beyond the conventional protest of the organized Left (including the New Left of the sixties). Though largely suppressed in West Berlin by the end of the eighties, the Autonomen movement was partly revived after the *Wende* in the former GDR. East German dissidents and artists in the run-down (but gentrifying) neighborhood of Prenzlauer Berg now share this district with Autonomen who have taken over several buildings there.—Trans.

In the GDR era he had hated the SED* regime, and he had known who his opponents were. He had been firmly convinced that the system would collapse eventually. When he was facing his interrogators, this certainly gave him moral support. To have resisted the system unflinchingly gave him self-confidence and an inner core. Now, after the old-boy networks have returned, his inner strength has fizzled out, and he feels empty. In therapy, his thoughts and words constantly and repeatedly circle around how the former persecutors and perpetrators are regaining strength: the Stasi officers waited for two years after the *Wende*, until everything had calmed down, and now they are "creeping out of their holes again," sitting in official positions, are in politics or business, or are cashing in on their pensions, while the former inmates are living on welfare (e.g., while at the Employment Office, he encountered a former MfS† officer who now held a high position there). Today these gentlemen reappear on TV talk shows as if nothing had ever happened, while former civil rights activists are driven to the minority corner by what is said in these discussions. Each vote by a high-ranking politician in favor of amnesty or for closing the Gauck files, each acquittal of a perpetrator, costs him two weeks' sleep. He is especially pained by the fork-tongued duplicity of West German politicians, who pat the civil rights activists on the back, praising them as "heroes of the *Wende*," though these same politicians have long since allied themselves with the former GDR's nomenklatura.‡ The constant speeches about reconciliation pass right over the heads of the victims. There can only be reconciliation when injustice has been exposed and the perpetrators have been brought to justice. As a victim, he should not be forced to sit down at the same table with a perpetrator for as long as the latter does not at least admit that he had committed an injustice. Some of his former fellow inmates had landed in right-wing radical groups (where they didn't even really belong), simply because these people took the

---

* The SED—Sozialistische Einheitspartei Deutschlands, or Socialist Unity Party of Germany—was the official name of East Germany's ruling party. Originally a forced merger of Social Democrats and Communists in the Russian-occupied zone, the SED was dominated by the latter and, for all practical purposes, a Communist party in all but name.—Trans.

† Ministerium für Staatssicherheit, or Ministry for State Security, another designation for the Stasi.—Trans.

‡ A Soviet term applicable to all East European Communist regimes, "nomenklatura" refers to the roster of Communist Party members and loyal technocrats who occupied positions of power in the state and the economy.—Trans.

law into their own hands now and again. The stability and credibility of democracy were at stake here; in Germany it had already happened once that the victims of a dictatorship were passed over, namely after 1945. There would be payback for this. There would be a second 1968, this time in the East, and compared to this one the '68 revolt in the West could look like child's play in retrospect.

He can no longer enter the building that housed the former Stasi headquarters, in which he had an office for two years. If he even gets close to the building, he has an anxiety attack and starts to shake. During a visit to his native city, he met a cousin who had made a career for himself with the Volkspolizei* and had hastily distanced himself from his dissident relative when the latter was arrested, so that his job with the police would not be jeopardized. Now Mr. N. had to learn about how his cousin is doing swimmingly again, enjoying a lucrative high-level position in a company, playing the bigshot, and letting his "little" cousin feel that the latter has never really amounted to anything in life. At the same time he met an old school buddy who, owing to his own critical attitude toward the regime, did not have a career and now sits in isolation again, in the same town where the old Stasi and party bosses run the show again. In moments like this he is overcome by a profound sense of resignation, a feeling that all the struggles and stamina of the last several decades have been in vain. Bouts of depression alternate with phases where he is overcome with rage and fantasies about arming himself and taking the law into his own hands. In moments like this, his voice becomes harsh and relentless, and his face hardens.

Mr. N. feels irresistibly drawn to political meetings dealing with the GDR past and to gatherings of Stasi victims. He absorbs each newspaper report, each television broadcast. Here he continues to find confirmation that the perpetrators are the winners and the victims the losers. It is as if he is obsessed with this topic, and he torments himself with it. Like a captured tiger, he circles inside his cage and finds no exit. Resigned to this fate, he asserts that whoever was a victim once remains a victim forever.

In therapy, Mr. N. talks hastily and without pausing. His words constantly circle around the same topic, and it seems impossible for him to break out of

---

* The national police force of the GDR, literally, "People's Police."—Trans.

this circle. It is as if he were holding fast onto his cage and guarding against any offer to open the door to the outside, even just a crack. As his therapist, I feel beaten and crippled, because I am hardly in a position to change anything about the developments in society from which Mr. N. is suffering. I suggest that he take a vacation from his obsession just once, that he refrain from attending all his political events, from paying attention to the media reports, from the enormous political-moral pressure that he's loading on himself. But in his eyes this would amount to surrender. Just the fact that he has sought help from a therapist was a capitulation for him. His comrades in the victims' associations have already been asking unpleasant questions about why he so seldom shows his face any longer. For him there are just two alternatives: to emulate the IRA or the RAF,* or to withdraw from politics altogether, make money, and become a cultural philistine. His self-image as a hero of the *Wende* does not tolerate what he sees as shirking his responsibilities. The thing that sustained him for all those years, his fighting spirit—how could he discard it now?

During a six-week treatment program at a clinic specializing in psychosomatic rehabilitation, he breaks out, for the first time, from his obsessive circle. There, at last, he reveals to a therapist the secret of his trauma: his sexual abuse at the hands of a female prison guard. He portrays the incident in all its details, after which he collapses. It makes him miserable, and he wants to die. His hallucinations about the shadowy men in gray who want to arrest him come back to haunt him. The therapist gradually succeeds in building him back up, in strengthening his self-esteem, by offering this message: he's now in the last quarter of his life, he has achieved a great deal in his life, he's a historic figure, and he's made history. At a stage like this it's completely normal and legitimate to take things more slowly, and it's certainly no shame that he no longer has the same energy and zest for struggle that he had at age 35. He is exhausted and has the right to get some rest. It is suggested that he apply for a pension, but he tears up the application and throws it in a corner. He rears up, saying that now he really wants to get going, he'll fight, he'll tear trees out of the ground. Shortly thereafter would come the next crash.

He comes out of rehabilitation doing much better. He has swallowed the

* The Red Army Faction—sometimes known as the Baader-Meinhof group—was a West German terrorist cell (now known to have had East German backing) whose peak of activity was in the seventies.—Trans.

bitter pill of the pension application. He is able to sleep better, and his out-breaks of rage against friends and family have become rarer. Compared to how things were earlier, he frequently succeeds in breaking out of the circle. He's finally able to turn toward the pleasant things in life, like music, literature, and nature—wellsprings from which he had earlier drawn a great deal of energy. He wants to rediscover his center. But a short time later he suffers a setback. Politics has caught up with him: a newspaper report about large pension pay-ments going to former Stasi operatives throws him for a loop for days. He seems really depressed, saying he feels powerless and full of hate. This time he goes so far as to wax nostalgic for his old "niche"* in the GDR, in the cultural field where he had hibernated, remained true to his ideas, and hadn't needed to conform. Those were the good old days, when he knew who his opponents were and where he belonged.

Then he has an accident and he suffers from a brain concussion. For ten days he is bedridden and cut off from the world. This quarantine inevitably uncouples him from the circle of his obsessions and gives him a moment to relax. Afterward he seems much less obstinate than usual, as if this break had done him good. He is now striving for a certain "philosophical sublimity," an above-it-all stance. Impishly he remarks, "Better to go down big than have a mediocre success." He proudly relates the story of his son, who is now writing a doctoral dissertation about the citizens' movement in the GDR, a thesis in which the son cites him, his father, as a leading witness. A verse from a folksong about Florian Geyer, a figure from the Peasant Wars, occurs to me: "We'll head home defeated right after this bout, our grandsons will do better at fighting it out." This verse really speaks to him, and he has the words written down. In moments like this, the paralytic tension of the circle is relaxed, and it's fun to be philosophizing with him.

The Dynamic of the Victim's Role

The swing of the political pendulum back in the direction of restoration, some-thing that seems to take place (to a greater or lesser extent) after every social

---

* Historians of the GDR nicknamed East Germany a "society of niches" (*Nischengesellschaft*) because of the way its citizens withdrew from public life into small groups and subcultures.—Trans.

upheaval, drives victims up against (and puts their backs to) the wall. It gives them the feeling that their struggle against dictatorship, the years they spent in jail, and the liabilities they deliberately risked incurring were all in vain. Behind all the justified criticism (of how the old-boy network was restored and how there was discrimination against victims), however, there lurks a trap. To be united in lamentation, and to appear before society as an ever-changing accusation, does not help find a way out of that vicious circle in which victims accuse their countrymen of collective guilt, then in turn react defensively against the charge—and the victims remain in social isolation. It seems as if the victims use this attitude to perpetuate their victim status, to remain passive, and to let the resources they had mobilized during the upheaval waste away. The lamentations become background music for a fade-out of the victims' historic accomplishment—that of finally being able to live in a relatively free system, instead of under conditions where people are spied on, censored, surrounded by a wall and barbed wire, and forced to disappear behind prison walls for years.

As the story of Mr. N. and many other former dissidents shows, being a resistance fighter against a dictatorship provides energy and identity. One is elevated above the masses, one is also admired for one's courage, and one can see oneself standing in a long line of historic insurrectionary heroes. When the restoration sets in after the fall of the old regime, this aura fades away, and one becomes just a face in the crowd.

The Therapist's Role

When the therapist comes into the picture after the revolutionary spring is over and encourages the patient to take a vacation from pressures (both internal and external) and to sort things out for himself, this only intensifies the patient's feeling of defeat and his loss of identity. The therapist finds himself playing a role in which he represents a terrible reality trying to "disarm" the patient. Hatred against the system was one of the patient's mainsprings. The energy mobilized by this hatred is now free-floating, without a new object. Uncontrollable aggression breaks out against partners, children, and friends, against the therapist, and against oneself. In moments of desperation, Mr. N. goes so far (at least in his imagination) as to long for a return to the era of the dictatorship, a time when he could distinguish between good and evil, when he knew where he belonged and who his enemies were, whereas now the enemy is no longer tangible for him. With the status of eternal victim, Mr. N. has something to lose. Now that freedom has deprived him of his source of energy and identity as a resistance fighter, he clings to his identity as a victim, drawing a secondary gain from perpetuating his state of illness and his suffering. "At least I'm still a hero in my suffering." The physician and psychotherapist run the danger of getting caught up in this dynamic, of letting themselves be forced into the role of an accomplice to laments about the terrible reality, and so of helping to cement his victim status.

In the course of therapy, however, Mr. N. also found that he gained something with the loss of his "eternal victim" status: composure, waggishness, the ability to laugh at himself, joy over the little things in life, access to buried resources like hiking and listening to music. It took exceptional situations, like his stay at the clinic or his bed rest after his accident, for him to escape his private imprisonment within the circle. Now he is able to delegate part of his mission to his son. It eases his mind and is encouraging for him to know that maybe someday the grandchildren can take care of neglected business. This way not everything will have been in vain.

Public Coping Rituals

In Germany there is a highly pronounced insurance culture. People are insured against all kinds of risks. When it comes to compensating the GDR's victims, too, the justifiable demand for compensation has meanwhile displaced the idea of recovery from the aftereffects of dictatorship, which compensation alone cannot accomplish. At public events over the last few years (sponsored by the Gauck Authority, the Bautzen Forum of the Friedrich Ebert Foundation,* and the churches), a constantly repeated ritual may be observed: a circle of experts on the podium, made up of prominent ex-inmates, lawyers, and physicians, talks about the aftereffects of the dictatorship, the suffering of the victims, and their lack of recognition by society. In the open discussion that follows, countless numbers of victims show up to speak their minds. Encouraged by the circle

---

* The Friedrich Ebert Foundation is an organization for political education close to the Social Democratic Party. Its Bautzen Forum deals with the history of the GDR. The city of Bautzen in Saxony was the site of a jail for political prisoners.—Trans.

of experts, they relate their personal stories of suffering, tell about how their applications for compensation are brushed off, how they keep encountering the old Stasi and SED comrades in some official capacity. This gets worked up to such a high pitch that an atmosphere of fury, outrage, powerlessness, and despair starts to pervade the hall, usually scaring the circle of experts into contemplating the kind of dynamic their statements have unleashed. There then appears a politician who, riding the wave of the auditorium's stirred-up mood, poses loudly as the victims' self-appointed advocate, denounces high-level politics for its dereliction of duty, and promises to stir things up in Berlin. Drowned out by the roar of applause is the fact that he is only compounding the illusions of those present and preprogramming the inevitable disappointment to come. Usually none of the experts has the courage to tell the people the truth, which is that they are in the minority of society, that there is hardly any prospect of changing the laws in their favor, and that it would perhaps be better to contemplate other political strategies and forms of working out their suffering.

One exception to this rule was a representative of the organization HELP at the Bautzen Forum of the Friedrich Ebert Foundation in May 1995, who held a critical lens up to the victims present in the auditorium, telling them that in a pluralistic society, the only ones who get what they're entitled to are those who organize around their interests and proclaim them loudly. The perpetrators' lobbies grasped this long ago. Instead of just lamenting their situation, the victims should get a grip on reality. In Berlin alone there live thirty thousand former political prisoners, but there are only about two hundred who are organized in the various competing victims' lobbies. And not even all of these two hundred regularly pay their membership dues.

At public events like this, the psychiatrist or psychologist is confronted with high expectations; in public he is supposed to use his professional authority and the expert opinions he issues to supply the victims' lobbies with ammunition in their struggle for better legislation. Furthermore, he is supposed to grant individuals therapeutic help and make up for their lack of social recognition. After the event is over, he is surrounded by many of the affected victims, whose cause he is expected to take up. The effectiveness of medical and psychotherapeutic action rests precisely on professional independence and on independence from societal interest groups. If the therapist, out of sympathy for the victims, allows himself to get carried away by the mood of these public events and to become a political spokesperson for a lobby, then he loses his independence and his weight as a neutral, professional authority.

However, collective rituals at public forums like this do have a constructive side. Along with individual therapy, or in place of it, they can exercise a healing function. They enable grieving and other processes of working things out to take place in large groups. The Enquete Commission of the Bundestag for Investigating the History and Consequences of the SED Dictatorship (which is in some ways comparable to the Truth Commission in South Africa) had such an effect. In numerous public meetings, victims got the chance to speak out, along with representatives of the citizens' movement, historians, and politicians. Newspapers and television reported documented instances of human rights violations, and the minutes of the commission's meetings were published (Enquete-Kommission 1995). The forums held by other associations perform a similar function. These are public hearings where victims get to speak out and where those who lack the courage to speak publicly can identify with what their fellow sufferers are reporting. One may characterize some of these public events as a kind of gigantic group therapy session. Equally important elements of self-healing are symbols like the memorial sites (both for chastisement and for commemoration), where victims gather on occasions like anniversaries, or the documentation centers that gather evidence of human rights violations and show them to the public.

After Therapy and Social Coping, What Remains Is Tragedy

In analyzing the experiences of therapists working with posttraumatic stress disorder (PTSD), Wilson and Lindy see an especially common form of countertransference involving overidentification with the victim, which they call "enmeshment." The therapist is overengaged, overidentified with the victim, and he forgets where the boundaries of his role as a therapist lie. He wants to relieve his own unconscious guilt feelings about having stood by and tolerated violence and injustice. By "rescuing" the patient, he attempts to come to terms with his own trauma. Therapists who themselves have been victims of violence, abuse, or political persecution are especially susceptible. A secondary victimization can be the result, meaning that the patient can be turned into a victim again, namely the victim of the therapist. The therapist makes the patient dependent on him and thereby repeats the dynamic of repression and incapacitation inherent in persecution (Wilson and Lindy 1994).

The goal of treatment for PTSD is to help the patient wrench loose from his victim status, to make possible the kind of autonomy and self-determination in his life that was taken from him by jail and persecution. Judith Herman sees a decisive step toward healing in the process of grieving. Victims resist grieving out of pride, or they refuse to admit their suffering because they believe that this concedes a victory to the perpetrators. According to Herman, grieving is not an act of humiliation but one of courage; in grieving the victim regains access to petrified feelings and to his own inner life (Herman 1994). Taking tiny steps, the patient Mr. N. succeeded in wrenching himself loose from his fantasies of revenge, from his fixation on the perpetrators, and from the rigidity of the victim and martyr roles.

Helping the patient free himself from the chains binding him to the perpetrator, accompanying him on his journey, following the hidden and encoded tracks he has laid down, decoding the puzzles he offers the therapist, shedding light on the thicket of one's own enmeshment with the patient through transference and countertransference—this is a long haul with plenty of setbacks. It goes right up to the boundaries of the therapist's own world, to the fundamental questions of human existence. It pains us to become conscious of the imperfections of our existence, to know that, in spite of all our efforts at coping, what happens was and remains a tragedy, that there is no absolute justice, and that there will not be any catharsis. Patient and therapist both want a better world that cannot be realized in their lifetime, or that may perhaps never be realized, because violence is an inherent part of human existence itself.

CHAPTER EIGHT

There, Where Words Fail, Tears Are the Bridge

Thoughts on Speechlessness in Working with Survivors of Torture

Britta Jenkins

According to Duden,* the definition of *speechless* is "being unable to speak for the moment." What is it that "leaves us speechless"? It is situations brought on by shock, physical or mental injuries, strong emotions, major pain, or anxiety. What's striking about this list is that while strong emotions can be triggered just as easily by moments of joy as by threatening occasions, all the other concepts enumerated here are unambiguously charged with negative feelings. In daily life we've all experienced how words can fail us for a much longer time after sorrow has been inflicted on us than after we've received a message eliciting jubilation. Jubilation is something we can't hold back: it dissolves the momentary speechlessness, whereas after an injury it can be very difficult learning to rediscover language and put sorrow into words. Many of us, however, have also experienced the salvation that can come from finding someone who knows how to listen, who can endure what is heard, and who can believe our words. Listening, enduring, and believing all depend to a large measure on how taboo-

---

* Duden is the standard reference work for the German language. "According to Duden" is like saying "according to Webster's" (or the OED).—Trans.

laden the issues are for the listener—in other words, if they have rendered the listener speechless.

An article in the German weekly *Die Zeit* (no. 29, July 14, 1995) states: "Knife to the throat—men who have been raped: A once taboo issue is raised . . . Rape against men is just as taboo-laden as raping women or the sexual abuse of children was twenty years ago." That last sentence is, in our experience, misleading. Sexual abuse remains a very difficult issue, even if a great deal has been written and discussed about it in the meantime. Those affected by it can still run up against a refusal to deal with this topic (even among therapists), in which case the victims are left to cope with it alone, since they can't find a single therapist able to tolerate listening to them.

Sexual abuse in different forms is one of the applied practices that our patients have been forced to suffer under torture. Through our work we have learned that the goal of torture is usually not to extract confessions or information. The brutal torturer and the "friendly" torturer—the one who feigns intervening in order to help the person under torture, who shows understanding, whether in word or deed—both have the same goal: to destroy the integrity of the human being in front of them, to isolate him from society, by using different methods of torture that deprive him of his fundamental trust in humanity and make him look crazy in the eyes of society. These human beings come to us with issues like mistrust, betrayal, rape, humiliation, ostracism, anxiety, and self-rejection.

The ramifications of torture are like the ever-widening circles made by tossing a stone into the water. As soon as you come into contact with the issue, you find yourself inside these circles, whether you like it or not. In my work with patients at the Treatment Center, I belong to the outer circle.

First, I would like to report my own experiences with speechlessness in the contacts that are part of my administrative work. I can be struck speechless because of an initial consternation on the telephone, when a call comes from a person overwhelmed by the pressure of his suffering or his story. What are the right words, if it is even possible to find them? How do I draw the line when my interlocutor becomes too demanding, too pushy, or (in extremely rare cases) even outrageous? Do I have the right to set my own boundaries when talking to someone who has been persecuted or, as a last resort, to end the conversation by hanging up? From a safe distance, the answer might be "Of course." In the practice of that circle of helpers to which I belong, however, it is considered a learning process to weigh, on the one hand, how much I can lend an ear to the hard-pressed without getting swept away myself and, on the other hand, to accept that there can be moments when aggressive feelings will well up in me, times when I have to limit the conversation myself. In most situations, even when considerable pressure is being applied, I still try to find a way to give the caller the feeling that he has received a hearing.

I also feel my own speechlessness on the phone when patients speaking a foreign language constantly repeat their request in the hope that I will finally understand. Others repeat just one word over and over, the name of whichever one of my colleagues speaks their native language. This leads, in part, to nonsensical "conversations," which sometimes can only be ended by hanging up. Since therapists are not to be disturbed in the middle of therapy sessions, I (as a staff member who is not providing treatment) often don't have an opportunity to make things easier on myself by transferring the call to one of the therapists. There are also people who call up basically in order to be heard, in order to unburden themselves of their story, and who often unleash such a torrent of words that at first there is no opportunity for interrupting. It may take me several tries before I'm able to get a word in edgewise, if only to transfer the call.

The category of speechlessness on the telephone also includes the many calls we get from members of the various helping professions like medical doctors, psychotherapists, pastors, and teachers. They call because their work suddenly confronts them with severely traumatized people whom they either want or are supposed to help. They often feel helpless and overburdened, and they hope to get advice from us about dealing with or treating these people, advice they can apply right away. When, for example, reports were circulating throughout the world in the summer of 1992 about the first mass rapes of Bosnian women in the Serbian camps, our telephone did not stop ringing. Inquiries came from every corner of the Federal Republic, from professionals who were on the spot trying to help and seeking advice, or even from well-meaning helpers who couldn't stand the pressure any longer and just wanted to "do something." But this "something" was what we were supposed to put into concrete terms for them. How often can one human being on the telephone try in a single day to offer advice to those seeking help? How often can a person talk about camps, rapes, murder, and forced expulsions, without himself wanting to throw down the receiver, simply because he can no longer stand hearing a single one of these words any longer? This is a question every person has to answer for himself or herself. In the meantime, in order to relieve at least some of this pressure from the telephone, we have installed an answering machine that makes the office more accessible and less chaotic.

We are subject to a similar kind of pressure from the personal inquiries we get from those affected by torture. Since Germany has many more refugees in need of treatment than we or the other treatment centers can possibly absorb, we unfortunately (and in spite of the horrible experiences just mentioned) often have to put off prospective patients by postponing their appointments. These people expect a lot from us, and they make us speechless because we, instead of fulfilling their expectations, have to initially disappoint them. They urgently and repeatedly tell us about their suffering, and they cannot understand the provisional No with which we have to resist their wish for treatment. Often they are hesitant and slow to take their leave of us. Setting necessary limits often proves difficult. Since, by now, we have all become familiar with this situation, we help each other out in establishing these limits.

As someone who is not providing treatment, furthermore, I am with patients immediately before and after treatment, when they register for their appointments and when I offer them something to drink. Speechlessness turns up in different situations here. Once more I am not able to make myself understood to many patients, except through words like *çai* (tea), a word that our patients from Eastern Europe and from Afghanistan to Morocco all use and understand, or *rojbas,* which means "good day" in Kurdish. The language that is missing gets expressed in other ways, through gestures and facial expressions; we smile, use humor, and sometimes even laugh together.

In spite of this, the "unspoken"—the reason for their visit—always hovers over us. I become especially conscious of this with patients to whom I can make myself understood. When one of these patients finds himself in an especially difficult situation—whether it's because there's a threat to his legal status for asylum in Germany or because what he's experiencing in therapy renders him speechless and paralyzed—then this also paralyzes me in my dealings with this person. There is perhaps an unspoken agreement between those of us who are not treatment providers and the patients to talk about other subjects, to reserve the unspoken for the therapists. By way of friendly greetings and a pleasant back-and-forth about the weather or other harmless subjects, we create an external framework around the inner circle in which "the other" is (or can become) the subject. Now and then, when I learn that a patient is in danger (so much in danger that his despair even leads him to harbor thoughts of suicide), the words stick in my throat, and my speechlessness gets translated into an especially friendly smile and show of concern.

But there are also other situations, as, for example, when one patient came to us completely frozen and speechless. A patient who refused any kind of friendly communication and who therefore also left us silent. Who first accepted an invitation to therapy but then stayed away, only to return later on. Who then, at some point, was on the telephone sobbing like a little child and had to be calmed down. Who now won't miss an appointment, often smiles while he waits, and then, as he's leaving, suddenly comes into the office to say "Bye!" before he goes. A wonderful moment, when the inner dedication of therapeutic work also takes an outward turn, so that I simply sit there and smile myself. Or there is the cheering moment when a patient arrives at our center and waves in front of us the letter officially recognizing his resident status. This kind of news always disseminates widely throughout the entire team, spreading joy. What especially strikes me is the joy over asylum prevalent among patients with whom I can't communicate by language. In the months immediately preceding the granting of asylum, most of these patients had waited for their appointments with shrunken shoulders and expressions of pain on their faces, behaving with a courteous reserve. Then, one day, when they arrive unexpectedly, suddenly walking through the door with an incredible glow in the face and a piece of paper in hand, I understand that finally the pressure of an uncertain situation in exile has been lifted from them.

Speechlessness also reaches me in the kitchen, the room we use as a lounge, when one of the treatment providers comes in after a therapy session paralyzed or distraught after what he or she has heard and simply has to recover. Then it is important to try to feel what this person needs: Is it words, touching, being allowed to cry or be left alone, or just having us there? It is a matter of contact with a fellow human being, of accompanying him or her in coming around again.

Speechlessness also catches up with me as a translator whenever language (either oral or written) somehow confronts the issue of torture. Elaine Scarry (1995, 43–44) writes:

> To attach any name, any word to the willful infliction of this bodily agony is to make language and civilization participate in their own destruction; . . . In all these cases the designation of an intensely painful form of bodily contortion with a word usually reserved for an instance of civilization produces a circle of negation: there is no human being in excruciating pain; that's only a telephone; there is no telephone; that is merely a means of destroying a human being who is not a human being, who is only a telephone, who is not a telephone but merely a means of destroying a telephone. The double negation of a human being and a symptom of civilization combine to bring about a third area of negation, the negation of the torturer's recognition of what is happening, a negation that will in turn allow the first two to continue. The torturer's idiom not only indicates but helps bring about the process of perception in which all human reality is made, no matter how screamingly present, invisible, inaudible.

Scarry is referring to the perception of the torture victim, who has been ostracized and whose familiar world and civilization the torturer has wrecked with different methods. The concepts under discussion are words like *telephone, submarine, swing,* or *parrot swing.* These harmless-sounding words conceal some generally well-known and frequently applied methods of torture. "Telephone" means repeated blows to the ears. "Submarine" designates submersion (close to the point of suffocation) in stinking liquid, often in urine and excrement as well, and the "swing" or "parrot swing" designates tying hands and feet behind the back of a person who is then hung up in this position.

These and other designations are not, however, only part of the torturers' vocabulary; they are also standard usage among the relevant circles who have declared war on the torturers, such as Amnesty International or one of the treatment centers. In publications and lectures, we introduce these torture methods with these very words, even if they are immediately followed by description and explanation. Why do we do this? Our goal is to inform society about the unimaginable that is taking place in the name of societies, even if it lies outside our normal values and imagination. Our hope here is not only to inform but also to invite vigorous action, so that the perpetrators find it harder to torture and the public becomes more willing to confront the damage inflicted on the survivors. When the attempt is made to present torture just as brutally as it really is (be that presentation verbal or visual), most people will immediately try to block it out, because they don't want to have anything to do with something that really ought not be. When such broadly known concepts are used, however, there is always a possibility that the precise, objective description of the act of torture will be suppressed, and that the metaphor—for instance, a word like telephone—is what will end up making an impression. This could then mean that when someone uses this apparatus, it might lead them to think about how torture exists and about the associations this word elicits for a person who has actually been tortured. In this process, feelings of guilt play a role, as does the wish to make the whole thing bearable. Guilt feelings arise because torture is a social problem. A person who needs therapy because of some personal misery is easier to dismiss as crazy, too unstable, someone with only himself or herself to blame. A torture victim, however, suffers from the consequences of collective violence. I am firmly convinced that confronting or even just encountering this issue unconsciously raises the following questions: Am I also to blame, and if so, where does the blame begin? What would I have done in such a situation? How would I have dealt with betrayal, mistrust, and isolation? Whom if anyone might I have betrayed? What could have helped me to understand and survive the unimaginable?

In her book, Scarry writes: "The act of verbally expressing pain is a necessary prelude to the collective task of diminishing pain" (9). The terrible problem of a tortured human being is that we are initially too preoccupied with our own unease (pain) to even turn to his pain or get involved. Our own pain stands like a wall between us and those who have been tortured.

In this connection, let me mention something I noticed while editing the English translations of our annual reports: in these translations (which we had contracted out), certain subject matter that made the translator too uncomfortable was unconsciously toned down, so that it became expressed in a "more articulate and acceptable" manner. Here are some examples:

"Feelings of shame and guilt that are so painful that they must not reach his consciousness" becomes *"feelings of shame and guilt that are so painful that he must not become aware of them."*

"People whose persecution aimed at robbing them of their right to self-determination" becomes *"robbing them of their ability to decide for themselves."*

The English term (used in the German text) PTS, *"posttorture syndrome"* becomes *"posttrauma syndrome."*

"Frequently raped women" becomes *"female rape victims."*

"So long as people have to leave their homeland because of persistent threats and persecution, treatment centers in 'countries of exile' will be necessary." "Countries of exile" becomes a *"host country."*

In the first translations I edited, I consistently turned "trauma" into "dream" (*Traum* in German). At first it didn't occur to me that I had done this; only as I was revising the English version did I stumble across the word "dream." It took a "foreign" language to provide enough perspective for me to recognize that the "foreigners" who come to our treatment center are rarely describing their dreams. Instead, nightmares is what they usually describe.

What do all these translations have in common? Except for my obvious mistake of transforming trauma into a dream, the statements made are not really false. Apparently the translators have tried to take situations that are consistently extreme (and which could prove painful to them) and bring them to the point where they are average (and bearable). From this point of view one could interpret the aforementioned examples as follows: When feelings of shame and guilt cannot even be perceived, then they also cannot enter consciousness. When it is self-evident that a person can make his or her own decisions, it becomes unbearable to harbor the thought that their "self-determination could then be destroyed." Rape, a taboo issue with different nuances in all cultures, is unbearable enough. Perhaps that is why "frequently raped women" became "many female rape victims."

It is also interesting that this tendency to "make it bearable" also encompasses situations involving us, in the country of exile. For we are the country of exile and not a "host country," as translated. Host country would mean that we are hosting and honoring the guest, showing him hospitality. But we are silent about the injustice he has suffered; we don't want to hear anything about it.

My concern here is not picking the translator's work to pieces. The translator could be a stand-in for us all, for our attempts to protect ourselves from speechlessness. Basically, anyone who lets himself "go part of the way through hell" must have the opportunity for debriefing, as a way of returning to a condition of normality. When I translate, I understand more about the therapeutic work with people who have been traumatized, but I also reach the limits where language alone no longer suffices as a protection. The subject matter begins to force itself on me. I need debriefing.

While I was proofreading our 1994 annual report, I noticed that in one case study the initial letter of the name of one of our patients had not been altered. I changed the first letter to a *U*. To me the *U* means "unspeakable," because the case study of this particular Bosnian patient triggers dread with each new reading. "Unspeakable" comes from speaking. Speaking = speech = a translator's tools. But who relieves a translator, who already has to render a variety of translations (from instruction manuals through complicated professional texts), and who is now supposed to translate one of our texts? He or she, too, needs an offer for debriefing whenever certain passages prove too "unspeakable."

In order to close the cycle of speechlessness, here is one more observation: In my professional life, I have never worked in an environment where so many Freudian slips are so close to being part of the daily routine as is the case at the Treatment Center for Torture Victims. When we mention our establishment's full name on the telephone or in personal conversations, people react by saying: "Oh, what do you do there? I get tortured on my job; can I also come to see you?" On the hospital grounds where we are located, we're called *Torture Center* for short. These examples are not Freudian slips in the true sense of the word; rather, they express unease at mentioning the word. There are usually two reactions to this: the "witty" or the "choked up." Both often imply an unspoken desire not to pursue this subject any further.

But in the meantime we have noticed that even people who certainly are familiar with our work talk about the *Torture Center* without being conscious of what they are saying. A pastor who phoned us to get advice about an asylum applicant asked me several times during our conversation, "And what do you do in a situation like this at the *Torture Center?*" I used to just pass over this slip of the tongue, but now I point it out. This might also be the place to mention that the acquisitions editor for the German edition of this book addressed one of his first letters to us to the *Torture Center.*

While composing this article, I wrote, "So long as people have to abandon their 'marriage' because of persistent threats and persecution." Of course, that should have been not "marriage" with an *r* (*Heirat* in German) but "homeland" with an *m* (*Heimat*). Here's how I interpret that mistake: most of our patients often do abandon their marriage, their relationship with their spouse, along with abandoning their homeland, because the partner cannot come along, is missing, or is already dead. Even when they're able to live together with their partner here, the marriage is still often abandoned, since unfortunately the experience of torture has all too often made it impossible to have the kind of relationship that existed before.

In one expert's report, I read about a diagnosis of "posttraumatic amusement reaction" (in German, *posttraumatische Belustigungsreaktion*) instead of "posttraumatic stress reaction" (*posttraumatische Belastungsreaktion*). I am convinced that this "professional expert" skimmed right over this and therefore read the correct term. Only what is the correct term? At the moment the report was typed up, had its content possibly become so unbearable and strange that the tension had to be loosened by turning a disorder into an amusement? It is well known that people apparently laugh "for no reason" in extreme situations when their personal unease becomes too great.

Working with survivors of torture can prove very burdensome, because one often runs up against one's own limits. Although many people are absolutely astonished to learn that torture is still practiced nowadays—that's really something from the Middle Ages—they still want nothing to do with it, if you please. But they do occasionally use expressions like "keeping on tenterhooks," which is derived from the practice of torture in the Middle Ages; today, however, the term is completely misappropriated when it is used as an expression "of excited anticipation." One is not necessarily "kept on tenterhooks" when one experiences something unpleasant; instead, the occasion would be anticipating a surprise or news of some kind.

After these first four years of practical work, we know that torture is certainly going to be around for as long as there are human beings. It seems as if the human imagination for inflicting torment on other human beings knows no bounds. Speechlessness often catches up with us when we hear about horrible acts, like the systematic slaughter of human beings. What do we do in situations like that? In order not to be paralyzed into speechlessness, we cry, either with patients or with colleagues coming straight out of a therapy session. One colleague once put it very nicely: "When I can no longer bear what has been said, I cry, with or without the patient." Since words fail, tears are the bridge that connects us.

In the work we do, trying to help people change from being victims of torture to becoming survivors, we have to be conscious of the speechlessness accompanying the subject of our work and learn to handle it. We must do this, on the one hand, in order to build bridges between the pain of the person who suffered the unspeakable and the society that shuts itself off from the unspeakable to avoid feeling any pain itself. Yet, on the other hand, we must do this to put up resistance against our own speechlessness. The therapeutic task is to accompany the patient on the road through a hell that one has never experienced oneself, but which one still attempts to bear along with him. But in order to avoid suffocating on the truly unspeakable and unimaginable oneself—the way our patients do, since nobody else can or wants to hear about this—we must repeatedly go before the public to tell what we have heard. Torture was and continues to be possible because it is quietly tolerated by the states and communities in which it takes place. Even in the countries of exile, people do not want to hear anything about it, because the horrible and unspeakable things we hear exceed our imagination. Change will only come about when the unspeakable is accepted—even if not understood—as the experienced reality of another human being, when more people are prepared to listen and perhaps also to cry. This could lay the foundation for people who, as Jean Amery says, "can no longer feel at home in this world after torture." This foundation may not provide all the support that is needed, and it may be quite fragile, since it is weighted down with our anxiety and defensiveness. Still, it is a foundation for keeping those who have been tortured from falling back into the abyss into which torture had once cast them.

CHAPTER NINE

Two Hundred Blows to the Head

Possibilities and Limits in Evaluating the Physical Aftereffects of Torture

Sepp Graessner

As the Treatment Center's therapists gained experience (something that inevitably could only have happened via an arduous learning process), there was also a growing demand on our staff to act as expert witnesses offering professional evaluations. More and more, the experiences of torture to which refugees testified at official hearings led to inquiries—from administrative courts, lawyers, and advising centers—as to whether we were prepared to conduct interviews, investigations, and certifications about the aftereffects of torture.

In a therapeutic institution, providing officials with expert opinions is only of marginal importance, since our priority is offering therapy. Severe traumas get treated regardless of whether they were caused by government institutions or originated in the private, family sphere. The aftereffects—that is, the variety of ailments displayed—cannot be easily categorized. A therapeutic institution that, after due consideration, calls itself a Treatment Center for Torture Victims is firmly committing itself by name to a group of human beings, refugees predominantly. This self-selected specialization is something it cannot escape.

Within the framework of the asylum procedure in different European countries, torture suffered in one's homeland does not count as grounds for asylum;

it can, however, serve as a barrier to deportation. Germany's criteria can be found in Article 16a in the Basic Law (Germany's constitution), as amended in 1993.*

Ethical Considerations

Before we put our evaluations of the aftereffects of torture into writing for the first time publicly, we were plagued by the same ethical problems faced by corresponding institutions in the rest of Europe, though we all try to resolve them in different ways. Given our outlook on the practice of socially responsible medicine, we should be able, in a fundamental and specific way, to confirm instances of torture.

If one is trying to work primarily with severely traumatized people who exhibit signs of torture trauma, an initial question that needs to be clarified is whether we can verify that the trauma resulted from torture. Therapists employing long-term therapy require a certain measure of certainty here, because they need and want to incorporate a plan for deliberately getting closer to the trauma as part of the treatment process. It is therefore necessary to distinguish between the symptoms resulting from torture and those that arose from other causes (or that already existed at an earlier time). Both cases can require treatment.

Therapists could certainly also use the patient's subjective depiction as the foundation for a therapeutic relationship; this would be a way to dispense with forensic considerations. This is the attitude prevalent among institutions like ours in neighboring European countries. As a result, they only work with survivors of torture who have a secure resident status, in other words, with patients who can't be affected by overwhelming fears of deportation. In these institutions, therefore, nobody even seeks treatment without exhibiting trauma from abuse.

Germany's experience with National Socialism and confrontation with its aftereffects prompted our Treatment Center to decide that it should offer se-

---

* West Germany had a very liberal guarantee of asylum in its Basic Law of 1949. Three years after unification, the Federal Republic restricted this right by constitutional amendment.—Trans.

verely traumatized refugees treatment even if they are in the middle of the procedure for seeking asylum. The Founding Fathers and Mothers of Germany's Basic Law granted the constitutional right of asylum. We take their motives seriously.

For refugees who are not sure of receiving asylum, it is off-limits to engage in treatment that probes and reveals too much, since the fear of deportation is quite real. The severely traumatized refugee is generally pushed into the very center of therapeutic interest, which militates against favorable conditions for long-term therapy *during the asylum procedure.* Intensive therapy must therefore be reserved for refugees with secure resident status. To be sure, a growing percentage of patients do become recognized as refugees fleeing political persecution while in treatment, although over 50 percent of the patients in the Treatment Center are still going through an asylum procedure when we first admit them.

An additional reason for our decision to offer treatment to severely traumatized refugees lacking a secure resident status has to do with the difficulty survivors of torture have finding appropriate and attentive treatment from doctors established in a health plan. This proves difficult because treating the aftereffects of torture within a health-plan practice is both extremely time-consuming and expensive, owing largely to language barriers. In addition to practical, financial, and legal problems, there are also psychological ones. Dealing with torture and tortured people requires targeted support, reflection by therapists about their own experiences, and supervision. When episodes of torture are portrayed, typical human reactions include downplaying it, denying it, avoiding it, and tuning it out.

The aftereffects of torture are often expressed as chronic psychological and psychosomatic complaints. Following the most recent restrictions on medical care for refugees, treating complaints like these was struck from the catalogue of services, a restriction rejected by the Federal Chamber of Physicians as an unethical instance of second-class medicine. This prevents doctors from treating emotional ailments earlier (and presumably more successfully). Even before these recent cutbacks, however, physicians were not taking the need for psychological support and psychotherapeutic procedures into consideration. The earlier treatment for torture trauma takes place, the more effective are the medium-term results. Not only does it benefit the survivor, but early treatment makes it easier to prevent the generation of refugee children from becoming infected by their traumatized parents. Timely treatment would therefore have a beneficial impact on refugee children as well as on their parents.

After one has decided to work with severely traumatized people whose resident status has not been clarified, however, it becomes essential to support them through their legal procedure. This means, above all, that we bear witness to human rights violations. Yet such legal testimony, or even just support for forensic argumentation, can also be apprehended as a form of distancing: the more responsibility I shift to others (i.e., the legal system) through my observations, the less I retain myself. The same mechanism can be seen at work whenever the Treatment Center is solicited for an opinion. The extremely burdensome issue of torture is passed on to specialists so they can clear up any details: health-plan and hospital doctors, lawyers, judges, and social workers try to avoid the issue by referring it to the Treatment Center.

Since we are well acquainted with these mechanisms for disposing of burdensome problems, we have let ourselves become increasingly willing to submit medical and psychological opinions. By implication, we are also more amenable to making these opinions a major component of the asylum procedure. Among other things, an essential objective behind issuing an expert opinion is to make it easier for judges trying to answer questions about details of torture and barriers to deportation.

Centers for psychological welfare in the Federal Republic and other countries operate much like the Treatment Center in Berlin. There are also, to be sure, institutions that insist on not becoming part of any procedure for obtaining resident status, since their view is that it would damage their effectiveness to become the instrument of a governmental procedure. They are afraid of being subjugated to a procedure prescribed for them: accepting limited definitions of trauma and restrictive diagnostic schemes, using a provisional information base, and losing the confidentiality that is the very foundation of a therapeutic relationship. These are all serious considerations, which one should ponder before making a quick decision in support of refugees; otherwise, one runs into a trap. For what is a physician supposed to do when he hears episodes of torture described to him but cannot confirm their traces, either by direct visual identification or through some kind of derivative evidence? He then becomes a participant in a juridically defined procedure for uncovering the truth, in contrast to the therapeutic relationship, where one can follow a different, existential concept of the truth, a biographical truth depicted in the fullness of its creative subjectivity. In pursuing this subjective truth, we also allow ourselves a certain leeway in interpreting symbols and fantasies, owing to our ignorance of other cultures, which may lead to problems of translation, mistakes in interpretation.

Here is a dilemma to which there is no satisfactory resolution. In many cases, the Federal Social Welfare Assistance Act demands medical opinions with a strict health-promoting rationale in order for certain hard-won services (an apartment, work, transportation subsidy, orthopedic aids) to be approved. Just undertaking to provide this kind of support on a daily basis makes it necessary for the physician to balance his professional vow of confidentiality against the practical need to get aid from public funds. As a result, Sigmund Freud's recommendation from 1920 cannot be implemented one hundred per cent: "The physician chiefly has to be an advocate for the patient, not for someone else. When the physician enters into someone else's service, his function is disturbed."

For the ethical reasons just mentioned, *expert witness* opinions should only be commissioned by courts (as a matter of state jurisdiction) in those cases where there is either no therapeutic relationship or where none is intended.

In all cases where the team in charge of admissions at the Treatment Center has ascertained a need for treatment, a therapeutic relationship is initiated. *Medical and psychological* opinions about possible torture episodes and their aftereffects are then viewed as part of treatment and, accordingly, introduced into the asylum procedure only after the refugees (having been informed and advised) agree to this. This means that each exchange of letters, even with attorneys, has to be approved in writing by the patient.

A similar kind of ethical problem cropped up in one case where certain organizations acting as guardians wanted to determine the ages of some young people whose own statements about their age were not believed by representatives of one public authority. These young and, for the most part, severely traumatized refugees had (by their own account) left their homeland as "unaccompanied minors." Other authorities, in charge of determining guardian status, were of the opinion that they had to be even younger than they were thought to be, and that the representatives of the public authority had therefore estimated wrongly.

Since it really did look as though the estimates made by the first public authority's representatives were questionable and couldn't help but be somewhat arbitrary, we agreed to draw up papers stipulating the minors' ages. In every case our determination departed from the official estimate. Since our opinions were issued in a spirit of advocacy for the minors on behalf of guardians, and not for the authorities, we believed it was permissible to take part in this legal procedure. Our papers represented a kind of counterexpertise. Cases from the state of Hesse, in which the x-ray of a minor's hand was ordered by officials, prompted a faction within the Hessian Chamber of Physicians to issue a report about the evidentiary value and ethics of stipulating age. The experts issuing the report came to the conclusion, both on ethical grounds and because they feared a danger to patients' health, that x-rays for administrative purposes should be ruled out. Their reasons were conclusive, so the age assessors working for the authorities in Berlin were persuaded by the Hessian doctors to withdraw their case, albeit at the price of continuing the practice of arbitrarily and imprecisely assessing the age of unaccompanied minors lacking identity papers.

Evaluating the Aftereffects of Torture

Every organ in the body can be affected by torture. This makes it necessary to request evaluations from a variety of professional colleagues. To the extent that one runs up against the limitations of one's own knowledge and experience, it becomes necessary to draw on evaluations of torture's aftereffects by dermatologists, neurologists, otolaryngologists, urologists, orthopedists, radiologists, gastroenterologists, cardiologists, and others. As a rule, our relationship with colleagues who work for clinics and health plans may be characterized as agreeable. In nearly all cases, we have encountered patience and sensitivity toward our patients affected by torture. Thus, our opinions are frequently a synopsis of different professional evaluations.

Socially responsible medicine whose context is the treatment of torture survivors resembles forensic medicine in the way that it seeks (among other things) to connect recognizable traces of torture with the acts of torture described (or to reject any such connection). In our field it also seeks to elucidate the cultural and political conditions behind human rights violations.

Confirmation of a torture episode rests on different complex factors:

1. *General conditions in the homeland* Through repeated encounters with survivors of torture from the same jails and police stations, we have come to acquire intimate knowledge about special features in the construction of jails, basement torture chambers, and cells. From patients' descriptions, we know all about the thickness of cell wall coverings and the chief forms of torture used in the widest range of places throughout the world. Information from Amnesty International has also contributed to broadening our information base. We now have fairly exact knowledge of whether and how physicians participate in torture, and of where blindfolded prisoners are tortured.

2. *Local peculiarities and political rivalries* Only growing experience has allowed us to assign the various types of violence in a place like Lebanon to the different groups operating there. Since (in the context of a civil war) all the groups active there were engaged in abuses of various kinds, and since each regional leader was also in charge of a secret torture unit, our operating assumption here could not be that we were dealing with a case of torture by the state or a quasi-governmental unit. Where those affected by torture (and their health) are concerned, who is doing the torturing is admittedly of little consequence. A similar kind of brutality in the application of torture can also be confirmed in cases such as Angola, Sierra Leone, Liberia, and Ethiopia.

3. *The appearance and form of the patient's depiction* Since it is not easy for refugees to size up our Treatment Center, a certain mistrust prevails at the outset of our communication with patients. The mistrust is aimed at the interpreter if he comes from the same country as the refugee. But it is also aimed at the treatment provider, who usually does not understand a single word the patient says, and who can only register what the patient means by way of facial gestures, intonation, and body language.

In the course of a conversation about traumatic experiences, vehement emotional outbursts are sometimes displayed. In this way, suppressed rage comes out into the open. Many patients cry when talk turns to forms of torture that have injured their dignity. Some patients suddenly turn mute and slump into their pain; some patients jump up, become restless, sweat, and tremble as they describe what happened. There are other involuntary symptoms (which we view as symptoms of struggle) under which the story of persecution is recalled. In one treatment center in Sweden, which is primarily concerned with confirming cases of torture, video films are made during the interviews with the permission of the patients. If the patient agrees, these can be introduced into court proceedings. On the videos one can see these involuntary reactions, as well as facial and bodily gestures, that accompany the patient's own depiction of abuse. These are intended to facilitate a judgment about credibility. So far not a single judge has made use of the films.

4. *Simple questionnaires allowing for a self-assessment of current ailments* The Harvard Trauma Questionnaire and the Hopkins Symptom Checklist are generally shown to the patient in his native language. In these surveys, the patient checks off his ailments and the degree to which he suffers from them. This gives us a first approximation of the symptoms of posttraumatic stress disorder. The results of the questionnaire are entered in the patient's case history. Processing the questions can, however, lead to an intensification of symptoms.

5. *The medical examination* It is obvious that an external examination provides, more readily than anything else, material for testimony about the aftereffects of torture. Injuries to the sense organs can be correlated relatively easily with the methods of torture described. Thus, perforations in the eardrums can often be the result of two-handed blows to the ears. Trauma from sudden loud noises is also typically indicated by how the holes are arranged. Damage from electric current frequently leaves behind characteristic scars. The *falanga* method of torture (blows to the soles of the feet) practiced in several countries leads to changes in the soles and in the stress patterns of the lower legs that are easily verified. From Syria we are familiar with the scar tissue formations characteristic of burning with heated plastic. In refugees from numerous African countries we find obvious traces of stab wounds from bayonets. Forced confinement in cages for weeks on end leads to painful changes in the joints and muscles. Cigarette burns leave behind typical scars on the skin. One man from Lebanon exhibited seventy-two of these burn mark scars. Torture in hanging positions results in head injuries, because the victims are suddenly dropped onto the ground. Nerve damage to the wrists is often the result of being tied up. A large number of blows to the body can make it look "like an eggplant" (in one patient's description). The buildup of blood effusions from the skin

and muscles can flood the kidneys with so much protein that a dialysis becomes necessary, as we have learned from Iran. Signs of hunger and participation in hunger strikes are relatively easy to read based on ruptures in the tissues under the skin. Torture using objects shoved under fingernails and toenails can be confirmed even after a long time.

Internal and psychological examinations can sometimes provide verifiable evidence of torture. Verifying sexual abuse, however, often depends on the time that has elapsed since the trauma. Long-lasting social deprivation or sensory deprivation leaves behind diminished cognitive capacity, which can only be described by someone who has experienced it. Blindfolding before, during, and after torture can favor psychosislike conditions resembling the experiences of people who have gone through an eye operation followed by several days of having their eyes covered.

While confirmation can be relatively securely obtained for numerous forms of torture, there are also several kinds of ailments resulting from abuse for which our state of knowledge is insufficient, or where we find ourselves moving into a speculative realm. What kind of long-term aftereffects are caused by two hundred blows to the head if they are executed with fists and different objects when the victim is blindfolded? How does constant anxiety affect the function of memory? Can numerous blows to the head that repeatedly leave the victim unconscious lead years later to hemorrhages in the cerebral cortex? Are abuse and prison conditions responsible for tuberculosis diagnosed months later? How should unusual EEG results be interpreted? Should hemorrhoids be linked causally to rectal abuse? Or are they the result of prison conditions where using the toilet was forbidden or hindered by feelings of shame in overcrowded cells? Was an HIV infection deliberately caused in Myanmar? Here we are presented with many unanswered questions that require systematic investigation and simultaneously limit the value of evidence that might confirm traces of torture.

"Common sense" may regard such connections as obvious; exact proof is often hard to establish, even if one cites the entire literature. For many of the earth's countries and regions, there are simply no basic investigations available. From the vantage point of Europe, with its causality criteria, an assessment can therefore only be made stating different degrees of probability.

In accord with other European treatment centers, we have adopted the following criteria for assessing an individual's description of torture:

1. The biography and experience of torture described, as well as verifiable traces, exhibit internal consistency.

2. Between the experience of torture portrayed and the verifiable traces there exists a relationship of high probability.

3. With a probability bordering on certainty, we know that this is a survivor of torture.

The smallest bit of evidence often tells us that we have not found any traces or that the available traces were insufficient to establish a clear-cut causal relationship, which might be attributable to our lack of knowledge or to the increasing tendency of many states to apply mental torture (i.e., without visible traces). In and of itself, evidence at the first level does not constitute a statement about the credibility of the patient. Yet when the Federal Office for the Recognition of Refugees brusquely rejects an application, it is lack of credibility, above all else, that plays a central role. The charge that credibility is lacking hits especially hard at asylum applicants from sub-Saharan countries, who often depict extremely odd-sounding prison and flight conditions, which go beyond the comprehension of Europeans lacking intimate local knowledge. A flight from prison with the help of a certain Monsieur X, or aided by a prison guard or soldier from the family or tribe of the inmate, simply triggers disbelief on the part of European officials. Yet how liberating it could be for people all across the world not to operate in line with the legalities of a provincial town in Germany! Other cultures aren't simply European cultures at a lower level, as official misunderstanding wants to suggest, but rather wholly different systems of experience, communication, and action. Since we lack detailed knowledge of local peculiarities—of culturally determined relationships, dictates of silence, oaths, and obligations—our statements to credibility should not be based on rigid ethnocentric standards.

There are many ailments that we cannot causally assign to the experience of torture. Diffuse images of pain especially come to mind. Pain that shows up predominantly when it is cold, or when the patient thinks about his traumatic experiences, or when he encounters them in a nightmare may be understood as part of a psychosomatic complex, but that does not mean that it can be explained (at least not for the time being). In cases like this, what one can do is describe. Even when it comes to physical injuries, however, patients and treatment providers are often confronted with the reproach that the refugee might have incurred these injuries—or even deliberately inflicted them on himself—working in the field or in an accident. How often have scars following slashes by a machete been dismissed as ritually acquired scars! (Of course it is possible for a person flagellated in religious rapture to have scars.) Even if these official reproaches often represent transparent attempts to deny or avoid the reality of torture and its aftereffects, they do amount to a forensic challenge.

A Case Study

By way of illustration, part of a medical evaluation will be depicted in order to clarify the variety of physical effects torture can have on health, and also to show the cultural and political character of that damage. By no means is the case of Mr. A. an exception; instead, it should be seen as typical of torture and the aftereffects of torture as we encounter them daily. His case cannot be related without including some extreme practices of mistreatment.

Following an inquiry by one of the judges on Berlin's Administrative Court, we were expected to determine whether there was evidence for the torture that Mr. A. claimed had been inflicted on his hands and genitalia. Naturally, taking a history of a torture episode cannot be restricted to two parts of the body alone, because only a compilation of all symptoms and traces permits testimony with any degree of certainty.

For scheduling reasons, only three sessions took place, each of which extended over several hours. When squeezed into a hurried schedule, interviews and investigations can harbor the danger of retraumatizing the patient. Consequently, Mr. A. was alerted to the possibility of experiencing flashbacks and associative panic reactions. Support was offered in the event that this happened.

The case concerned a 27-year-old man, a Kurd from Turkey. In 1980, the year of the military coup, this man turned 13. That year, a state of emergency was declared in the provinces of Turkey inhabited by Kurds, and latent anxiety became the only lesson learned by millions of boys and girls. Mr. A. was beaten by his teachers for speaking Kurdish. His daily life and social contacts became characterized by permanent mistrust of everyone. Since nothing is so infectious as violence, he was inevitably infected by the violence of the police and military. Relatives were arrested. Mr. A. wavered between grief and desires for revenge. When the armed struggle started to take shape, Mr. A. saw this as a challenge for him to support the resistance with food, clothes, and money. Increasingly, he became conscious of how he was being infected by the violence of the resistance in the form of "punitive actions," and of how he was in the midst of a tragic conflict: if he were to join the village guardians cooperating with the Turkish military, he would become suspect in the eyes of the armed resistance. If he were to reject the role of village guardian, he would automatically be viewed as a supporter of the rebels. Freely choosing a position in between was not an option that existed for a man of his age.

He resolved to flee to Germany. The first attempt failed.

Following his arrest he was brought to Diyarbakir, where (by his account) he was tortured almost daily for four months straight. He had already been mistreated on the prison transport. He was accused of cooperating with forbidden organizations. Why else (suspected the Turkish officials) should he have wanted to leave the country illegally, as a Kurd without a passport or visa?

According to his depiction of the spatial configuration in the rooms where he was interrogated and tortured, it is evident that this had to be a case of the Type E prison found in Diyarbakir. Depictions by other patients, especially their drawings of the building and cellars, warrant this conclusion.

The forms of torture laboriously portrayed by Mr. A. yield an overall picture that we know to be characteristic of this prison:

Mr. A. was forced to enter a room whose floor was strewn with shards of glass. After the soles of his feet were badly cut, he was shoved into a room lined with salt. He was repeatedly beaten on the soles of his feet, then forced to stand in a room ankle-deep in water.

At the time of the evaluation, these events in Diyarbakir lay three years back, so we had to look for scars on the soles of the feet roughly three years old. On the left sole I found thirteen, and on the right sole twelve distinct scars, darker than the surrounding skin. Their age can be verified based on experience. The fatty cushions underneath the soles are significantly reduced, which can be diagnosed as the aftereffect of *falanga*. The tendons of the soles can just barely be tensed, and the big toes are overstretched. We are indebted to our Danish colleague Skylv for his pathophysiological explanations of these findings. The aftereffects of these symptoms are pain and walking disorders.

Mr. A. indicated that he had been hit on the hands with a bayonet. He also described having been tortured on the backs of his hands by heated pliers or a similar instrument. During an examination we found one irregular scar on the back of each hand, which can correspond to squeeze wounds. In addition there is a secondarily healed cut wound over the surface of the right hand, which can be seen as the result of bayonet lashes to the hands. In his interview Mr. A. had reported being scalded by hot water. During an examination one could see areas of scalding in typical configurations over the backs of fingers 2 through 5 on both sides. His hands had been scalded while he was tied up, which explains why the thumbs were spared. Another striking finding from the examination was an irregular, bulging scar on the shoulder, which Mr. A. explained as a spontaneous bite from one of his torturers. While being scalded, he reacted and hit the torturer, whereupon the man bit him fiercely. And, indeed, bite marks from two rows of incisors are recognizable. Since bite wounds often result in infections, the scarlike distentions can also be explained.

By his own account, Mr. A. was subjected to torture of his penis by electric shock. His depiction of how the electrodes were applied corresponds to the standard procedure. There is a characteristic scar that, for obvious reasons, was not given a tissue-optical examination. We have encountered torture survivors who have insisted on being examined with tissue samples from their earlobes and hands.

The most common forms of abuse, according to Mr. A.'s account, were blows made by fists and other objects to the body and especially to the head. They repeatedly resulted in a loss of consciousness. On the scalp there are seven distinct scars of the same age. Three of these indicate surgical intervention. Furrows from the stitch marks can still be seen. We pay special attention to indications of physician participation in any actions surrounding torture. These cases get special documentation.

According to Mr. A.'s account, he regained consciousness twice and noticed that his scalp had been sewn up. He had been blindfolded and therefore couldn't report any details. No one spoke during the surgical operation. According to Mr. A., it could have been a nurse. An injured person who has been blindfolded (as those in charge know) can only have suffered this kind of damage under torture.

Episodes of abuse that induce shame and feelings of dishonor cannot be read from the skin. In the process of remembering, however, they are revealed through speaking habits, facial expressions, grief, and silence.

Mr. A. was always tortured with his clothes off. Objects were stuck into his rectum. He was forced to drink his torturers' urine. Mostly, Mr. A. experienced interrogations while blindfolded. He noted that torture was going on in the neighboring rooms. The experience of passively overhearing screams from other prisoners leaves behind deep traces.

The purpose behind these torture methods injurious to the sense of honor is not confession; rather, its aim is the dissolution of personal identity. The greater the horrors portrayed, and the more fragile the remnants of identity, the greater the likelihood that the victim will lack credibility. Simon Wiesenthal once told about the pleasure taken by SS people in the concentration camps as they cynically kept their eyes on prisoners: "Just imagine that you're arriving in New York and people ask you: 'How was it in the concentration camps? What did they do with you there? . . . You'd tell the people the truth. . . . And you know what would happen? . . . They would think you're crazy, maybe put you in an insane asylum." Mr. A., too, was released from prison with a farewell message telling him he would not find a soul who would believe his story. There would be no prosecution, no trial, no judgment, no written document. Just a confession signed by Mr. A. in which he expressed gratitude for his friendly treatment.

His experience of being sexually abused in a humiliating, dishonoring way prompts Mr. A. to articulate the feeling that he would rather be dead. At our institution, there really isn't a single patient, male or female, from this region who hasn't complained about sexual abuse or mistreatment violating their sense of shame. In the jail at Diyarbakir, many people have already died under torture. These cases have been documented by Amnesty International as well as by the Turkish Human Rights Foundation.

Theoretically, an alternate story could be construed for each one of the scarlike changes that we confirmed and properly dated. To come up with a different story would require little more than a dose of maliciousness or of trust betrayed. In the aforementioned case, the only conclusion to be drawn from an overall look at the evaluative criteria was this: with a probability bordering on certainty, we are dealing with a survivor of torture.

After he succeeded in fleeing to Germany, Mr. A. had the reasons for his flight scrutinized by the Federal Office for the Recognition of Foreign Refugees and the Administrative Court. The Federal Office rejected the reasons pertinent to a grant of asylum. So the only question that came to matter for issuing an expert opinion was whether deportation could be prevented because of the torture described. That is, the question that counted for the court was whether there was a plausible danger of more torture in case of deportation. Against this background, reaching a decision from a moral point of view can occasionally be difficult. In the case just described, there were no doubts.

A medical evaluation of torture's physical traces cannot neglect the question of suicidal tendencies. Some patients depict themselves as endangered; their daily fantasies revolve around different ways to take their own lives. Some patients have a history of suicide attempts. Yet others (in spite of manifest depression and a sense of resignation) deny that this option is open to them; their religion forbids it. The threat of suicide puts heavy pressure on the physician submitting an opinion, pressure that can become so massive that the professional neutrality expected in an opinion proves impossible to maintain. A merely superficial depiction of suicidal tendencies is therefore out of the question. When signs of suicidal tendencies can be clearly recognized in a patient, and when he isn't under regular medical supervision or enclosed within a dense network of social control (which is frequently not the case among unmarried refugees), the need for therapy is obvious.

Suicidal intentions that are both seriously meant and taken seriously require that a person be supported. For this reason, it is imperative that the possibility of suicide be introduced into the formal asylum procedure, since a suicidal tendency that seems to be in earnest has to be evaluated as a barrier to deportation. Of course, this applies not just to survivors of torture. In 1994 alone, there were twenty suicides among those in detention pending deportation, which should be warning and admonishment enough. The goals behind offering professional opinions and expert testimony are these: being a witness to torture that was suffered (an important aspect of treatment!), providing a therapeutic orientation within the traumatic event, being able to plan long-term treatment, and answering the question of whether eventually (years later) claims for compensation can be raised. The justice of such claims has to be determined with a certain clarity, so that reparations cannot be lightly denied. Reparations can be actionable in international courts of law. Even if compensation cannot be achieved in many countries that allow their military and police to torture, confirming that torture did take place can assume overwhelming importance for some countries' inner peace after a regime of torture has been toppled (and if a society faces its history and tries to work on its past).

An informed person certainly would now have to pose the question: Is the effort exerted in providing professional opinions, in interviewing, and in investigation ever justified? Is it really necessary? Aren't there other ways to obtain a refugee's history? Might not the method of interviewing and investigating induce retraumatization? Should one even publicize one's methods for verifying the aftereffects of torture? Doesn't this lead to a refinement in the methods used by torturers? Questions like this occur to us as well. They are part of our ongoing ambivalence toward our role in the current asylum procedure. Completely lacking in ambivalence, however, is our attitude about the need for traumatized refugees to be protected and treated.

CHAPTER TEN

"Like a Drop of Water"

Everyday Life for Asylum Seekers and Social Work with Survivors of Torture

Frank Merkord

A social worker's job basically consists of telephoning, writing letters, getting information, advising, establishing contacts, and negotiating with officials in a never-ending tug-of-war. The work is laborious and accompanied by disappointments. The greater the joy, then, when things go right, when a patient wins asylum or finds housing. In order to elucidate the kinds of difficulties social work has to contend with, I start out by depicting the background conditions under which refugees live in Germany. Special living conditions were created for refugees by way of laws regulating foreigners and asylum, and through administrative rulings. Their everyday life is so very different from our own that I would like to describe it in some detail.

Refugees are at a turning point in their lives. Persecution, war, and violence at home, followed by flight abroad, mean social and cultural loss, separation, and rupture. Refugees are often in surroundings that are new to them. They haven't mastered the language, and they are not familiar with the unwritten rules in their country of exile. The result is personal disintegration and loss of identity.

Admission Procedures

Refugees who reach Germany are housed in institutions especially created for them. These include the institutions where they are initially admitted, which are communal or collective accommodations. For asylum purposes, unaccompanied children and minors under the age of 16 are in a special situation. They are accommodated in supervised institutions. The institutions where initial admission takes place are linked to the authorities that deal with refugees, meaning police stations and the federal border police. The goal of asylum policy is to clarify, as much as is possible within three months, the residency status of asylum seekers, so that those who are not going to be admitted can be expelled, deported, or placed in detention pending deportation. If the authorities do not meet this deadline, the refugees are transferred from the initial admission camp to collective camps. Both kinds of camps can barely be distinguished in character from each other. Only after a year has passed does an asylum seeker get the chance to be accommodated in a smaller institution. Unfortunately, the going trend is in the direction of abolishing the smaller institutions.

Asylum applicants have to hand over their passports and other personal and travel documents. This is accompanied by a short, formal inquiry concerning place of origin, travel route, and stops along the way. There may be a body search leading to the confiscation of cash and jewelry meant to finance legal proceedings. Personal data are collated and stored in the Central Register for Foreigners, and then a place of residence is picked by a centralized computer system. From that point on, they may no longer leave the place of residence assigned to them without the authorities' permission. Requests to join relatives living in Germany are usually not given any consideration. The process of being committed to the camp begins with taking the refugee's fingerprints and a photograph. A schedule is then distributed with appointments for the next several hours and days (examination by the official doctor, a hearing, brief instructions on the refugee's own responsibilities). This is followed by the allotment of sleeping quarters.

The administrative personnel in charge of the refugees are employed by different authorities and operations (hierarchically organized) and have different tasks. To the refugees, however, the individual components of the administration look like a whole, like the "other" side, all lumped together under the name "police."

The admission procedure and the method used in the first inquiry largely ignore the motives of the people who have fled their countries. They are not asked about their state of health. The authorities are interested in how they got to Germany and in relatives who have already arrived. To the refugees, this kind of procedure signals a lack of interest in them as persons and a lower social status. This kind of treatment calls into question the refugees' self-image as people who have been persecuted and are seeking aid, and it shakes their self-confidence.

In the country where they are trying to gain admission, asylum seekers are confronted by an administrative apparatus that displays a kind of technocratic perfectionism that is unfamiliar to them. Thus, refugees are repeatedly surprised at how lawyers, social workers, and doctors are unable to exert greater influence over the procedure.

The Hearing

In the asylum procedure, the hearing that is supposed to take place within the first three days after arrival is an event of central importance. In this hearing, relevant facts for the asylum request must be presented and there is no time left over for any advising about the procedure. The applicant is asked to say everything right away. Here is where, among other things, problems like not knowing the language and illiteracy arise. Many refugees never had a chance to attend school; their ability to express themselves is accordingly limited. Not enough consideration is given to this problem during the asylum procedure. This is obvious in an especially crass way during the "airport procedure," where the hearing takes place immediately after arrival.

As of now, more than 90 percent of all asylum seekers have their applications rejected. Time pressures, the alienating nature of the whole situation, and the character of the hearing rule out any kind of trust. For many refugees this situation evokes memories of other situations they faced with the police and in their native countries' jails, and this rejection frequently triggers a severe psychological crisis.

Camps

Although the refugee camps are different depending on their location, size, and former use, they are very similar in their technical-administrative construction and internal organization. The big welfare organizations divide up the task of finding accommodations among different private operators who, owing to special opportunities for making money, are increasingly engaged in this business. To the refugees, their accommodations situation is the situation of inmates in a camp.

Refugee camps may be designated as "total institutions," following the definition of the American sociologist Erving Goffman. A large number of people are thrown together and forced to live in these places at the beginning of their stay in Germany. The camp situation is the social milieu in which refugees spend their daily lives. They have only limited room for maneuver and no opportunities to organize anything. Life in camp is shaped by having others provide for you and by regimentation.

In the camps, refugees lead a life largely cut off from the rest of society. This comes from being settled in out-of-the-way places or in industrial regions, from terrible public transportation, residency requirements, fences, barbed wire, and guard teams. Being committed to a camp, then, means relative loss of freedom. From this moment on, asylum seekers can no longer determine for themselves where and how they live. It can happen that they suddenly get transferred. People who live in camps and are put under the supervision of a camp administration are comprehensively observed, controlled, and assessed. The spaces they inhabit can be entered at any time by staff or police and can even be searched. Receiving visitors is limited to certain times and is only possible with proper identification and registration on a list of names. Staying outside the camp is fraught with difficulty. There is a lack of money for participation in social life. Getting to know the surroundings and establishing relations with the German population is barely possible under these conditions.

Since life in the camps does not suit most of the refugees, they want to leave there as quickly as possible. Only outside the camps do they have any opportunity of making contacts. Contacts with compatriots, new relationships, and friendships are a precondition for leading a dignified life. Therefore, in spite of the residency requirement and especially in rural areas, a number of inhabitants live outside the camps.

With the buildup of the camps and after several reforms of the Asylum Procedure Law, police powers have been bestowed on camp managements for the first time since the end of the war. The official justification for the existence of camps is the need to create residential space and therefore to avoid homelessness. Accommodation in a camp cannot be legally classified under the category of residency; therefore, according to current law, this kind of accommodation does not fulfill the minimum residency requirements.

Lost Time

During their stay at camp, refugees are at the beck and call of the authorities. Boredom is the prevailing mood: each day resembles the next, and the inmates spend most of their time waiting and pondering their future. They are homesick and keenly miss their families. Nothing is offered in the way of activities and ways to fill leisure time. Being forced to do nothing leads to permanent stress. For asylum seekers there is a de facto prohibition on working; however, for a direct payment of 2 DM per hour (or even without compensation) refugees can be put to work by the camp administration on jobs that help run the camp. Even though this is extreme underpayment, many inmates would gladly undertake this kind of work in order to escape the boredom. There are, however, only a few who are put to work in service jobs like translating, doling out food, and organizational activities. In the long run there is a danger that acquired aptitudes atrophy and that personal aptitudes for coping with reality are lost. In every achievement-oriented society, individual inactivity means a decline in social status and stigmatization.

Deprivation

In camps with up to a thousand beds, people with different languages, religions, and political views spend their daily life in close quarters. Any possibility of withdrawing does not exist. Toilet and shower doors often cannot be locked, or else the barriers separating one stall from another may be missing. The right to a protected private sphere, which is so important in our society, does not exist. Camps require compulsory community; individual differences and needs are leveled.

Refugees are under the jurisdiction of the Asylum Applicants Benefits Law. Its authors wrote this special law to make it clear that refugees are not entitled to what is defined as a minimum standard of living in Germany. Thus, asylum applicants have no claim to benefits in the form of cash. They are entitled to provisions in kind on the basis of a limited set of needs, and beyond that they can get a monthly allowance of 40 to 80 DM. Telephoning family members at home or lawyers is practically out of the question. When they arrive they usually do not have enough clothes. Outfits cannot be purchased in stores but have to be assembled from what the refugees find in clothing storerooms. Similarly, a book or a newspaper to keep in touch with their own mental world or with the homeland becomes an exorbitant luxury, as are letters (because of the cost of postage). For people with children the situation is even more of a burden, since no child allowances are paid.

In most cases refugees have lost their property. People tend to have an emotional attachment to their property, and an assortment of personal belongings always has a special meaning for someone. Furnishing one's immediate surroundings with personal things is one way to appropriate a place of one's own. This is even more important because the camp accommodations are mostly rooms containing several beds within a narrow space, where several people have to construct a private sphere using the remnants of their belongings. In this context it can even become a matter of importance whether a closet with a key is available next to the bed.

Many asylum seekers experience having their name changed, since staff are often unable to comprehend the refugee's correct name. Titles are mostly ignored.

Since asylum seekers are only allowed to get benefits in kind, they receive vouchers or food in the form of packages or meals assembled by wholesale delivery companies. This "one-size-fits-all" approach to eating diminishes individual and social customs as well as patterns of self-affirmation. Eating is more than nutritional intake. In preparing a tasty meal and in eating familiar dishes there is a link to the lost homeland. In devaluing nutrition and eating, the social role of women, who are responsible for feeding the family, is also devalued. In recent years the question of meals has been responsible for inflaming the greatest discontent in the camps. In all of Germany's federal states, it has gotten to the point where there are sometimes bitter conflicts between asylum seekers and staff.

A Limited Claim to Healthcare

According to law, refugees have only limited claims to assistance when they fall ill. This results in a willful endangerment of their health. Treatment is only allowed for acute illnesses and severe pain. Usually an asylum seeker who has fallen ill has to go to the welfare office in order to obtain a treatment certificate good for one doctor's visit. Treatment for chronic illnesses or symptoms of torture and abuse is only rarely approved. Dentures and prostheses are usually denied. Social services and psychological care and counseling are not offered. Many refugees are physically or mentally handicapped from persecution, war, or torture. Many are missing limbs, others are scarred with burn wounds, and many are frightened. In a society where being strong and demonstrating achievement are preconditions for recognition and success, handicaps like these are often regarded as defects and weaknesses. This often leads those affected to avoidance behavior and withdrawal from social contact.

Another major health problem for all the camp inmates is sleep deprivation. Refugees, who are constantly worried about their own future and that of their relatives at home, find it hard to get rest, and perpetual inactivity means they cannot get tired. Since there are only a few square meters per refugee in the camps, nobody gets regular sleep at night anyway. In conditions like these, many inmates develop anxiety about nighttime and sleeping.

Another affront to dignity and danger to health comes from the uncleanliness or insufficient cleanliness of spaces like hallways, showers, and toilets, of mattresses and linens. Thus, in the camps one usually comes across hygienic conditions that are deplorable. The common use of bedding and sanitary facilities means forced social contact. Not infrequently, inmates report feelings of disgust, extending all the way to a feeling of internal uncleanliness.

Interpersonal Relations

Relations with spouses or children are strongly influenced by conditions in the camp. The opportunity to express love or have satisfactory sexual relations is strongly constricted, since there is no privacy in the crowded spaces where all the activities take place. Families live constantly together with their children in a single room. This can lead to cramped and burdensome situations that, over the long run, favor brutal forms of sexuality, impotence, and other sexual disorders.

In these compulsory communities, with their mixtures of cultures and genders, female refugees are often subjected to latent and overt sexual threats. Women are in the minority. Obtrusive behavior, sexual harassment, and attempts at rape are not infrequent occurrences. In order to avoid these humiliations, women are forced into withdrawal. Although the problems of sexual oppression and violence (along with their consequences) are well known, refugee women are rarely offered any space where they can find protection. Gender-specific reasons for fleeing a country are not recognized as grounds for asylum. As a result, the fact of sexual threat is barely taken into consideration in finding accommodations for female asylum seekers. Refugee women are also burdened by their traditional role of caretaking, to ensure that compromise and smoothing things over prevail. For this reason they often do not safeguard their own interests.

Men and women complain about marriage and child-rearing problems. Fathers and mothers have frequently lost their traditional influence within the family; they experience themselves as helpless. The father's role has been abolished. In this context the kind of violence that not infrequently emanates from men and fathers simply amplifies existing difficulties. Here, alongside pretensions to dominance, a feeling of inferiority is often at work, a feeling amplified by the father's own loss of potency and his helplessness. For the children, life in the camp offers neither conditions appropriate for a child nor opportunities for personal development. There are no playrooms, and children romp around in the hallways, are dismissed by adults, or are kept in their families' rooms. Fathers and mothers often do not dare to let their children go outside into a strange environment. The children learn to speak German more quickly than their parents, so they often serve as their interpreters. This role reversal often places a responsibility on the child that is overtaxing and forms a major potential for conflict.

Social Behavior and Resistance

Camp residents, like other compulsory communities, form their own society with a hierarchy and specific information channels. In this society certain forms and patterns of confrontation, solidarity, and even collaboration take shape. Under conditions of inadequate provisions and privation, it is hard to summon up understanding for others. The other person tends to be seen as a competitor and a disruptive element. Refugees frequently do not trust each other because things get stolen and because the law of the strong prevails. The ones who suffer the most from this are women and those who are least valued in the social and ethnic hierarchy. Thus, Roma and Sinti experience discrimination from other refugees too. It may be said that conditions in a total institution get in the way of forming socially appropriate behavior and solidarity among the inmates. What is more, fraternization among inmates quickly gives the impression of resistance and is viewed with suspicion by the staff. Offsetting these negative conditions, overcoming cultural, situational, and even personal barriers in a counteroffensive against living conditions in the camp can lead to a revival of refugees' energy resources and capabilities. Refugees again perceive themselves as people taking action. They are able to see that their environment can be changed and their external isolation broken. Examples of this are common defense against racist attacks and common protests against the food they're given.

Deportation and Illegality

During their stay at camp, refugees experience rejections, expulsions, and police raids when arrests for detention pending deportation are made. Deportation is the major issue during the time the refugees spend waiting. The threat of being picked up can drive refugees into the illegal world, which means greater existential insecurity. In this situation, refugees become dependent on getting assistance from their fellow countrymen or establishing contacts with Germans. Illegality means violating the laws on foreigners and, by so doing, criminalizing those concerned. Illegals can no longer get welfare benefits. Inevitably this leads to petty crimes that, like the violations of the laws on foreigners, flow into the criminal statistics and "confirm" the high proportion of foreigners involved in crimes. As suspects, refugees are repeatedly victims of inappropriate police measures. Detention pending deportation can last up to eighteen months, even if the asylum seeker has not committed any crime. Detention is arranged to clear up a refugee's identity or to prepare the return home of rejected asylum applicants. In this extreme situation, the fate of the asylum seekers lies completely in the hands of the federal German authorities. For some, it is subjectively a matter of life or death. Suicides are common during detention pending deportation.

The Personnel

The staff members working in the refugee administration do not form a homogeneous group, but they have a common mission: to facilitate a smooth work process and efficient movement through the stages of the asylum procedure. To achieve this, the personnel were concentrated in central walk-in offices, data transmission was expanded, and administrative cooperation was intensified. A primary mission of personnel is to implement and justify restrictive treatment. There is a general climate of overwork and mental burden from confronting refugees, against whom the personnel also have to protect themselves. In certain circumstances, the staff find it helpful to adopt the perspective of the authorities and regard their own activity as necessary. "If I don't do it, someone else will," or "What matters is putting a stop to the abuse of asylum." This automatic identification with the process is a fundamental means of social control. In the refugee administration, however, some employees are able to summon up understanding for individual refugees and their undignified situation. Repeatedly, it is these staff people who help asylum seekers get justice.

The Impact of Asylum Status

Most refugees bring along a false image of the situation in Germany, which interferes with achieving insight into their new situation and frequently leads to severe disappointments. In the stereotyped image of the refugee held by the German, the "inferiority" of the refugee is already predetermined. Rejection, prejudice, and misjudgments can lead to embitterment and elicit psychological disorders and illnesses. The feeling of being superfluous promotes loss of the sense of self-worth and self-esteem. Forcing refugees to linger in the purgatory of the asylum procedure objectifies them, treats them like children by depriving them of personal autonomy. Being forced to conform to a camp world characterized by inactivity and emptied of meaning promotes regression to earlier stages of development. The results are a feeling of helplessness and, frequently, inappropriate behavior. Refugees describe their most common problem as irritability and depression, up to and including thoughts of suicide.

Anxiety is a constant companion in the life of refugees. Beyond that, the feeling of inadequacy and uselessness and their uncertain prospects create permanent inner turmoil. In addition, it is impossible for asylum applicants to contribute toward supporting family members back home who have often helped defray the costs of their escape and who expect repayment. This intensifies feelings of guilt and self-blame. Too, refugees often berate themselves for having survived when family members continue to be subject to persecution and danger.

Treatment and Relationship

I have described what life is like for refugees seeking asylum because medical doctors, therapists, and especially social workers are confronted in their daily work with the effects of these living conditions. We see how our patients' suffering results in part from the pressure of current conditions. Changes in personality caused by torture make it harder for them (on the one hand) to be flexible enough to come to terms with their living situation during the asylum procedure. On the other hand, this very situation can intensify and solidify feelings of powerlessness and other symptoms caused by earlier torture.

The task of social work is to find ways to improve the patients' social situation and provide them with the benefits and services to which they are legally entitled. What's involved are problems relating to residency status, finding lawyers, living situations, freedom of movement around the country, the question of material provisions, obtaining healthcare with doctors in private practice, finding language courses, gaining access to social institutions and cultural offerings, obtaining education, enrolling children in schools, overcoming personal isolation, gaining protection against xenophobic attacks on foreigners, and learning about social, political, and cultural life in the country of exile. This work also involves being available in an advisory and mediating capacity for patients in every kind of social conflict. Not infrequently it even becomes necessary to intervene, vis-à-vis officials, in family conflicts or marriage problems. Patients are usually not in a situation where they can satisfy bureaucratic demands and meet scheduled appointments regularly. Ideally, staff in public offices and other contact persons would receive special training so they could better understand the difficulties faced by refugees.

It is important to make this part of the work as clear as possible to the patients and to include them in it. Thus they should learn how applications are submitted, how official responsibilities are distributed, and how one talks with whom. Patients should gradually be given the opportunity to make decisions for themselves again. Frequently social work is what first creates the right preconditions for psychotherapy. For example, patients from other federal states come to us to apply for a transfer to Berlin so that continuous treatment becomes possible. Social work support in securing residency, improving living conditions, finding small pleasures, and gaining certainty that one is not alone—these are frequently the preconditions for defusing and stabilizing the situation enough to make trauma-focused therapy possible. Our patients, who find themselves in a no-man's-land far from their familiar surroundings, need help in resolving their residency status so they can anchor themselves in the new reality. Knowledge of the language plays an important role here.

Among almost all our patients, the sense of basic trust has been significantly violated. This loss of trust has also diminished the capacity to enter emotional relationships. Regaining trust and building up a relationship between social worker and patient are among the essential goals of treatment, for which personal and political openness on the part of the social worker is a precondition. Political openness means taking a strong stand against the torture that has devastated the patient's life. It also means taking a clear position on living conditions in exile. Personal openness means empathizing and getting involved. In an atmosphere like this, bridges can be built. Naturally, one's own psychological boundaries and limitations have to be taken into consideration.

The relationship starts taking shape at the very first meetings establishing contact. At first the patients do not know what kind of institution the Treatment Center is. Some patients arrive with the notion that we are part of the state-run refugee administration. In general, patients do know that we offer a special kind of help, so they address their initial expectations to our doctors. Psychotherapy, however, is something unknown to many. Frequently the patients see the offer of psychotherapy as a sign of their own failure. It is therefore very important at the outset to make clear what our understanding of torture is and to portray the different kinds of help we have to offer. Afterward we search for an already available support network to which we can connect them. We respect and accept the people who come to us. We listen to them. We show that we can bear to hear them out as they tell their stories, and that we believe them. A certain measure of sympathy and empathy is important. We know that refugees are having this kind of experience for the first time with us.

We often have to describe our limitations vis-à-vis our patients' expectations. We cannot promise anyone that he will receive asylum. We also cannot release our patients from their often inhumane camp accommodations. Of course, in cases where a history of a patient's illness or persecution has not been recognized, we write up supporting statements for the authorities (with the patient's approval). Clarifying our patients' expectations and our limitations is part of our work and must be continually restated. Avoiding disappointments that result from our lack of clarity regarding what we can and cannot do is a fundamental precondition for the relationship of trust we seek.

In relating to the patient I often try to create a place where he or she can feel secure. In this place it should be possible to conduct conversations about experiences and feelings in exile. If the patient brings up feelings of helplessness and powerlessness, for example, he can experience here that I believe his feelings and reactions are normal and appropriate. I try to let an image of the country of exile emerge that helps the patient fit his subjective experiences into a context and simultaneously evaluate them. In this way I expand his room to maneuver. In order to do this, it is also important to undertake a joint search for the patient's strengths. The smallest steps that the patient takes on his own can lead to a sense of achievement and thereby strengthen self-esteem.

In my meetings with patients I invite them to talk about themselves, how they used to live in their homeland and with whom, what they enjoyed doing, and what political conditions exist there. Conversations like this about memories are, in my experience, an important wellspring of personal resources. Frequently their state of mind changes spontaneously, and I experience them as active, exciting, and competent people. Furthermore, this provides a good opportunity for me to become informed about what is going on in the world firsthand and from different perspectives. In the process I have become acquainted with many interesting people whose experiences and points of view have enriched my own.

It is important to expand the patient's system of social contacts. To the extent that this is possible, contacts with family, friends, and other patients from the same village (or, if necessary, from the same organization) should be activated. For the healing and stabilization process, having exchanges with persons from the same background and getting reacquainted with one's own social identity are very important.

During the period of treatment there may be periodic personal misfortunes that upset the patient's equilibrium, for example, a rejected application for asylum, a change of dormitory, an especially upsetting form of personal harassment, xenophobic attacks on foreigners, or bad news from home. In psychosocial crisis situations like this, the stability and strength of the relationship between treatment provider and patient are put to the test. Conversations must leave room for disappointment, sadness, and despair, and together treatment provider and therapist must search for any ray of hope.

The social worker's problems also include his own difficulty in dealing with the subject. How much openness and understanding do I have? How much pain can I bear without buckling? How can I set limits for myself? In doing this work, I have to protect myself against getting so entangled in the problems of the patients that I become crippled in my capacity as a treatment provider. It is not easy to find the appropriate distance at which the capacity for empathy can still be maintained. Time and again I keep running into my own traps, prejudices, and defense mechanisms.

Sharing in the daily experience of the impact of tougher asylum laws on refugees presents a special burden and demands constant confrontation with conditions in one's own country.

> My life is like a drop of water that rests on my hand. The hand trembles and wobbles, and the droplet slides around and threatens to fall. My hope is that my hand comes to rest here and that I become healthy again.
>
> —A PATIENT FROM LEBANON

CHAPTER ELEVEN

Everything Forgotten!

Memory Disorders among Refugees Who Have Been Tortured

Sepp Graessner, Salah Ahmad, and Frank Merkord

> And whether it is a matter of social or personal iden-
> tity, false representation claiming that one is what
> one is not may be distinguished from false representa-
> tion seeking to prove one is not what one is.
> —ERVING GOFFMAN

Asylum applicants who were jailed and tortured in their native countries and who desire treatment for the resulting disorders and illnesses often refer to the minutes of their hearing with the Federal Office for the Recognition of Foreign Refugees. We read these frequently truncated records only after the first, relationship-establishing conversations we conduct with patients, assisted by interpreters. Usually, elements of patients' stories as they appear in the hearing minutes are shot through with contradictions and vary from what they have told us. Those deviations that can be ascertained from the details provided in the minutes for the hearing become more conspicuous the longer a relationship with us has existed. Although it seems obvious to us that a story of persecution would contain inconsistencies, it inevitably irritates hearing examiners and judges. How is it possible that such different versions of a personal biography can be told? Doesn't it follow that the officials are right to impute a lack of credibility?

The first thing to prompt suspicion, however, would be if two completely different situations, with different techniques of conversation and questioning, were to result in one and the same version being presented. The minutes frequently reveal a questioning technique that differs significantly from ours in its form and aims, especially where respect for the refugee's whole personality is concerned. Dignity and culturally bound honor are often the only characteristics that refugees are able to take along with them. This has prompted us to offer some reflections on the causes and significance of factors influencing mental disorders—factors that emanate from the applicants and their life histories, cultural backgrounds, and forms of memory, but that also have other origins—that force their way into the refugees' presentations before German authorities.

Refugees who have survived imprisonment, torture, and flight are required to undergo a formal hearing in Germany during which they are supposed to present their personal story of persecution coherently and convincingly. When the hearing examiners and judges become convinced that the presentation appears contradictory or incoherent or contains imprecise data, the applicant's plea for asylum is rejected. The asylum applicant can then appeal this decision to an administrative court.

We proceed from the assumption that asylum applicants who can demonstrate that they suffered massive individual persecution, with all the associated posttraumatic disorders, are not in any position to offer details about their experiences that are precise and free of contradiction. In numerous cases we have documented, therefore, we find that attempted deception and excessive demands are falsely attributed to them.

The Hearing and Disorienting Influences

Disturbing and disorienting influences creep into the hearing. In general, the interviews are mediated by language differences, with their considerable potential for misinterpretation and misunderstanding. The interpreter does not, a priori, enjoy the asylum applicant's confidence. Further, the background conditions framing the hearing are stress-laden because the applicant suspects that his future residency situation depends on what happens within the next hour. A repeatedly interrupted self-presentation often lasting forty-five minutes decides the applicant's life chances. Subjective anxieties cannot be dissolved in so short a time. Finally, the interviews rarely take place in a relaxed atmosphere. They occasionally remind the applicant of interrogations to which he was subjected at home. Those interrogations at home were often characterized by the applicant's wish not to say anything that might implicate others or lead to a withdrawal of the interrogators' goodwill. At the hearing with the Federal Office, refugees certainly are meant to implicate others while simultaneously securing the interviewer's goodwill.

Prior to their hearing the applicant has usually had some contact with officials: for example, with the office that deals with foreigners, the welfare office, or the housing administration. In these situations, he runs up against the unwritten laws for dealing with authority, and he encounters mistrust, defensiveness, and emotional aloofness. He experiences himself not as a person but as the object of an administrative act. In short, he learns all too well that officials are a microcosm of an entire society.

Among the recent changes narrowing the scope of Germany's asylum law was the establishment of a Central Processing Center. Now the orientation process takes place in a camplike setting (as a total institution, in which every aspect of living is subject to administrative control), which calls up associations that are retraumatizing in nature. Registering and checking out at guarded gates, the prohibition against leaving the assigned district, cramped living quarters, house regulations, and all the controls on visitors—these things immediately remind torture survivors of their prison conditions. These memories, however, do not influence the refugee's trauma history in the direction of greater precision; instead, they tend to have a confusing effect. Every total institution creates mental disorientation and stigmatizes the inmates.

All of this means that the applicants are inclined not to cause any "difficulties" for the interviewers. They submit to a ritual that they are only able to encounter with vague expectations. When the applicants are thoroughly prepared or have backing from an attorney as they enter the hearing, they will reel off the essentials of their persecution story, and their statement will shape the course of the hearing. They will also supply their own catchwords for the questions posed to them in the inquiry.

If, however, applicants come to the interview poorly prepared because they are convinced that their statement will speak for itself, they are in for some nasty surprises. Here "poorly prepared" also means that the applicants will have exchanged their story with compatriots from their homeland and will have received numerous bits of information on events back home that (mediated by these compatriots) intrude into their own stories in a disorienting way. This kind of information can (without anyone's intentions having to be second-guessed) displace authentic autobiographical details and distort exact recall (to the extent that exact recollection is even possible).

Examiners "Infected" by the Applicants' Stories

It is a fundamental fact that examiners—just like executioners—are confronted with monstrosities that push them into a conflict of interest: between, on the one hand, encountering the torture survivor with empathy and, on the other hand, responding to what they hear by establishing taboos, by relativizing, or by identifying with the perpetrators.

As treatment providers for torture survivors, we know that we can become infected by the cumulation of the "unspeakable" to which we subject ourselves, so that an inappropriate distancing from what we have heard can set in:

"It couldn't have been so awful; otherwise the person affected by this would not be sitting in front of me. Some things are certainly being exaggerated. Torture couldn't be undertaken without some reason for it—who knows what the asylum applicant's share in this might be? Maybe he had been mistreating someone earlier. Every victim also displays aspects of being a perpetrator. Yes, in this country and that country things can get pretty gruesome, but there are always people who latch on to the history of the truly persecuted."

A frequently observed reaction to the terrible things described consists of interrogating the applicant in a confrontational way so as to make it apparent that things could not have happened the way he said. In order to accomplish this, contradictions about the time, place, and substance of testimony are readily recorded in order to relativize the burden of those experiences by turning the examiner into a witness. This way the examiner, without consciously realizing it, gradually identifies with the perpetrators. This inevitably has an impact on the applicant. In the questioner he no longer finds an impartial ear but, rather, a doubter.

It is not just individual officials who get caught up in this kind of defense mechanism; entire societies do too. The portrayals of mistreatment, trickery, and unfair trials in the GDR were believed—as human rights violations—by only a small portion of society in the West German Federal Republic. Victims hardly got a hearing; only a few wanted to bear witness. Among the victims, this led to exaggerated claims in their own stories of suffering. These exaggerations were summarily exposed and relegated to psychiatric categories. The result was a subtle complicity with the GDR's regime.

Applicants comprehend very clearly whether they are receiving sympathy during the hearing or whether the judges are unsympathetic. News about the mechanical side of the administrative process is the first kind of story to get around in asylum applicant circles, and this does not contribute to conversations based on trust during the hearings. We have read minutes and decisions rejecting asylum whose stereotyping was enough to destroy anyone's faith in the possibility of individual examination. A refugee from one African country was rejected with an argument inaccurately describing the applicant's nationality, as if the judge had previously rejected one asylum applicant from another country and was then no longer in any position to adjust to the circumstances surrounding this case.

Mistrust on Both Sides

One cardinal symptom showing up conspicuously among a number of refugees is their own mistrust. Even in a relaxed atmosphere it often takes weeks or months before they are in any position to tell their tale of persecution in detail. Even in the therapeutic situation, painful events going back a long way can remain hidden.

This mistrust first and foremost affects the interpreter, who usually comes from the same culture as the applicant. The politically persecuted suspect that interpreters have a relationship with their countries' embassies, something that should not be entirely ruled out in some cases, especially where the interpreters were themselves refugees and have family members back home, on whose behalf the interpreters are vulnerable to blackmail. But the mistrust also affects the interviewer: Will my reports be treated confidentially? Is there an intra-agency exchange of files? Who has access to them?

Mistrust simultaneously affects the selection of what gets brought into evidence. The examiners expect that everything related to asylum will be presented by the applicant conclusively and within a short period of time. In general this expectation is articulated by the examiner. It affects an applicant who does not know what is regarded as relevant to asylum. An apprehensive applicant would rather present scenes of his persecution bit by bit, in the hope that he will get some indication of when he has told enough. The less he offers on his own, however, the more likely it is that he will be confronted with questions. These inquiries often have the goal of obtaining detailed information about the escape route and individual persecution. In general, when an applicant who was tortured does not mention this experience because the memory is painful and he refuses to recall it, he is not expressly asked about it, because proven traumatization could have some relevance for his residency status later on in court.

It is hard to see why questions about prison conditions and methods of interrogation are not posed, even though the answers could provide clues about human rights violations suffered firsthand whenever the applicant is prepared to describe them. The problem of human rights, to be sure, would then be pushed into the foreground, where apparently the examiner (following the rules and regulations) does not want to have it placed. Suffering from torture does not, per se, count as grounds for asylum. It must be a source of additional confusion to the applicant that human rights—invoked on everyone's tongue so freely in the Western world—only assume importance when the applicant conveys them doggedly. Indeed, the fact of repeatedly experienced human rights violations turns out to be irrelevant in asylum law if it cannot be demonstrated that these violations have been deliberately aimed at the person actually pleading for asylum.

Consequently, there is also no leaflet about the hearing to be handed out to the applicant when he applies for asylum and in which the requirements of the interview are laid out in the applicant's native language. This is why so many proceedings end up in administrative court, since there is at least a procedural order there.

No interviewing civil servant is free of the judgments and prejudices that society produces. He may try as hard as he likes, but he will not depart from the preexisting grid, largely derived from the executive, the Foreign Ministry. The examiner, too, develops mistrust. It sickens him to be deceived—and he is not infrequently deceived. Therefore his mistrust clashes with that of the applicant. What emerges are the conditions for a duel. Who really wants to be defeated? In its own way, this situation places a burden on the examiner; therefore some kind of supervision has to be promoted that can back up both examiner and judge. The examiner, who only rarely has any decent knowledge about the applicant's country of origin, evades this strain by emphasizing contradictions in testimony about places and especially about dates.

Psychomedical Considerations

There is, from a medical and psychological standpoint, a series of disruptive influences limiting an applicant's capacity for recall. These have been established in a number of experiments dealing with witnesses' memory that, simultaneously, have made a contribution to research on memory function and its mode of operation.

The precision with which memory traces are played back depends on several factors, including the applicant's age, the amount of time that has transpired since the event that is supposed to be recalled, the circumstances under which memory traces are supposed to be reproduced (or, to be more precise, produced), the scope of damage to the brain, distractions after the event, and the applicant's cultural framework.

If we take a closer look at these factors, which can lead to mnemonic disorders, it becomes clear that traumatized people are subject to greater risks of distortion. We have known administrative judges in asylum proceedings who were familiar with the literature on disruptive influences on memory, who therefore took into account minor contradictions in the applicant's story and who assessed these in favor of the applicant when they were persuaded about the traumatization itself.

It is a truism that memories are harder to retrieve among the elderly than in younger people. Deleting mechanisms are activated, or else access to stored memories is blocked. This even applies to autobiographical details, though not to traumatic experiences, which tend to be memorized more deeply under the influence of adrenaline and other stress hormones. Traumatic experiences can therefore enter consciousness spontaneously or turn into dream images. Even in old age they can surface again after a long latent period, as if they were leading an autonomous existence. To be sure, in many cases the details accompanying these memories have been buried, for example, dates, times of day, or names. If the traumatic experience is recounted over and over again, in many cases the effective memory trace of one's own story is the one most recently laid down. In the case of events bound up with shame and guilt, the memory becomes fainter, because it is either not articulated or only expressed in therapy. The silence and forgetting of German society as a whole, soldiers and civilians alike, after World War II might be taken as one indication of this phenomenon. The repeated telling of the same story (starving and freezing during the siege of Stalingrad) to friends, relatives, and therapists heightens the person's belief in the truth of what was told, independent of its objective truth content. Selective memory traces suppress significant details so that the part is taken for the whole truth.

The malfunctioning of memory is heightened in people who link a concrete desire to their story. Traumatized refugees certainly do have a concrete desire: they want a secure residency status in exile. To be sure, only in the rarest of cases are they able to tell their story of persecution, torture, and escape. Instead, they affect their hearing examiners in a manner similar to people with a war or pensioner's neurosis: they frequently concentrate on insignificant details, on a general portrayal of the situation in their homeland, on their anxieties, on events that have happened to other people, or on the costs arising from escape using an organization of professional refugee haulers. At the end, they appeal to Germany's democratic tradition. The minutes from some of these hearings often leave the reader speechless. The actual history that is relevant to asylum, by contrast, tends to be given a hesitant or inadequate presentation. The farther back an event to be recalled actually lies, the more uncertain the memory and the greater the possibility of being made to feel insecure by doubts and impatience articulated by the examiner.

After many years of research in the area of memory distortions and a vast number of experiments with an equally impressive number of different methods, what remains is astonishingly little in the way of uncontested or barely contested facts, according to psychologist Wolfgang Hell (Hell 1993). Even if attempts at explaining false or distorted memories are far from complete, at least some building blocks are generally recognized. For example, the degree of distortion is dependent on variables that influence the quality of memory, such as the time of storage and the quality of coding of the information to be recalled. If the memory trace for the information to be recalled is weak, the distortion is strong, as Wolfgang Hell explains. Hence it actually makes sense that the years in which events took place tend to leave behind very weak traces, since events are not engraved in memory in connection with dates but rather with external perceptions and the accompanying emotions. "There is no neuro-physiological function for storing memories of objective environmental representations," according to brain researcher H. R. Maturana (1982).

By contrast, it is still not clear what happens to memory under torture. It is a fact that memory becomes disoriented under hostile interrogation and that torturers aim at deliberately confusing recall. It is the torturer who not only determines real units of time under torture but who also damages historical orientation. The unit of time for torture remembered under intense emotions becomes stretched out and thus distorted. In the brain, fear of annihilation leads to a slowdown in the experience of time—similar to the impact of hallucinogens—that changes the synchronization between time as it is lived out and calendar time. Similarly, even anxiety about deportation, coupled with fears of repressive measures back home, can bring about a similar kind of disorientation. Anxiety anticipated in the brain is real anxiety. As a result of this kind of renewed disorientation, a young Turkish man almost threw himself off the sixth floor of the Berlin administrative courthouse. The twenty suicides alone during 1994 by asylum seekers in detention pending deportation should be taken seriously, as any human being's death deserves to be taken.

Subjective and Objective Memory Losses

Changes in memory resulting from extreme traumatization have been noncontroversial since systematic research was done on Holocaust survivors. They are part of basic knowledge for everyone who deals with torture survivors in therapeutic situations. As a result, therapists also know that traumatic experiences cannot simply be examined in the context of an administrative hearing without simultaneously pointing the way toward some prospect for joint processing with therapists. The (re)production of painful experiences in front of an examiner is not something that offers this prospect. It leaves an applicant in an unreal state of suspension whose consequences are not foreseeable. Even in a therapeutically supported situation, the dynamics of these consequences are not always predictable. To this extent, every hearing runs the risk of ending catastrophically. Under these circumstances, some hearings therefore have to be characterized as irresponsible.

A variety of mechanisms lead an applicant to refrain from telling about his traumatic experiences. The main reason is that he would like to forget. The hearings take place so soon after his escape that they actually occur in a period of exhaustion or depression. In this phase, there is a pronounced unwillingness to reflect on the conditions impelling escape. Basic traumas are hidden under a blanket of shame, which may be, but is not always, culturally determined. Torture by forcing objects into the anus is laden with shame in any culture. And we should remind ourselves about how upset we were when we learned about the mass rapes of women in Bosnia. Although even the presence of female civil servants is no inevitable guarantee that the hearings of female applicants will be conducted with the required sensitivity, for this reason alone their hearings should not be conducted by men.

In the context of processing their traumas, not a few refugees will unconsciously employ denial and avoidance. Their form of processing understandably hinders a detailed investigation of their traumatic memories. When the traumatic experience goes back years, protective coping mechanisms will have set in during the interim.

Cultural Aspects

According to Jan Assmann, "forgetting" is determined by a shift in framework, by a complete change of living conditions and social relations (Assmann and Harth 1991). These preconditions obviously apply to refugees, and they always apply to damaged people who come to us from completely different cultures. When asylum applicants come from cultures in which oral tradition carries the main burden of communication, they become overwhelmed by questions about dates, since they do not have a date-linked way of memorizing experiences. In cultures that operate by writing, connecting an event to a detailed time is customary; however, there are numerous people on this planet to whom this form of remembering is alien.

The French sociologist Maurice Halbwachs, who was murdered in Buchenwald, developed the thesis that there is no memory that is not social. Even the process of recall, the act of remembering, is linked to social conditions. If exile causes these to slip away, remembering is disturbed. Remembering means creating meaning for experiences in one's own framework; forgetting means changing the framework, in the course of which certain memories become disconnected and are therefore forgotten, while others enter into new connective patterns and are therefore remembered (Jan Assmann's explanation).

It may seem evident that the experience of torture cannot be integrated through remembrance: torture cannot acquire meaning through individual experience; it remains meaningless. Consequently, the attempt at remembering torture is a labor of Sisyphus. But simply mentioning a torture experience is not enough for some examiners—they want details. When these are mentioned hesitatingly, however, or only slip out in catchwords, persistent questioning follows. Good examiners, by contrast, call for a break in the face of all this emotional effort.

A special problem arises when asylum applicants run into conflicts of loyalty while presenting their history. Some refugees have sworn loyalty to a particular organization by oath. In order to protect their organization or party, they have agreed to say nothing about their own possible involvement in human rights violations. Their portrayals, therefore, often seem unconvincing and full of gaps. Behind their portrayal hides a secret they cannot reveal; therefore they need more time before this secret can emerge in a discernible way from behind their obviously superficial story. Even then, to be sure, it is often not possible to comprehend the "true" story. All that remains is the prevailing impression that something essential remains hidden. We have to come to terms with this and not attempt to fill the gap with our own imaginations.

Special Restrictions on Memory

When the Treatment Center and its professional staff (or a comparable institution) are brought in to provide a professional opinion, this guarantees that things will proceed in a trauma-centered manner and that a torture victim will not be viewed from the outset as a potential swindler. How a person remembers, how he formulates, and how he concentrates depends, after all, on the type of traumatization. We do not even need to look at the forms of sexual abuse that affect the deeper levels of the psyche. It suffices to take into consideration the widespread use and consequences of blows to the head and the back of the neck.

Among a major group of our patients, repeated blows to the head and back of the neck led to multiple losses of consciousness; consequently there may be repercussions from the beatings or disturbances in consciousness via heightened breathing (hyperventilation). Both forms often show up simultaneously. Wherever we have to assume loss of consciousness caused by beatings to the head with various objects, symptoms of repeated concussive blows to the head (*commotio cerebri*) show up. Bruises of the brain are not uncommon. Since those who have been tortured have often lost consciousness and suffer a retrograde or posttraumatic amnesia, they will not even be able to remember certain events that preceded their torture. Two-handed beatings against the ears create an enormous number of eardrum perforations with a characteristic arrangement of lesions (similar to noise trauma). The social consequences consist of communicative mistrust similar to cases we find among the hearing-damaged.

It is incontestable that blows reaching certain portions of the inner brain layers not only can lead to a collapse of the electrical activity of the brain but can also result in circulation changes within the cerebral cortex. This mechanism has been reconstructed in macabre animal experiments. The consequences can include different disorders in the capacity to remember, especially when pressure waves hit the area of the hippocampus. The delayed effects of boxing have a strong resemblance to the symptoms of torture survivors.

As a result, it is important to investigate the trauma exactly, in order to evaluate changes in the asylum applicant's ability to remember and recall. Evaluating traumatic aftereffects and the restrictions that ensue from them is something that physicians and psychologists, not lawyers, have to undertake.

Furthermore, estimating the effects of torture by means of electricity on the ability to remember is a very uncertain enterprise. In most cases, loss of consciousness resulting from electrical torture is likely to be caused by hyperventilation, induced by screaming and intensified breathing under torture. Altogether, there are several forms of torture that are either hard to prove or can only be established based on a patient's complete presentation. One should not, however, make the error of dismissing a particular form of torture and its consequences simply because one has not heard of it before or has run into extreme difficulty explaining it. Torturers vary their methods, and our proofs inevitably lag behind. This is especially true for those states that are increasingly replacing physical torture with refined forms of psychological torture.

We can be more certain about our testimony concerning memory disorders when we combine our experiences and those of experts in starvation cases following the Holocaust. From these we can see that poor nutrition caused by hunger or a hunger strike and its effects on the performance of memory should not be underestimated. Shortages of protein, vitamins, or calories have a critical impact. The nervous system, and by implication also its performance, suffers from their withdrawal.

Mere isolation from sensory impressions can decrease the blood flow to the brain, which causes a disorder in cognitive capacities, including the capacity to remember and concentrate.

Taking psychotropic medications in the country of exile, as well as poor treatment in prison back home using medications whose application is forbidden in the Western world, can influence memory at a hearing or in court. Studies of this are legion.

Epidemiological Research

So far only a few epidemiological studies are available in Europe that have investigated the frequency of torture experiences among refugees. A Danish investigation (Montgomery and Foldspang 1994) of arbitrarily chosen refugees from the Near East, using structured and semistructured interviews in 1994, shows that 30 percent of this sample had suffered torture. The underlying definition of torture experience used there comes from the Tokyo Declaration of the World Medical Association. A Swedish study (Norström and Persson 1988) that medically investigated and interviewed 187 newly arrived multiethnic refugees in Sweden in 1988 came to the conclusion that 25 percent of the refugees had experienced torture. Baker (in Basoglu 1992) estimates the frequency of torture experience among multiethnic refugees in England in 1992 at 5 to 30 percent.

Statistically speaking, one may expect every fourth refugee in Germany to also have experienced torture. One should be conscious of this if one does not want to overlook torture experiences. On the whole, one has to concede that traumatized asylum applicants are subject to numerous influences that have a disorienting impact on their memory and ability to recall. This becomes evident when one approaches from the perspective of trauma the mistaken or incomplete details they report at a hearing or an administrative court proceeding.

CHAPTER TWELVE

What Does This Work Do to Us?

Johan Lansen

Like all intensive work with "man-made disasters" (when humans are tormented by human hand), therapeutic work with torture victims leaves no one untouched. It is work that, in many respects, requires very personal participation by the therapist. This is not just about the serious aspects of psychological illness, the stories of misery, or specific challenges of treatment. (It is also not about something else, about some kind of "professional enmity" toward people of a given ethnic background.) Torture and psychotherapy are antithetical to each other. Where therapy aims at liberating people from pain, torture wants to oppress fellow human beings and consciously cause pain. Therapy promotes personal autonomy, while torture aims at total dependence. Therapy means growth; torture, deprivation of the psyche's brilliance and mutilation of the body. For that very reason, therapists and torturers are each other's mortal enemies. Normal therapeutic work helps the human being who has had bad luck, has fallen victim to illness, or has an unhappy story in his past.

As bad as this can be, it usually cannot compare with what we find among torture victims: the woman, the child, and the man who have been systematically mistreated or tormented have experienced this by *human hand.* We belong to the same species as the torturers; we are neither devils nor angels. The total antithesis derives from how they have "treated" fellow human beings diabolically, while we, by contrast, try to be guided by ethical precepts.

Can One Stand It?

"How can you stand all this?" "How can you keep listening to these stories?" These are questions often posed to us. As we shall see, there are professional answers, or at least attempts to respond professionally. To personal questions like this, however, one cannot offer answers as professionals; one senses that such answers are not valid in a personal context. Naturally, this work does something to us. It can deprive us of our sleep, and it can cause burnout. It can influence our behavior at home and among colleagues; it can turn us into annoying people. We can develop the same symptoms as our patients: tension, depression, and severe anxiety.

This work, however, can also elevate us above everyday trivialities, nurture our spirit and creative energies, and reconcile us to the inadequacies of others and of ourselves. It can turn us into warmer and wiser human beings.

But the torture victim—as a human being who has experienced the unspeakable, who carries this trauma around inside himself like a foreign body, whose "self" has been partly ruined—can (sometimes on his own accord, but usually with the help of others, such as therapists) lead a life that, ultimately and in spite of everything, is more differentiated, richer, and possibly even happier than if he had never had these experiences. In this respect, clear parallels to the torture victims show up among us therapists (even if we need to be on the alert about keeping our professional distance).

When therapists come into contact with torture indirectly, they may not be able to process their experiences for a while; identifying with the person who was unable to digest his experience of torture can have an impact that is shattering. But, just like victims, therapists (in principle) can always achieve some distance in order to reach the point where they can cautiously approach the horror again. For this process to work, therapists also require meaningful assistance. Gradually they learn to comprehend the horror, to endure it, and they become containers for feelings of grief, pain, and humiliation; together with their client, they can digest the latter's traumatic experiences.

Difficult Work

Therapeutic work is not easy, neither for those on the receiving end nor for the therapists. Treating clients who suffer from the effects of persecution and torture is essentially treatment of people who suffer from a form of extreme psychological trauma. As we experienced with Holocaust victims, the clinical picture of this kind of trauma explodes the narrow classification of posttraumatic stress disorder as defined in *DSM-IV* (American Psychiatric Association 1994).

Perhaps I can prove just how difficult intensive work with torture victims can be by looking at some sobering clinical facts. Here are a few clinical aspects that make treatment difficult:

— Persistent symptoms appear ("Complex PTSD," after Herman 1994).
— There are additional diagnoses besides PTSD, such as depression, compulsive behavior, etc.
— Even the diagnosis of depression seems not to reach far enough. Dutch colleagues speak of an "existential emotional syndrome" (Blijham 1992).
— Affects are severely disturbed (regression, reduced tolerance, anhedonia, loss of the ability to register feelings and perceptions and to find meaning and words for them) (Krystal 1988).
— As a result of heightened vulnerability, new traumatizations can be triggered by completely normal life events.
— The internal mental world can be permanently injured by an attitude of victimization, displayed in patterns of aggression and mistrust.

These structures can be hidden under the surface of social conformity. In intrahuman relations, however, they can damage those within the sphere of intimacy (partners, children). In a similar way, therapists working with the tortured can be indirect victims of the trauma.

Burnout

Every intensive kind of work with groups of deeply suffering, injured patients carries the risk of burnout. Burnout symptoms (to pick just a few) are apathy,

feelings of hopelessness, rapid fatigue, disillusionment, melancholy, forgetful-
ness, irritability, experiencing work as a heavy burden.

The phenomena of burnout manifest themselves not only among the therapists who treat torture victims. Other staff, such as administrative personnel,
secretaries, telephone receptionists, and translators can be affected by burnout
over the course of time. In this respect, treatment centers for torture patients
are not essentially different from other institutions working with the intense
pathologies and problems of clients, such as with AIDS patients, victims of
racist or sexist discrimination, or drug-addicted youth.

Professionals and volunteers doing this humanitarian work often get involved not only in every aspect of their clients' emotional problems but also in
their institutional (Herman 1992) or organizational problems because the outside world often displays minimal insight into and little understanding of these
latter difficulties. In a treatment center for torture victims, problems often turn
up that go beyond the experience of torture. There are major difficulties ad-
justing to a foreign country and a foreign culture. Language problems and
difficulties with residency status crop up. Beyond that, refugees have suffered
heavy losses, such as the loss of friends and family, of work and social status. In
many families there are complicated problems with relationships and health.

The treatment centers and their sponsoring organizations frequently have
to use limited resources for completing extraordinary assignments in which
therapists are also enlisted. The centers—and this is how it is across almost the
entire world—often exist outside the regular systems of healthcare and social
assistance. Instead of receiving public subsidies—as ought to be the case in any
respectable social welfare state such as Germany—one has to raise money oneself and, in addition, worry about the organization's public relations. At the
same time there are demands on such a center, not only to care for torture
victims, but also to conduct research, to receive visitors from other branches of
the healthcare field, and to take positions on numerous things that happen in
society and on social policy.

In this way, highly motivated therapists and other staff can become heavily
burdened. Symptoms of exhaustion become apparent among individuals and in
teams. In a team where burnout is present, there is a gradual loss of energy. Energy
is dissipated in nagging and whining, in complaints about management, in dis-
putes about workload. One's own jobs are in danger of being neglected.

Being Affected Goes Beyond Burnout

Therapists who treat victims of persecution and torture can themselves develop classic symptoms of the kind described under the rubric of posttraumatic stress disorder, for example, intrusive nightmares in which one is confronted by violence oneself, or where one is tortured oneself. Upon waking, one feels very vulnerable. Anxieties can appear in which something in everyday life that normally has no particular meaning is experienced as a threat, for example, a barking dog, a man in a uniform, a slamming door, or the sight of a large knife. These events can elicit inappropriate reactions of horror, flight, or paralysis.

Among the more long-lasting mental aftereffects is a growing feeling of alienation, of isolation. One feels that one is no longer understood by friends and family members and loses confidence that anything good is possible in this world. Personal happiness is lost; at home one becomes quiet and reserved; one cannot regain one's previous sense of security; one is disillusioned with humanity.

The concept of burnout, therefore, does not suffice to describe the possible aftereffects of working with torture victims. Therapists are constantly exposed to emotionally disturbing images of torture and terror and cannot avoid their influence.

An attempt has been made to provide a different explanation for the specific effects on therapists treating torture victims or other severely traumatized victims of man-made disasters. For example, the cause has been sought in the especially vulnerable personality of individual therapists (idealists with a good heart taking on too much grief). Probably this only applies to a minority of cases. The cause is also sought in especially suggestive effects that horrifying stories of human cruelty and unbearable losses have on therapists, effects that can be distinguished from the rather unspecific effects of burnout. Another explanation of a more classical nature aims at therapists' feelings of counter-transference: a reaction to the story that the therapist can no longer control, to the thoughts and to the behavior of clients that derives from the therapist's own vulnerabilities. Finally, another cause cited is a too great identification with (and not enough distance from) clients.

Before I review some of these explanations, I would like to give a brief overview of how these difficulties become apparent at the level of behavior in therapeutic practice. How can the phenomena be described in relatively simple words? Here, with some slight variation, I follow the description of Van der Veer (1991), who described three stages of reactions in therapists: during the session, then shortly thereafter, and finally after a somewhat longer time.

While the therapist and client are engaged in conversation. Listening to a victim can lead to surprising reactions on the part of the therapist. The client can tell his story so movingly that it makes the therapist shudder or feel choked up with tears. Of course, the aspects that turn out to affect the therapist depend on his personality. Listening to a moving story can also create an intense closeness to the client. Other possible reactions to a client's experiences are as follows:

— The therapist avoids asking a series of questions that obviously should be posed.
— The therapist fails to notice certain statements made by the client, or else a particular statement's emotional charge eludes him.
— The therapist unconsciously changes the subject during a conversation when the subject unnerves him. This can easily be the case when the victim himself has also been a perpetrator in his native country.

The therapist has to be able to deal with any strong emotions aroused in him, so he can concentrate on the client. But what goes on between client and therapist can also have a very positive value: the therapist may cautiously take this as a sign that he, too, is a human being making an effort to deal with this story, yet able to endure it.

Shortly after the session. The therapist will have to get over the trauma material within some period of time. If he cannot shake off this story, it will also become difficult for him to concentrate on other things. At home people might ask him: "What is preoccupying you? You're so distracted."

The need to share the trauma story with someone can be intense; sometimes this is possible during short breaks between sessions. Deliberately planned case presentations would be quite useful in this regard, but usually they cannot be immediately organized in critical moments. When there is an extremely burdensome story, it can prove helpful to let the therapist undergo an immediate emotional debriefing (cf. Mitchell and Everly 1993).

It is conceivable that a therapist might not be able to shake off the feelings he experiences in therapy sessions, such as powerlessness, pessimism, profound rage, and aggression. These feelings are not always easy for the therapist to recognize, and for that very reason they remain disturbing; the therapist can then become tense and tire easily. These disturbances can also, for example, express themselves in a refusal to write up a record of a conversation, or else there could be dissatisfaction regarding the next conversation that takes place with the client, so that the therapist feels greatly relieved when the client calls and cancels the next session.

Even treatments that are going well can often be upset by current events: an asylum request is rejected; a house in which asylum applicants live is attacked by racists; bad news arrives from the home country. The therapist then feels frustrated and partly responsible for the decision of the authorities or for the behavior of his fellow countrymen; he feels powerless in the face of this misery.

In the long run. Repeatedly being confronted with human evil, with horrible forms of suppression and injustice, can fundamentally change a person's images of self, humanity, and the world. So, too, it may lead to a lasting change in the therapist's attitude toward his work. A strong temptation can arise to step back too far, to stop writing up records, to develop prejudices against certain categories of clients, or to keep a distance from clients with difficult problems by conveying a less inviting attitude. An inclination can develop to investigate clients less thoroughly, as a result of which appropriate therapeutic steps in extremely difficult cases can no longer be taken. The therapist can also become inclined to cease consulting with experienced colleagues. In brief, a lowering of professional norms sets in.

This distancing often happens as a reaction to prior intense involvements in treatments. Most therapists have chosen this kind of work for idealistic reasons, and initially they throw themselves into it. When they can no longer take it anymore, this is often followed by reactions having the character of avoidance (cf. Wilson and Lindy 1994).

Some Data

Teams that treat victims of torture and persecution are often aware of these dangers. I sent out a questionnaire to the treatment centers that are connected to the IRCT in Copenhagen (Lansen 1993), and I got back twenty-three questionnaires that were filled out by treatment centers worldwide. The goal of the questionnaire was to gain an impression of the phenomenon of vicarious traumatization.

Approximately 10 percent of the roughly three hundred therapists in these centers were affected by the ailments described above. Methodologically this investigation has its weak points. It is interesting, though, that the majority of these centers were clearly aware of the risks of working with torture victims and that they also had clear ideas about the measures required to combat these. The major recommendations, in order of preference, were:

—external supervision by an experienced therapist
—peer group supervision (collegial support)
—limits on workload; control of the number of cases

The phenomenon was empirically investigated in the Netherlands by Hafkenscheid and Lansen (1993). All the therapists investigated were treating traumatized as well as other kinds of clients. Ninety percent experienced work with a traumatized client as the most difficult. Approximately 20 percent of these therapists were themselves traumatized by this work. The therapists were, as a rule, not predisposed this way owing to traumatic experiences of their own; instead they developed symptoms as a result of working with the victims.

This investigation's results allow one to assume that the phenomenon of vicarious traumatization is empirically verifiable.

Explanatory Models

Three explanatory models for vicarious traumatization are the most current in therapeutic circles:

—the model of vicarious traumatization developed by McCann and Pearlman (1990)
—a model based on psychoanalytic object relations theory (elaborated by the author)
—a model that stresses special empathy and identification (Wilson and Lindy 1994)

Within the context of their theory, McCann and Pearlman attempt to classify the reactions of therapists to traumatic material revealed by clients. They call these reactions vicarious traumatization, but perhaps "transmitted" or "induced" traumatization would be better designations. Therapists suffer from nightmares, anxieties, and intrusive images. They become mistrustful because they experience the ruinous effects of stories that traumatized people tell. These stories undermine the basic security about oneself, about fellow human beings, and about the world that a therapist has acquired in the course of his development. The basic ideas (also called schemata, or patterns) that are ruined include feelings of secure attachment to fellow human beings, of trust, the very feeling of security in life. These fundamental ideas may be at least partially eroded, and in their place there emerges an awareness of abuse and the vulnerability of human life. The therapist loses his feeling of power and competence—the powerlessness of clients may lead him to feel that it is an illusion to think it is possible to control one's life. Everything can be destroyed in a second by unanticipated events.

The victim, with his damaged body and mind, can confront and embarrass the therapist with his own anxiety about the loss of personal freedom. The therapist can go on to become an embittered and cynical person and lose all respect for his fellow human beings. Confrontation with a cruel reality alienates the therapist from his family, friends, and colleagues.

Therapists can also take over their clients' memory pictures, whereby their own memory can be temporarily or permanently changed. In this way visual images of the client's traumatized material can show up without having any meaning in the context of the therapist's own life. These alien images intrude in the form of flashbacks and nightmares. (The authors cite the example of a therapist who had a nightmare in which the rape of one of her patients takes place.)

In the authors' theory, these images turn up especially in those mental domains where the therapists themselves are vulnerable. A therapist for whom security is very important will probably experience images associated with whatever is life-threatening. A therapist for whom the subject of respect is more important will probably experience threatening images that contain humiliation and cruelty. In short, McCann and Pearlman emphasize the power of cognitive elements in transmitting the patient's trauma history to the therapist. In principle, clients' experiences can affect all therapists.

The second explanatory model looks not so much at the client's horrible stories as at the *injury done to the client's inner mental world.* Here we are dealing with a kind of deep inflicted wound to the client's self, which, in turn, profoundly moves and involves the therapist during an intensive therapeutic relationship, through a process of protective identification.

During an episode of torture, early images from childhood are reawakened. It is seen as a repetition of cruel incidents that had been experienced as anxieties and fantasies in the pre-Oedipal period, at a time when the distinction between self and external world was not yet even possible. This seeming repetition is like a regression, a return to a level of diminished differentiation among cognitive schemata. In the torture cell, castration anxieties are revived, but also feelings of total powerlessness and worthlessness as they used to exist (which is something we know from, among other sources, observations from child analysis and treating adult patients with borderline personality disorder).

The victim learns again to think, to feel, and to classify the world at a very primitive level. These cognitive schemata are not only cognitive, but they also have a strong affective charge. They are usually polarized into simple oppositions like "persecutor (aggressor)-victim," "good-bad," "strong-weak," or "superior-inferior."

Among people who have been tortured severely over a longer period of time, these regressions later fail to abate: they remain as a form of injury to the self. This injury takes on a lasting role: it structures, in a certain sense, these people's new experiences. The major liability is that it plays a special role in the sphere of intimacy (torture can be seen as a perverted act of intimacy). The influence on relations with one's partner and children can be quite strong. This is something we also find among Holocaust victims: partners who were not persecuted and the children born after liberation, the so-called second generation, can be strongly affected indirectly.

Something similar also happens in the therapeutic relationship. The client unwittingly engages the therapist in aspects of relationships that are repetitions of the traumatic torture stories. Even without an exact cognitive representation or knowledge of the torture story, the therapist can be sucked into a pattern whose content is a repetition of the persecutor-victim theme: for example, a pattern of persecution behavior can emerge in therapy. Both therapist and client can assume the role of persecutor. Patterns of powerlessness, guilt, and incrimination can emerge. With respect to the client's experience, roles can change in the course of repetition. The therapist can thus be seen as "very good and wise," but also as "very bad and mean."

Relationship patterns of this kind can be destructive in therapy when they are not adequately recognized and taken up as a theme. In this way, therapists are exposed to the experiences of the torture cell.

This explanation picks up on modern conceptions of psychoanalysis. Today one sees in every kind of intensive treatment a dimension of pre-Oedipal character that goes beyond the classic relationship of transference to countertransference (the latter affects the Oedipal level). One can certainly view the pre-Oedipal relationship as the "primary relationship" (de Jonghe, Rijnierse, and Janssen 1991). Especially among torture victims, this dimension of the relationship is therefore very important.

In simplified terms, this explanation does not put the client's horrible story, but rather his deepest injury, at the center. This leads to a repetition of the client's experiences in contemporary personal relationships. In these relationships, very destructive processes can develop in which injuring the self of one person (the victim) ultimately leads to self-injury for another (the therapist).

In the third model, Wilson and Lindy (1994) take up the theme of the special patient-therapist relationship in treating extremely traumatized clients.

Publications since the second half of the eighties have repeatedly and increasingly emphasized that traditional ideas and views of psychoanalysis are insufficient in this area of treatment. On a broad psychoanalytic foundation, Wilson and Lindy have developed a new theoretical approach.

In their view, the emphasis is on the capacity of the therapist for *empathy* with the client, for profound understanding and identification. At first this empathy is usually quite possible, but in the course of treatment it becomes more difficult, depending on how the trauma story develops. The empathetic relationship comes under pressure because the client himself has not integrated the traumatic experiences. The client is inclined toward projecting his trauma-specific transferences onto the therapist, because he unconsciously relates to the therapist in a manner affected by the unresolved, unassimilated, and ego-alien aspects of the traumatic occurrence. The torture cell's unnatural situation thus repeats itself.

The therapist will then identify with the client's painful memories and feelings. He must be able to empathize with feelings of humiliation and ruin, and he must clearly perceive this empathy. He has to unfold and enrich his empathy in a process of habituation and growth. If he cannot do this and cannot be conscious of it, then there is not only a possibility that the therapy will fail but also that the therapist will be injured.

Wilson and Lindy refer to two major ways in which therapists can go off the track. Type 1 is maintaining too great a distance: the therapist eschews empathy and tends to reflect this deficiency in his behavior; for example, by intellectualizing and withdrawing behind a façade of neutrality. When therapists then go beyond this to the point of giving up for personal reasons, they can even repress experiences from therapy and negate the emotional significance of the material. Type 2 reactions, by contrast, have to do with too strong an identification. When therapists feel insecure as a result of personal imbalance, they also lose sight of boundaries in the therapy. This can give rise to a very difficult situation with strong involvement and behaviors of excessive participation or mutual dependence.

The authors take the view that every therapist, regardless of his personality, is subject to the risk of going off the track. The consequences, however, are more serious for those therapists whose own psychological structure is unstable.

Both empathy and distance are necessary. Experiencing growing empathy while maintaining distance is an optimal condition for treatment. When the therapist understands the client's unique experience and the influences on his life, an essential therapeutic structure emerges, enabling a growth process for the client.

Some Recommendations

What does this work do to us? How and why do these processes happen? How can we best prevent burnout, entanglements, or the danger of too much distance? What lessons can we draw, and how can we put the problem to positive use? In the preceding, I have partially answered these questions. Much remains unclear, however, and should be investigated further.

I am hopeful that, by today's standards of psychotherapy, the kinds of feelings I have described will no longer be regarded as shameful. We are already beginning to talk about them calmly, and they signify an enrichment of the treatment process if they are recognized, understood, and personally processed correctly. This way we heighten our capacity for compartmentalizing in our therapeutic relationships. The more multifaceted and the deeper our resonance, the more latitude our client experiences.

It also becomes clear that we are in a better position, when we do not remain alone, to see the dangers in our feelings. Traumatized clients have to speak and must not remain stuck in the silence of what they have experienced, but it is just as important for therapists to talk and share their experiences. Where possible, they should do this in a working group, a team, for it is ill-advised to carry out this work alone. Forms of collegial support and/or supervision by experienced colleagues are necessary. In many cases, an acute emotional debriefing is also essential.

These measures cost time and money. It is essential that administrators, umbrella organizations, and sponsors see how worthwhile this effort is, since it has a positive impact on the quality of therapeutic work.

Furthermore, it is necessary that care be taken in building a treatment team. In addition to professional qualifications and work experience, the staff's personal stability is important.

Administrators knowledgeable about both questions of treatment and management have to pay attention to distributing work properly and to checking up on treatment goals, as well as seeing to it that these are appropriate to the clientele's changing needs.

In the restricted world of individualistically inclined therapists, it is too easily assumed that an idealistic attitude and good intentions will suffice. Although idealism is necessary, to be sure, it is not enough.

Even a team needs to have a compartmentalizing function, and needs to develop ways to keep client issues from splitting staff. For this, one needs a head as well as a heart; otherwise the danger arises that regressive and destructive team phenomena will emerge (Bustos 1990).

In today's world, torture is becoming more systematic and more "scientific." From an international perspective, there are many countries where—in spite of numerous human rights treaties—people are systematically tortured by the police, military, secret intelligence services, and others, and not just physically, but also and increasingly psychologically. There are indications that knowledge about torture methods and their effectiveness is shared and transmitted, that there exists a kind of international society of torturers with opportunities for learning from each other.

In democratic (but also in nondemocratic) countries, this group is confronted by another international society that attempts to readmit tortured people into human society. They form loosely structured healing networks. Their staff—therapists and others—are democratic and, therefore, frequently less battle-hardened, seemingly weaker and more vulnerable. By swimming against the current of destruction and tragedy, however, they gain experience and knowledge. They work within a circle that has an ethical foundation and is not dependent on the coercion of ruling dictators or an authoritarian clique. For these reasons, their power will become stronger than anything that takes place inside the coercive strongholds of concrete and steel, and they

> shall renew their strength;
> they shall mount up with wings as eagles;
> they shall run, and not be weary;
> and they shall walk, and not faint.
>
> —(Isaiah 40:31)

Legal Status, Living Conditions, and Health Care for Political Refugees in Germany

Christian Pross

Legal Status

The German Constitution of 1949, intending to overcome the heritage of the Nazi state, carries one of the world's most liberal asylum provisions, stating simply in Article 16a: "Politically persecuted persons enjoy the right to asylum." Asylum includes the right to enter the country and apply for asylum; to have one's case heard by the authorities; to have an interpreter present at the hearing; to obtain legal assistance and access to the court if the asylum authority rejects one's application; to be accommodated in a refugee camp on arrival; and to receive food, clothing, and monthly welfare payments.

Since the adoption of the constitution, large numbers of individuals from all over the world have sought shelter in Germany. In the 1970s and early 1980s they came from Eastern Europe, Vietnam, Chile, Central America, Lebanon, Sri Lanka, and Iran; in the late 1980s and early 1990s a Kurdish population also began to arrive from Iraq and Turkey. Germany has hosted large numbers of asylum seekers, rising from 107,800 in 1980 to 438,000 in 1992, at which time it hosted two-thirds of all people seeking asylum in European countries.*

* F. Nuscheler, *Internationale Migration Flucht und Asyl* (Opladen: Leske und Budrich, 1995), 48.

In response to rising xenophobia after the reunification of Germany in 1990 and championing of the slogan "the boat is full," a coalition across party lines in the Bundestag (the German Parliament) passed an amendment to the constitution in 1993 making it difficult for individuals to be granted asylum. Key to this amendment is the so-called third-country rule, which states that anyone who has passed through a "safe" third country on the way to Germany from a home country is not entitled to asylum in Germany. The bulk of asylum seekers in Germany fall under this category, because their escape routes generally led through Austria, Poland, the Czech Republic, France, or the Netherlands— safe countries bordering Germany where refuge could theoretically have been sought. Only individuals arriving directly from their home country by plane or boat or entering illegally with the help of "tugger gangs" (*Schlepperbanden*) have a chance of circumventing the third-country rule. As a result, the number of those granted asylum has diminished considerably since 1993.

The two largest groups in the patient population of the Behandlungs-zentrum für Folteropfer Berlin (Berlin Center for the Treatment of Torture Victims) are refugees from the former Yugoslavia (Bosnia-Herzegovina and Kosovo) and Kurdish refugees from Turkey. The Kurdish population in South-eastern Turkey is a suppressed minority living under martial law. They are not allowed to preserve their own culture or language or to govern themselves in some kind of regional autonomy. Instead, the Turkish government and the military having been fighting a "search and destroy" kind of low-intensity war against the Kurdish population, destroying villages and arresting and torturing large numbers of suspected members of the militant Kurdish liberation movement "PKK" and other opposition groups.

Since the military coup in Turkey in 1980 there has been a constant migration of political refugees to Germany, which since the late 1960s has seen a growing number of immigrant workers from Turkey. Thus refugees found a relatively large existing native community. Berlin hosts the largest Kurdish community of all German and all European cities.

Germany has accepted the largest number of Bosnian refugees (about 320,000) of any European country.* However, these individuals have not been

---

* Pro Asyl, *Keine Rückführung mit der Brechstange* (Frankfurt am Main: Pro Asyl e. V., with support from the European Commission, 1997). Pro Asyl is an organization for refugee aid.

granted asylum under Article 16a. Instead, like the refugees who came to Germany from Vietnam and Lebanon in the 1970s and 1980s, they have been accepted as asylees (*Kontingentflüchtlinge*) under the Geneva Convention.* As a result, since the Dayton Peace Accord of December 1995, Bosnian refugees have faced increasing pressure to "voluntarily" return to Bosnia-Herzegovina. Several thousand Bosnians have already returned voluntarily, and German state governments offer repatriation subsidies to encourage them to do so.† Although relatively few persons have been forcibly repatriated so far, the authorities have created "pressure to return"—as they call it—by, for example, suddenly arresting groups of Bosnians and flying them home under cover of darkness.

Living Conditions

Upon arriving in Germany, individuals are sent to centralized camps, which are usually deserted barracks or public buildings. These camps have many of the indicators of "totalitarian institutions" described in Goffman's classic study "Asylums." The camps are often located in isolated areas, hard to reach by public transportation and surrounded by barbed wire with guards posted at the entrance. Camp personnel are given authority equivalent to that of a police force. Individuals living in the camps can be subjected to body searches and their fingerprints forwarded to the state Central Register of Foreigners. Within a short time after arrival, a computerized distribution system allocates refugees to camps scattered in different German states according to a quota system. This anonymous bureaucratic procedure often ignores individual wishes, such as the desire to be located near relatives already settled in Germany. After their first year in Germany, individuals can be transferred to one of the many smaller hostels managed privately for profit. The owners of these hostels keep lodgers in overcrowded, extremely shabby conditions while taking high fees from the welfare department for each individual lodger. Among insiders these hostels are

* The word *Kontingentflüchtlinge* is usually translated as "contingent refugees"—victims of a civil war or a war within a particular country who are hosted according to the Geneva Convention as a group, not as individual asylum seekers.

† M. Mohr, "Traumatisierte Flüchtlinge und Bürgerkriegsflüchtlinge in Deutschland," *ZDWF-Schriftenreihe* 72 (1998): 37.

called "lice houses." The terrible living conditions in most camps, homes, and hostels certainly do not offer a traumatized person the rest or the privacy necessary for recovery.*

Individuals are given a hearing in front of the German authorities within the first few days after arrival. The asylum authorities must be given a detailed account of the reasons for seeking asylum and any other relevant details. This report is expected to be complete, and the authorities consider any new or supplemental information added later to be an aggravation. The hearings, held by an interrogator who is assisted by an interpreter, rarely last more than an hour. A hearing protocol is drafted, the interpreter translates it orally, and it is then signed by the applicant. The time for going over the protocol with the interpreter is often much too short to enable the applicant to make corrections.

A study of hearing protocols taken from patients of the Berlin Center has shown that interrogators rarely pay attention to clues indicating past trauma and torture.† The hearings often resemble police interrogations and may therefore have a retraumatizing effect on applicants who have been harrassed by the military or the police in their home country. In addition, this procedure ignores the fact that the main characteristics of traumatized persons and torture victims may be their shame and silence, their mistrust and their difficulty speaking about the trauma to a stranger. Memory loss and a tendency to avoid painful topics (a self-protecting psychological mechanism) can cause a person to confuse dates and produce blank spots in biographical data.‡ Cultural differences are also often disrespected in the hearings. For example, while the German authorities expect an individual to prove that he or she has personally been persecuted, applicants whose culture encourages them to think collectively may be more inclined to report the persecution of their people or political organization as a whole. German courts have begun to pay increasing attention to these issues and to accept "aggravation," omissions, avoidance behavior (e.g., reluc-

---

* See F. Merkord's chapter in this book.

† S. Graessner and R. Weber, *Umgang mit Folteropfern im Asylverfahren. Qualitative und Quantitative Auswertung von 40 Asylanhörungsprotokollen und Asylentscheidungen des Bundesamtes für die Anerkennung ausländischer Flüchtlinge* (Berlin: Republikanischer Anwaltsverein, 1996).

‡ See Graessner, Ahmad, and Merkord's chapter in this book.

tance to report rape), or contradictory statements as psychological symptoms that do not necessarily undermine an applicant's credibility.*

Individuals who find their asylum application rejected or who are denied legal status for some other reason may find themselves in "deportation prisons" while they await deportation to their country of origin. This is meant to be something like preventive detention. Care of these individuals does not fall under the jurisdiction of criminal law, but they are nonetheless often treated like criminals. The conditions vary from state to state. For example, North-Rhine Westfalia is known to try to provide humane living conditions in its deportation prisons, whereas the conditions in Berlin are scandalous. The Berlin facility is known to forbid refugees from occupying themselves, to allow them outside for only one hour each day, and to mandate that all conversations with visitors occur behind a screen. Medical services are provided by police doctors who offer only minimum care. An inmate must overcome considerable bureaucratic and financial obstacles in order to see a health care provider from outside the facility. Although most individuals are deported or released after a short period of time, some can spend more than a year in detention while awaiting a final decision in their case or because they lack the necessary identification papers. Not surprisingly, a number of suicides have been reported in deportation detention.[†]

Health Care

Physicians who wish to give adequate care to refugees feel handcuffed, as emphasized by a brochure edited by the Berlin Medical Association entitled "Medicine in Handcuffs."[‡] Different legal categories entitle people to different types of medical care. Employed individuals who have been granted asylum under Article 16a of the German Constitution receive the same coverage as a worker born in Germany. If unemployed, they fall under Federal Welfare Law,

---

[*] M. Mohr, "Traumatisierte Flüchtinge," 37.

[†] Flüchtlingsrat Berlin, Ärztekammer Berlin, and Pro Asyl e.V., eds., *Gefesselte Medizin: Ärztliches Handeln—abhängig von Aufenthaltsrechten* (Berlin: Flüchtlingsrat, Ärztekammer Berlin, and Pro Asyl e.V., 1998). It is to the credit of the Ärztekammer Berlin (the Berlin Medical Association) that such a brochure was published.

[‡] Ibid.

which grants health care to people on welfare. This law, however, denies foreigners health care coverage for such things as orthopedic surgery and devices,
visual and hearing aids, and dental care.*

Next in the hierarchy are individuals awaiting decisions from the asylum
authority or the asylum court. This waiting period can last for several years
because the authorities and courts are poorly staffed and equipped. During the
first year of their stay in Germany, asylum seekers fall under the Law on Services
for Asylum Seekers, which grants medical care only in the case of severe pain
or acute illness. In the case of a chronic illness, it is civil servants working at
welfare agencies or, in some cases, public health officers who judge whether
outpatient or hospital treatment is absolutely necessary to preserve health.
Since the summer of 1997, the Law on Services for Asylum Seekers has provided
asylum seekers and "tolerated refugees" with limited welfare payments and
health care up to the first three years of their stay. "Tolerated refugees" are those
who have been denied political asylum but who cannot be repatriated because
their country of origin is unclear, they do not have and cannot obtain passports,
or their home country refuses to take them back. Individuals who are in the
country illegally are by law not entitled to receive health care. Of course, some
may find a sympathetic doctor willing to treat them.[†]

Asylum seekers must obtain a health insurance voucher (*Krankenschein*) in
order to see a doctor. In Berlin, German welfare recipients receive vouchers
directly from the welfare agency. In contrast, asylum seekers are given a voucher
application which must be signed by their doctor. The patient then sends this
application to the welfare agency, which in turn sends the voucher on to the
doctor. This awkward procedure is intended to prevent abuse by ensuring that
individuals do not pass their voucher on to someone else. As a consequence,
doctors receive vouchers (which they need in order to be reimbursed by the
welfare agency) only after long delays. This leads many doctors to refuse to
treat asylum seekers or to demand a cash advance—something few asylum
seekers can afford. The end result is, of course, that many asylum seekers see
health care providers only in the emergency rooms of city hospitals, where the
care is given late, in a rather anonymous setting, and lacks follow-up. These

* Ibid.
[†] Ibid.

emergency room treatments are much more expensive than routine appointments with a family physician and cost the state much more in the end.*

Approximately 90 percent of the patients of the Berlin Center do not have full health insurance coverage, and of those approximately half are asylum seekers. Therefore, most of the treatment provided by the Center—physiotherapy, psychotherapy, art therapy, sophisticated orthopedic and plastic surgery—is not covered by the state and has to be paid for through grants and donations. A doctor or psychologist in private practice can rarely afford to treat traumatized asylum seekers, and, as a result, the few treatment centers that do exist have huge waiting lists.

In German culture, public life is overregulated by laws, decrees, and orders. It follows that the legal framework for refugees and asylum seekers is so complicated, and in part so illogical, that it is hard for nonlawyers to understand, let alone an asylum seeker or nonnative speaker. Political bodies and authorities have shown impressive creativity in inventing new laws every couple of years.[†] In addition, the administrative procedures required for the provision of health care to refugee and asylum seekers has resulted in inflated bureaucracy and excessive costs.

A comparison of European countries shows that Germany—although taking in the largest absolute number of asylum seekers in the 1980s and 1990s—is currently at the top of the list of hardliners with respect to asylum policies.[‡] It is followed by Switzerland, the United Kingdom, and the Netherlands. France and Sweden have the most liberal policies but have indicated they are likely to follow the German model more closely.[§]

* Ibid.

[†] This is demonstrated in the following three publications on health care for refugees: Ärztegruppe Asyl, ed., *Abschrecken statt Heilen, zur medizinischen Versorgung von Asylbewerbern* (Berlin: Ärztegruppe Asyl, 1986); C. Pross, "Apartheid in der Medizin? Zur Situation der Krankenversorgung von politischen Flüchtlingen," *Berliner Ärzte* 5 (1990): 27–28; and Flüchtlingsrat Berlin, Ärztekammer Berlin and Pro Asyl e.V., eds., *Gefesselte Medizin.*

[‡] B. Leuthardt, *Festung Europa* (Zürich: Rotpunktverlag, 1994), 150.

[§] Ibid.

Posttraumatic Stress Disorder (PTSD)

Posttraumatic Stress Disorder (*PTSD*), in German: *Posttraumatische Belastungs-störung* (*PTBS*). The English concept is in common use and has been classified as a diagnosis since 1980 in the *Diagnostic and Statistical Manual of Mental Disorders* (*DSM*) of the American Psychiatric Association (APA). Since torture victims were usually subjected, lengthily and repeatedly, to extreme forms of stress (years of persecution, frequently multiple incarcerations, persistent and/or repeated torture, flight, the shock of exile, retraumatization in exile), PTSD falls short as a concept. There is often no closure for trauma after it first happens; instead, the trauma persists (ongoing traumatic stress). It is advisable to consult the concepts of *complex PTSD* (Herman 1992) and *DES* (*disorders of extreme stress*) (Van der Kolk et al. 1996). It also makes sense to differentiate among

— man-made disasters (committed by human hand—torture, rape, attack, kidnapping, etc.);
— technological catastrophes (chemical accidents, nuclear power plant disasters, sinking ships, airplane crashes, etc.); and
— natural catastrophes (earthquakes, floods, volcanic eruptions, etc.).

For work with torture victims, the "by human hand" aspect has special significance with respect to the spectrum of illnesses going beyond the spectrum of PTSD symptoms (comorbidity) as well as for difficulties in treatment (mistrust, transference of perpetrators' features onto therapists, and destruction of assumptions about the self, other people, and the world). In practice it makes sense to connect the basic concept of PTSD with the more far-reaching concepts of complex PTSD and DES.

PTSD Criteria according to DSM-IV (APA 1994)

A. The person has been exposed to a traumatic event in which both of the following were present:

1. The person experienced, witnessed, or was confronted with an event or events that involved actual or threatened death or serious injury, or a threat to the physical integrity of self or others.

2. The person's response involved intense fear, helplessness, or horror. *Note:* In children, this may be expressed instead by disorganized or agitated behavior.

B. The traumatic event is persistently reexperienced in one or more of the following ways:

1. Recurrent and intrusive distressing recollections of the event, including images, thoughts, or perceptions. *Note:* In young children, repetitive play may occur in which themes or aspects of the trauma are expressed.

2. Recurrent distressing dreams of the event. *Note:* In children, there may be frightening dreams without recognizable content.

3. Acting or feeling as if the traumatic event were recurring (including a sense of reliving the experience, illusions, hallucinations, and dissociative flashback episodes, including those that occur on awakening or when intoxicated). *Note:* In young children, trauma-specific reenactment may occur.

4. Intense psychological distress at exposure to internal or external cues that symbolize or resemble an aspect of the traumatic event.

5. Physiological reactivity on exposure to internal or external cues that symbolize or resemble an aspect of the traumatic event.

C. Persistent avoidance of stimuli associated with the trauma and numbing of general responsiveness (not present before the trauma), as indicated by three or more of the following:

1. Efforts to avoid thoughts, feeling, or conversation associated with the trauma.

2. Efforts to avoid activities, places, or people that arouse recollections of the trauma.

3. Inability to recall an important aspect of the trauma.
4. Markedly diminished interest or participation in significant activities.
5. Feelings of detachment or estrangement from others.
6. Restricted range of affect (e.g., unable to have loving feelings).
7. Sense of a foreshortened future (e.g., does not expect to have a career, marriage, children, or a normal life span).

D. Persistent symptoms of increased arousal (not present before the trauma), as indicated by two or more of the following:
   1. Difficulty falling or staying asleep.
   2. Irritability or outbursts of anger.
   3. Difficulty concentrating.
   4. Hypervigilance.
   5. Exaggerated startle response.

E. Duration of the disturbance (symptoms in criteria B, C, and D) is more than one month.

F. The disturbance causes clinically significant distress or impairment in social, occupational, or other important areas of functioning.

Complex PTSD

J. Herman (1992) has developed a profile describing people who have been continually and repeatedly subjected to totalitarian oppression and control as suffering from *Disorders of Extreme Stress Not Otherwise Specified.* Examples include torture victims, victims of kidnapping, prisoners of war, concentration camp inmates, members of religious cults and sects, victims of childhood sexual abuse and other mistreatment as children, and victims of violence and rape in families and of sexual exploitation. These persistent and repeated traumas in the context of intrahuman relations (man-made) can have grave consequences in the following areas:

A. *Regulation of affect (feeling),* e.g.: persistent depressive moods, extremely pent-up rage and aggression, which, for some of those affected, alternates with other moods such as explosive outbreaks, blocking, and loss of sexual interest, perhaps alternating with exaggerated or inappropriate and provocative sexual behavior.

B. *Consciousness,* e.g.: memory loss (amnesia), detachment from memories, feelings, and emotions (dissociation), self-alienation (depersonalization), and brooding.

C. *Self-perception,* e.g.: feelings of helplessness, shame, guilt, self-blame, stigmatization, loneliness, and separation.

D. *Perception of perpetrator(s),* e.g.: continual thoughts of revenge, paradoxical gratitude toward perpetrators, and assumption of the perpetrators' value system or creed.

E. *Relationship to others,* e.g.: isolation and withdrawal, destruction of relations with partners and family, persistent mistrust, loss of ability to protect oneself, and search for a savior.

F. *Concept of meaning and purpose,* e.g.: loss of belief and trust, and feelings of hopelessness and desperation.

DES (Disorders of Extreme Stress)

Van der Kolk et al. use the DES profile to suggest a supplement to the PTSD concept, since the symptoms of persistent and repeated traumatization by human hand are not covered by PTSD. They augmented Herman's complex PTSD and transposed it into a special diagnostic profile (DES) for PTSD.

Inter alia, the following augmentations of PTSD need to be emphasized for torture victims: problems dealing with rage and anger, self-destructive and suicidal behavior, impulsive risk behavior, chronic pain (psychosomatic pains), idealization of the perpetrators, assumption of the perpetrators' values and of part of their world-view, incapacity to trust oneself and others, tendency to become a victim again, and inclination to make victims out of other people.

It needs to be emphasized that those victims who had been lengthily and repeatedly traumatized by human hand often develop a series of clinically significant reactions and illnesses that are not covered by the PTSD concept, for example: persistent depression, panic attacks, compulsive behavior, psychogenic eating disorders, suicide risk, alcohol and medication abuse, addictive behavior in general, somatization (transposition of feelings and emotions not lived into physical ailments, psychosomatic pain, and psychosomatic illnesses). The clinical picture for torture victims would therefore even support the idea of multimorbidity (multiple illness). At the very least, other striking clinical features (comorbidity) usually show up alongside PTSD.

Glossary

anhedonia: A pathological state of unhappiness, often an aspect of depression.

burnout: Burnout happens to helpers who are overtaxed, are having boundary problems, are overidentifying with or overnurturing clients. Major symptoms: depressive moods, hopelessness, loss of energy and drive, development of cynicism, reality loss, psychosomatic illnesses, and addictive behavior.

castration anxiety: An Oedipal phase—a special developmental stage at age 6 or 7, in which the child directs his or her sexual instinctual wishes toward the parent of the opposite sex.

compliance: The client's/patient's agreement to therapy or individual steps in therapy.

conditioning: Using conditions of reward or punishment to induce or modify behavior.

Conditioned behaviors can include internal events such as reflex movements, and physiological changes or complex patterns of thought and feeling, as well as externally observed complex reactions such as behavioral patterns.

countertransference: Conscious or unconscious feelings, thoughts, and fantasies that the therapist has about his patients.

debriefing: An initial, emotionally unburdening articulation of traumatizing feelings, emotions, and experiences. Debriefing may be conducted by competent "debriefers," who ask a series of probing, sympathetic questions, or it may be a kind of unburdening ritual involving sharing feelings and emotions with others. It should come after burdensome events as soon as possible; it is no substitute for dream processing or therapy (see, e.g., Mitchell and Everly 1993).

defense, defense mechanisms: This is how psychoanalysis characterizes unconscious psychological mechanisms that the ego uses to ward off (and relegate to the unconscious) the id's unconscious tendencies and drives that are in conflict with the superego's psychological authority. These include so-called more mature defense mechanisms against anxiety such as repression, displacement, rationalization, and identification, as well as less mature, early childhood mechanisms such as splitting, projection, and introjection (A. Freud 1936).

dissociation: The partial crippling of emotions, detachment or separation from perceptions, feelings, and emotions, often going hand in hand with feelings of self-alienation and detachment from aspects of one's personality.

empathy: The capacity for emotional identification.

flashbacks: Sudden images or thoughts that attack an individual after a traumatic experience is over. Usually these fragments of the trauma situation are so strong that they make the survivor relive the ordeal in his imagination. Physiological manifestations of anxiety and agitation usually appear similar to those that occurred in the original trauma.

hypervigilance: Heightened or exaggerated perception, alertness, and readiness to respond; a constant "being on one's toes."

introjection: An unconscious process by which one incorporates into one's psyche the characteristics of another person or object.

IRCT: International Rehabilitation Centre for Torture Victims in Copenhagen. Across the globe, the IRCT provides assistance in building treatment centers for torture victims.

object constancy: A child's capacity at the end of the pre-Oedipal phase to enter into a stable and trusting relationship with his objects (the central people in his life). Positive, wish-fulfilling, and drive-fulfilling aspects of experiences with parents or objects as well as bad experiences that trigger existential anxiety and rage are fused into a joint realistic image.

object relations theory: A theory originating in psychoanalysis (main representatives: Melanie Klein and Otto Kernberg) that, rather than placing drives, instinctual conflicts, and instinctual development at the center of psychological development, emphasizes the growth of ego consciousness and the ego function through ties to parents and close acquaintances as well as the spatial environment and landscape (objects) in childhood. In contrast to the psychoanalytic teaching about psychic hierarchy, object relations theory has the advantage of offering a theoretical model for narcissistic developmental disorders and deficits. Another difference from psychoanalytic theory is that the theory posits not fear of punishment (castration anxiety) as the decisive motor for resolving the Oedipal phase but rather love for the parent of the same sex.

object representation: The depiction of the objects (mother, father, etc.) in the child's forming ego consciousness.

objects: The persons and components of the environment to which one most closely relates in childhood.

regression or (better) *regressive transference:*   A concept from psychoanalytic theory, here used to characterize the phenomenon of the relationship between patient and treatment provider in which the patient is unconsciously taken back to early childhood development stages and develops feelings and attitudes toward the treatment provider that he had as a child with respect to parents or other important objects.

resources: Hypnotherapy according to Milton Erickson and neurolinguistic programming (NLP) in particular use the concept to describe life-preserving experiences and capacities from the unconscious. These are basically positive, "wise," creative, protective, and supportive.

retraumatization: Renewed traumatization of a victim through stimuli that are similar to the original traumatic situation or that stand as a symbol for the trauma. These stimuli can be meaningless in everyday life, but for the victims they have a traumatic charge because of a similarity or a triggering memory.

transference: A patient's conscious and unconscious feelings, thoughts, and fantasies about his therapist that have nothing to do with the therapist himself but rather with the patient's previous objects such as parents, siblings, friends, teachers, and the like.

Bibliography

Compiled by Leyla Schön. All titles are listed only once, even when they deal with several topics.

General

Adam, Hubertus. *Terror und Gesundheit.* Weinheim, 1993.

Ahrens, S., and M. Hasenbring, eds. *Psychosomatik in der Neurologie.* Stuttgart, 1995.

Amati, Sylvia. "Reflexionen über die Folter." *Psyche* 31 (1977): 228–45.

American Psychiatric Association. *The Diagnostic and Statistical Manual of Mental Disorders (DSM-IV).* 4th ed. Washington, D.C., 1994.

Amnesty International. *Jahresbericht* [Annual Report]. Frankfurt am Main.

———. *Wer der Folter erlag.* Frankfurt am Main, 1988.

———. *Examining Torture Survivors.* Copenhagen, 1992.

Arendt, Hannah. *Elemente und Ursprünge totaler Herrschaft.* 3d ed. Munich, 1993.

———. *Macht und Gewalt.* 8th ed. Munich, 1993.

Assmann, J. "Die Katastrophe des Vergessens." In *Mnemosyne—Formen und Funktion der kulturellen Erinnerung,* ed. A. Assmann and D. Harth. Frankfurt am Main, 1991.

Bettelheim, Bruno. *Erziehung zum Überleben.* Munich, 1982.

Blanck, G., and R. Blanck. *Jenseits der Ich-Psychologie.* Stuttgart, 1989.

Bloch, Ernst. *Das Prinzip Hoffnung,* 4th ed. Frankfurt am Main, 1993.

Bommert, Claudia. *Körperorientierte Psychotherapie nach sexueller Gewalt.* Weinheim, 1993.

British Medical Association. *The Torture Report.* London, 1986.

———. *Medicine Betrayed.* London, 1992.

———. *Verrantene Medizin.* Berlin, 1995.

Buber, Martin. *Das dialogische Prinzip.* Darmstadt, 1984.

Burgers, J. H., and Hans Danelius. *The United Nations Convention against Torture.* Dordrecht, 1988.

Danieli, Yael, Nigel S. Rodley, and Lars Weisaeth, eds. *International Responses to Traumatic Stress.* Amityville, N.Y., 1996.

Dieckmann, Hans. *Träume als Sprache der Seele.* Fellbach, 1978.

Dreyfuss, D. "Zur Theorie der traumatischen Neurose." *Internationale Zeitschrift für Psychoanalyse* 26 (1941): 122–41.

Egle, U. T., and S. O. Hoffmann, eds. *Der Schmerzkranke.* Stuttgart, 1993.

Enquete-Kommission. "Aufarbeitung von Geschichte und Folgen der SED-Diktatur in Deutschland." In *Materialien*. Baden-Baden, 1995.

Epstein, Helen. *Die Kinder des Holocaust*. Munich, 1990.

Fanon, Frantz. *Die Verdammten der Erde*. Reinbek, 1969.

Flor, Herta. *Psychobiologie des Schmerzes*. Bern, 1991.

Freud, A. *Das Ich und die Abwehrmechanismen*. Vienna, 1936.

Freud, S. *Gesammelte Werke*. Vol. 13, *Jenseits des Lustprinzips*. London, 1940.

Fromm, Erich. *Märchen, Mythen, Träume*. Reinbek, 1981.

Goffman, Erving. *Asylums*. Harmondsworth, 1971.

Gurris, Norbert. "Wie kann es gelingen den Mißbrauch zu beenden?" In *Monster oder liebe Eltern,* ed. K.-J. Bruder. Berlin, 1993.

Halbwachs, M. *Das kollektive Gedächtnis*. Frankfurt am Main, 1985.

Hell, W. "Gedächtnistäuschungen." In *Kognitive Täuschungen,* ed. W. Hell, K. Fiedler, and G. Gigerenzer. Heidelberg, 1993.

Heseding, Georg. *Menschenrechte und Folter*. Göttingen, 1991.

Hoffmann, S. O., and G. Hochapfel. *Einführung in die Neurosenlehre und psychosomatische Medizin*. 4th ed. Stuttgart, 1991.

Jacobson, E. "Depersonalization." *Journal of the American Psychoanalytical Association* 7 (1959): 581–610.

Jonghe, F. de, P. Rijnierse, and R. Janssen. "Aspects of the Analytic Relationship." *International Journal of Psycho-analysis* 72 (1991): 693–707.

Kernberg, O. *Borderline-Störungen und pathologischer Narzißmus*. Frankfurt am Main, 1978.

———. *Objektbeziehungen und Praxis der Psychoanalyse*. Stuttgart, 1989.

Knechtel, Rüdiger, ed. *Stalins DDR*. Leipzig, 1991.

Kütemeyer, Mechthilde. "Psychosomatische Aspekte bei Patienten mit Lumbago-Ischias-Syndrom." *Verhandlungen der Deutschen Gesellschaft für Innere Medizin* 85 (1979): 1384–87.

———. "Körperschmerz, Angst, Seelenschmerz als ärztliches Problem." *Zeitschrift für medizinische Ethik* 40 (1994): 3–13.

Langer, Marie. *Von Wien bis Managua*. Freiburg i.Br., 1986.

Maaz, Hans-Joachim. *Der Gefühlsstau*. Munich, 1992.

Maturana, H. R. *Erkennen: die Organisation und Verkörperung von Wirklichkeit*. Braunschweig, 1982.

Mitchell, J. T., and G. S. Everly. *Critical Incident Stress Debriefing (CISD)*. Ellicott City, Md., 1993.

Pross, Christian. *Paying for the Past: The Struggle over Reparations for Surviving Victims of the Nazi Terror*. Baltimore, 1998.

———. "Apartheid in der Medizin?" *Berliner Ärzte* 27 (1990): 27 ff.

———. "Breaking Through the Postwar Coverup of Nazi Doctors in Germany." *Journal of Medical Ethics* (suppl.) 17 (1991): 13–16.

Raess, Markus. *Der Schutz vor Folter im Völkerrecht*. Zurich, 1989.

Rauchfleisch, Udo, ed. *Folter: Gewalt gegen Menschen*. Zurich, 1990.

Reemtsma, Jan P. *Folter: zur Analyse eines Herrschaftsmittels*. Hamburg, 1991.

Reinecker, H. *Grundlagen der Verhaltentherapie.* 2d ed. Weinheim, 1992.

Scarry, Elaine. *The Making and Unmaking of the World.* New York, 1995.

Schliephacke, Bruno P. *Märchen, Seele, und Sinnbild.* 3d ed. Münster, 1986.

Schultz, Hans J., ed. *Schmerz.* Stuttgart, 1990.

Schulz-Hageleit, Peter, ed. *Alltag, Macht, Folter.* Düsseldorf, 1989.

Stolze, Helmuth. "Selbsterfahrung und Bewegung." In *Die Konzentrative Bewegungstherapie,* 2d ed. Berlin, 1989.

Uexküll, Thure von, ed. *Psychosomatische Medizin.* 5th ed. Munich, 1996.

Vollmar, Klausbernd. *Farben.* Munich, 1991.

Wagner-Simon, Therese, and Gaetano Benedetti. *Trauma und Träumen.* Göttingen, 1984.

Wicker, Hans-Rudolf. *Die Sprache extremer Gewalt.* Bern, 1991.

Wirtz, Ursula. *Seelenmord.* Zurich, 1989.

History of Torture

DuBois, Page. *Torture and Truth.* New York, 1991.

Helbing, Franz, and Max Bauer. *Die Tortur.* Berlin, 1926. Reprint, Aalen, 1983.

Mannix, Daniel P. *The History of Torture.* London, 1970.

Maran, Rita. *Torture: The Role of Ideology in the French-Algerian War.* New York, 1989.

Quanter, Rudolf. *Die Folter in der deutschen Rechtspflege sonst und jetzt.* Dresden, 1900. Reprint, Aalen, 1970.

Rauter, Ernst A. *Folter in Geschichte und Gegenwart.* Frankfurt am Main, 1988.

Villeneuve, R. *Grausamkeit und Sexualität.* Berlin, 1988.

Methods of Torture and Case Studies

Agger, Inger. "Die politische Gefangene als Opfer sexueller Folter." *Zeitschrift für Sexualforschung* 1 (1988): 231–41.

———. "Sexual Torture of Political Prisoners." *Journal of Traumatic Stress* 2 (1989): 305–18.

Amery, Jean. *Jenseits von Schuld und Sühne.* Munich, 1988.

Arce, Luz. *Die Hölle.* Hamburg, 1994.

Behnke, Klaus, and Juergen Fuchs, eds. *Zersetzung der Seele.* Hamburg, 1995.

Bro-Rassmussen, Frede, and Ole Rasmussen. *Torture by Phalanga.* Copenhagen, n.d.

Domovitch, Edward, et al. "Human Torture." *Canadian Family Physician* 30 (1984): 827–30.

Dorfman, Ariel. *Der Tod und das Mädchen.* Frankfurt am Main, 1992.

Erzeren, Ömer. *Septemberspuren.* Reinbek, 1990.

Gurris, Norbert. "Die sexuelle Folter von Männern als weltweit systematische Methode der Folter." In *Multikulturelle Gesellschaft—monokulturelle Psychologie?* ed. Iman Attia. Tübingen, 1995.

Karlsmark, T., et al. "Tracing the Use of Torture." *Nature* 301 (1983): 75–78.

Konuk, Abdul A. *Folter.* 2d ed. Frankfurt am Main, 1990.

Kosteljanetz, Michael, and Ole Aalund. "Torture." *Interdisciplinary Science Reviews* 8 (1983): 320–28.

Rivabella, Omar. *Susana: Requiem für die Seele einer Frau.* Frauenfeld, 1987.

Rosencof, Mauricio, and Eleuterio Fernández Huidobro. *Wie Efeu an der Mauer.* Hamburg, 1990.

Suedfeld, Peter, ed. *Psychology and Torture.* New York, 1990.

Timerman, Jacobo. *Wir brüllten nach innen.* Frankfurt am Main, 1982.

Zana, Mehdi. *La prison,* no. 5. Paris, 1995.

Zilli, Timo. *Folterzelle 36.* Berlin, 1993.

Aftereffects of Torture among Survivors

Agger, Inger. *The Blue Room.* London, 1994.

Allodi, F., and G. Cowgill. "Ethical and Psychiatric Aspects of Torture." *Canadian Journal of Psychiatry* 27 (1982): 98–102.

Åstrøm, Christina, et al. "Sleep Disturbances in Torture Survivors." *Acta neurologica scandinavica* 79 (1989): 150–54.

Basoglu, Metin, ed. *Torture and Its Consequences.* Cambridge, 1992.

Behandlungszentrum für Folteropfer Berlin. *Jahresberichte* [Annual reports]. Berlin, 1993–.

Bendfeldt-Zachrisson, F. "State torture." *Radical Journal of Health* 3 (1988): 56–61.

Bettelheim, Bruno. Afterword to *I Didn't Say Good-bye,* by C. Veigh. New York, 1984.

Bittenbinder, Else. "Krieg, Verfolgung, und Folter überleben." *Systhema* 6 (1992): 3–17.

Ehlert, Martin E., and Beate Lorke. "Zur Psychodynamik der traumatischen Reaktion." *Psyche* 42 (1988): 502–32.

Eitinger, Leo, Robert Krell, and Miriam Rieck. *The Psychological and Medical Effects of Concentration Camps and Related Persecution on Survivors of the Holocaust.* Vancouver, 1985.

Fischer, Gottfried, Norbert Gurris, Christian Pross, and Peter Riedesser. "Psychotraumatologie." In *Psychosomatische Medizin,* 5th ed., ed. Thure von Uexküll. Munich, 1996.

Gersons, Berthold P. "Therapeutic approach to PTSD." Paper presented at the fourth European Conference on Traumatic Stress, Paris, 7–11 May 1995.

Goldfeld, Anne E., et al. "The Physical and Psychological Sequelae of Torture." *Journal of the American Medical Association* 259 (1988): 2725–29.

Graessner, Sepp. "Tinnitus in Torture Survivors." *Torture* 4 (1994): 19–22.

———. "Forensic Considerations in Survivors of Torture with Craniocerebral Trauma and Postconcussive Syndrome." *Torture* 5 (1995): 50–53.

Haenel, Ferdinand. "Die Auswirkung der Langzeithaft und psychische Symptome bei Stasi-Untersuchungshäftlingen." In *Zur medizinischen, psychologischen und politischen Beurteilung von Haftfolgeschäden nach 1945 in Deutschland.* Magdeburg, 1994.

Herberg, H. J., ed. *Spätschäden nach Extrembelastungen.* Herford, 1971.

Hoppe, Klaus D. "The Emotional Reactions of Psychiatrists When Confronting Holocaust Survivors of Persecution." In *Psychoanalytic Forum,* vol. 3, ed. J. Lindon. New York, 1969.

Hougen, Hans-Petter, et al. "Sequelae to torture." *Forensic Science International* 36 (1988): 153–60.

Initiative für ein Internationales Kulturzentrum. *Psychische und psychosomatische Folgen bei Folterüberlebenden.* Hanover, 1993.

Janoff-Bulman, R. *Shattered Assumptions: Towards a New Psychology of Trauma.* New York, 1992.

Juhler, Marianne, and Peter Vesti. "Torture: Diagnosis and Rehabilitation." *Medicine and War* 5 (1989): 69–79.

Keller, Gustav. *Die Psychologie der Folter.* Frankfurt am Main, 1991.

Kordon, Diana, et al. *Psychological Effects of Political Repression.* Buenos Aires, 1988.

Krystal, Henry, ed. *Massive Psychic Trauma.* New York, 1968.

———. *Integration and Self-Healing.* Mahwah, N.J., 1988.

Lök, Veli. "Bone scintigraphy as Clue to Previous Torture." *Lancet* 337 (1991): 846–47.

Matussek, P. *Die Konzentrationslagerhaft und ihre Folgen.* Berlin, 1971.

McCann, L., and L. Pearlman. "Vicarious Traumatization." *Journal of Traumatic Stress* 3 (1990): 131–49.

Mollica, Richard F. "Assessing Symptom Change in Southeast Asian Refugee Survivors of Mass Violence and Torture." *American Journal of Psychiatry* 147 (1990): 83–88.

Montgomery, E., and A. Foldspang. "Criterion-Related Validity of Screening for Exposure to Torture." *Torture* 4 (1994): 115–18.

Niederland, William G. *Folgen der Verfolgung.* Frankfurt am Main, 1980.

Nordström, A., and A. Persson. "Fängelse och tortyr valinga orsaker till psykiska och somatiska symptom hos flyktingar i Sverige." *Läkartidningen* 86 (1988): 3560 ff.

Op den Velde, Wybrand, G. Frank Koerselman, and Petra G. H. Aarts. "Countertransference and World War II." In *Countertransference in the Treatment of PTSD,* ed. John P. Wilson and Jacob Lindy. London, 1994.

Orellana Aguirre, Daniel. "Das Ego im Kontext extremer Erfahrungen wie Folter." In *Das Prinzip Egoismus,* ed. T. Heckt. Tübingen, 1994.

Peters, U. H. "Über das Stasi-Verfolgten-Syndrom." *Fortschritte der Neurologie und Psychiatrie* 59 (1991): 251–65.

Petersen, Hans D., et al. "Psychological and Physical Long-Term Effects of Torture." *Scandinavian Journal of Social Medicine* 13 (1985): 89–93.

Pross, Christian. "Folter: Schweigen bedeutet Komplizenschaft." *Deutsches Ärzteblatt* 87 (1990): 3104–8.

———. "Folteropfer." *Dr. Med. Mabuse,* no. 79 (1992): 46–49.

———. "Gesundheitliche Folgen politischer Repression in der DDR." *Berliner Ärzte* 31 (1994): 19 ff.

———. "'Wir sind unsere eigenen Gespenster.'" In *Zersetzung der Seele,* ed. Klaus Behnke and Jürgen Fuchs. Hamburg, 1995.

Rasmussen, Ole V. *Medical Aspects of Torture.* Copenhagen, 1990.

Rehabilitation Centre for Torture Victims (RCT). Annual reports. Copenhagen.

Stiftung für Kinder, ed. *Children, War, and Persecution: Proceedings of the Congress.* Osnabrück, 1995.

Stoffels, Hans, ed. *Schicksale der Verfolgten.* Berlin, 1991.

Stover, Eric, and Elena Nightingale, eds. *The Breaking of Bodies and Minds.* New York, 1985.

Turner, S., and C. Gorst-Unsworth. "Psychological Sequelae of Torture." *British Journal of Psychiatry* 157 (1990): 475–80.

Van der Kolk, Bessel A., et al. *Traumatic Stress.* New York, 1996.

Wilson, John P., and Beverly Raphael, eds. *International Handbook of Traumatic Stress Syndromes.* New York, 1993.

Treatment of Survivors of Torture

Allodi, F. "Assessment and Treatment of Torture Victims." *Journal of Nervous and Mental Disease* 179 (1991): 4–11.

Amati, Sylvia. "Die Rückgewinnung des Schamgefühls." *Psyche* 44 (1990): 724–40.

Beaujolin, Marie-Hélène. *Modification of the Psychoanalytical Technique in Psychotherapy with Torture Victims.* Paris, 1991.

Becker, David. "Psychoanalytische Sozialarbeit mit Gefolterten in Chile." *Psychosozial* 12 (1989): 43–52.

———. *Ohne Haß keine Versöhnung.* Freiburg, 1992.

Besuden, Frauke. "Das Körperbild als Matrix des Körpererlebens." *Konzentrative Bewegungstherapie* 11 (1984): 1–7.

Blijham, H. "Het dilemma van het existentieel getraumatiseerd zijn." In *De actualiteit van het traumatisch verleden,* ed. J. N. Schreuder and A. J. de Ridder. Utrecht, 1992.

Bloch, Inge. "Physiotherapy and the Rehabilitation of Torture Victims." *Clinical Management in Physical Therapy* 8 (1988): 26–29.

Budjuhn, Anneliese. *Die psycho-somatischen Verfahren.* Dortmund, 1992.

Bustos, Enrique. "Dealing with the Unbearable." In *Torture and Psychology,* ed. Peter Suedfeld. Washington, D.C., 1990.

Cienfuegos, Ana J., and Christina Monelli. "The Testimony of Political Repression as a Therapeutic Instrument." *American Journal of Orthopsychiatry* 53 (1983): 43–51.

Dhawan, Savita. "Psychodrama in der therapeutischen Arbeit mit politischen Verfolgten." *Systhema* 6 (1992): 37–49.

Drees, Alfred. "Leitlinien in der Therapie mit foltertraumatisierten Patienten." *Systhema* 6 (1992): 26–36.

Edelman, Lucila, Diana Kordon, and Dario Lagos. "Impunity: Reactivation of Psychic Trauma." Paper presented at the Seventh International Symposium on Caring for Survivors of Torture. Capetown, 15–17 November 1995.

Fischer, Gottfried, and Norbert Gurris. "Grenzverletzungen." In *Praxis der Psychotherapie,* ed. W. Senf and M. Broda. Stuttgart, 1996.

Foy, David W., ed. *Treating PTSD.* New York, 1992.

Genefke, Inge K., and Peter Vesti. *Behandlung und Wiedereingliederung von Überleben-den der Folter.* Dorsten, 1990.

———. "Hilfe für Folteropfer in der Türkei." *Berliner Ärzte* 27 (1991): 26.

———. "The Stasi Persecution Syndrome." *Torture* 1 (1991): 10–11.

Graessner, Sepp. "Behandlungszentrum für Folteropfer—erste Fallberichte." *Deutsches Ärzteblatt,* no. 21 (1992): 89.

———. "Regarding the Health of Bosnian Refugees." In *Care and Rehabilitation of Victims of Rape, Torture, and Other Severe Traumas of War in the Former Yugoslavia,* ed. UNHCR. Utrecht, 1993.

Graessner, Sepp, Salah Ahmad, and Frank Merkord. *Gedächtnisstörungen und Unsicher-heit der Angaben zur eigenen Verfolgungsgeschichte bei Flüchtlingen mit Foltererfah-rung.* Berlin, 1995.

Gurris, Norbert. "Folteropfer und Opfer politischer Gewalt." In *Therapie der posttrau-matischen Belastungsstörungen,* ed. A. Maercker. Berlin, 1997.

Haenel, F. "Traumatische und therapeutische Regression." In *Jahresbericht des Behan-dlungszentrums für Folteropfer.* Berlin, 1993.

Hafkenscheid, A., and J. Lansen. "Vicarious Traumatization." In *Therapeut en trauma,* ed. A. J. de Jonghe. Assen, 1993.

Herman, Judith L. *Die Narben der Gewalt.* Munich, 1994. Originally published as *Trauma and Recovery: The Aftermath of Violence, from Domestic Abuse to Political Terror.* New York, 1992.

Initiative für ein Internationales Kulturzentrum, ed. *Psychosoziale Versorgung von Flüch-tlingen und MigrantInnen.* Hanover, 1993.

Institut für Wissenschaft und Kunst. *Seelenmord—psychosoziale Aspekte der Folter.* Vi-enna, 1992.

Jacobsen, Lone, and Peter Vesti. *Torture Survivors: A New Group of Patients.* Copenha-gen, 1990.

Kepner, James I. *Körperprozesse.* Cologne, 1988.

Kinzie, J. D., et al. The Prevalence of Post-Traumatic Stress Disorder and Its Clinical Significance among South East Asian Refugees. *American Journal of Psychiatry* 147 (1990): 913–17.

Kleber, Rolf J., and Dany Brom. *Coping with Trauma.* Amsterdam, 1992.

Johan Lansen. Unpublished, 1992.

———. "Vicarious Traumatization in Therapists Treating Victims of Torture and Per-secution." *Torture* 3 (1993): 138–40.

Mohamed-Ali, Hassan. "Patient Folteropfer." *Berliner Ärzteblatt,* no. 27 (1990): 11–19.

Mollica, Richard, and Yael Caspi-Yavin. "Measuring Torture and Torture-Related Symptoms." *Psychological Assessment* 3 (1991): 581–87.

Ochberg, Frank M., ed. *Post-Traumatic Therapy and Victims of Violence.* New York, 1988.

Oesterreich, Sieglinde, and Sibylle Rothkegel. "Einführung in gestalttherapeutische Traumbearbeitung." Manuscript. Berlin, 1990.

Ortmann, Jørgen, et al. "Rehabilitation of Torture Victims." *American Journal of Social Psychiatry* 7 (1987): 161–67.

Pagaduan-Lopez, June C. *Torture Survivors.* Manila, 1987.

Peltzer, Karl, and Jean-Claude Diallo. *Die Betreuung und Behandlung von Opfern organisierter Gewalt im europäisch-deutschen Kontext.* Frankfurt am Main, 1993.

Perls, F. S. *Gestalt Therapy Verbatim.* Lafayette, Calif., 1969.

Perls, F. S., R. F. Hefferline, and D. Goodman. *Gestalttherapie,* New York, 1951.

Peterson, C. P., Maurice F. Prout, and Robert A. Schwarz. *Post-Traumatic Stress Disorder.* New York, 1991.

Petzold, Hilarion G. "Was nicht mehr vergessen werden kann." *Integrative Therapie* 3 (1985): 368–80.

Pharos Foundation for Refugee Health Care. *Health Hazards of Organized Violence.* Utrecht, 1993.

Prip, Karen, Lone Tived, and Nina Holten, eds. *Physiotherapy for Torture Survivors.* Copenhagen, 1995.

Randall, Glenn R., and Ellen L. Lutz. *Serving Survivors of Torture.* Washington, D.C., 1991.

Riquelme, Horacio, ed. *Zeitlandschaft im Nebel.* Frankfurt am Main, 1990.

———. "Die neuen Leiden Südamerikas: zur Behandlung von Folteropfern." *Systhema* 6 (1992): 18–25.

Somnier, Finn E., and Inge K. Genefke. "Psychotherapy for Victims of Torture." *British Journal of Psychiatry* 149 (1986): 323–29.

Somnier, Finn E., et al. *Medical Treatment of Torture Victims.* Copenhagen, 1982.

Stoffels, Hans, ed. *Terrorlandschaften der Seele.* Regensburg, 1994.

Tata Arcel, Libby, ed. *Psycho-Social Help to War Victims: Women Refugees and Their Families.* Copenhagen, 1995.

Van der Veer, Guus. "Getraumatiseerde vluchtelingen." *Maardblad geestelije volksgesundheid* 10 (1991): 1078–90.

———. *Counselling and Therapy with Refugees.* Chichester, 1992.

Vesti, Peter and Søren Bojholm. "Antithesis of Therapy." *Psychiatria Danubina* 2 (1990): 297–312.

Vesti, Peter, Finn E. Somnier, and Marianne Kastrup. *Psychotherapeutic Manual to Be Used as Part of an Integrated Approach in the Rehabilitation of Torture Survivors.* 3d ed. Copenhagen, 1992.

———. *Psychotherapy with Torture Survivors.* Copenhagen, 1992.

Weiss, Regula. *Therapie-Projekt für gefolterte Flüchtlinge.* Bern, 1993.

Wilson, John P., and Jacob D. Lindy. *Countertransference in the Treatment of PTSD.* New York, 1994.

Torturers

Adorno, Theodor W. *Studien zum autoritären Charakter.* Frankfurt am Main, 1973.

Amnesty International. *Folter in Griechenland.* Baden-Baden, 1977.

Arestivo, Carlos. "Die perverse Allianz zwischen Folterer und Opfer." *AI-Info,* no. 1 (1992): 28 ff.

Boppel, Peter, and Monika Held. "Warum foltern Menschen?" *Süddeutsche Zeitung Magazin* 23 (October 1992): 12–18.

Crelinsten, Ronald D., and Alex P. Schmid, eds. *The Politics of Pain.* Leiden, 1993.

Deile, Volkmar, and Peter Boppel. "Schulen der Bestialität." *Der Spiegel,* no. 27 (1994): 124–26.

Milgram, Stanley. *Das Milgram Experiment.* Reinbek, 1992.

Tišma, Aleksandar. *Die Schule der Gottlosigkeit.* Munich, 1993.

Vesti, Peter. "Why Are Torturers Never Punished?" *Danish Medical Bulletin* 35 (1988): 493–95.

Weschler, Lawrence. *A Miracle, a Universe: Settling Accounts with Torturers.* New York, 1990.

Ethics

Amnesty International. *Standesregeln: eine Strategie, Folter undenkbar zu machen.* Bonn, 1984.

———. *Ethical Codes and Declarations Relevant to Health Professions.* London, 1994.

Amnesty International, French Medical Commission, and Valérie Marange. *Doctors and Torture.* London, 1991.

Danish Medical Association. "Doctors, Ethics, and Torture: Proceedings of an International Meeting." *Danish Medical Bulletin* 34 (1987): 185–216.

Gordon, Neve, and Ruchama Marton. *Torture.* London, 1995.

Kosteljanetz, M., and O. Aalund. "Torture." *Interdisciplinary Science Reviews* 8 (1983): 320–28.

Pross, Christian, and Lucas Torsten. "Menschenrechtsverletzungen und die Heilberufe." *Medizin und globales Überleben* 6 (1995): 28–40.

Sørensen, Bent, and Peter Vesti. "Medical Education for the Prevention of Torture." *Medical Education* 24 (1990): 467–69.

Journals

Anxiety, Stress, and Coping. Yverdon, 1992–.

Health and Human Rights. Cambridge, Mass., 1995–.

Forensic Science International. Amsterdam, 1994–.

Human Rights and the Health Professions [previously *News for Medical Groups*]. London, 1992–.

Journal of Traumatic Stress. New York, 1991–.

PTSD Research Quarterly. White River Junction, 1994–.

SOS-Torture. OMCT, Geneva, 1991–.

Torture. Copenhagen, 1991–.

The years refer to the Treatment Center's collection.

Contributors

Salah Ahmad, born 1959 in Kirkuk, South Kurdistan. Education degree (Diplom), trained as teacher in Sulaimani, worked in the villages of Kurdistan with children and promoting adult literacy. Fled Iraq 1981 for Germany. Studied at the Free University of Berlin, education department (adult education). Through 1992 special casework and work in family assistance. Training in family therapy. At the Treatment Center for Torture Victims since 1992.

Sepp Graessner, M.D., born 1943. Cofounder of the Treatment Center for Torture Victims. Worked in private practice, emergency medicine, tropical medicine. Interest in historical questions. In charge of forensic aspects of the Treatment Center's work.

Norbert Gurris, born 1948 in Oldenburg/O. Worked for the Berlin city justice department as clinical psychologist and psychotherapist in adult prisons, 1974–77, then in child, youth, and family therapy at special education centers for the city of Berlin, 1977–87; director of a conference center, 1987–90; family therapy for sexual abuse at "Kind im Zentrum" (KIZ—"Child in the Center"), Berlin, 1990–92. Additional training in behavioral therapy, conversational therapy, psychodrama, clinical hypnosis/hypnotherapy, systematic family therapy. At the Treatment Center for Torture Victims from 1992 to 1999.

Ferdinand Haenel, M.D., born 1953 in Mannheim. Studied mathematics and computer science in Freiburg i. Brsg. In Berlin since 1976. Research assistant at the Institut für Psychologie, Free University of Berlin. Professional training in psychiatry at the Krankenhaus am Urban, among other hospitals. Training in gestalt therapy and psychoanalytically oriented psychotherapy.

Britta Jenkins, born 1949. Bachelor of Arts, School for New Learning, DePaul University, Chicago. Lengthy stays abroad in France and the United States. Human rights work in Chicago with Amnesty International. Public relations manager and translator at the Treatment Center for Torture Victims since 1992.

Sylvia Karcher, born 1940 in Kiel, grew up in Austria, long stays abroad in Israel and the United States. Psychotherapist and physical therapist for concentrative movement therapy. Work in different clinics, in freelance practice, and in continuing training in concentrative movement therapy. Training in TZI and conversational therapy. At the Treatment Center for Torture Victims since 1992.

Johan Lansen, born 1933. Psychiatrist, psychotherapist, and psychoanalyst. Formerly medical director of the Jewish Psychiatric Clinic "Sinai-Centrum" in Amersfoort, Netherlands. Active in continuing training, supervising, and advising for the Treatment Center for Torture Victims in Berlin, the Rehabilitation Center for Torture Victims in Copenhagen, and for ESRA, the Association for Psychological and Social Assistance for Victims of Nazi Persecution and their Descendants, Berlin. Publications on therapy for Holocaust survivors, posttraumatic stress disorder, and traumatization in the second generation.

Dori Laub, M.D., F.A., P.A. Associate clinical professor of Psychiatry in the School of Medicine at Yale University and education advisor, Fortunoff Video Archive for Holocaust Testimonies, Yale University.

Frank Merkord, born 1952. Degree (Diplom) in social work and education; cofounder and staff member of various sociocultural projects in the 1970s and 1980s; experience with self-help initiatives and group work in the intercultural area; advising and caring for refugees since the mid-1980s; currently training in psychodrama. At the Treatment Center for Torture Victims since 1993.

Christian Pross, M.D., born 1948. Physician in general practice. Training in psychotherapy. Publications on medicine in the Weimar Republic and under National Socialism as well as on medicine and human rights. Cofounder and medical director of the Treatment Center for Torture Victims.

Sibylle Rothkegel, born 1947. Lengthy stays abroad in Paris and Cairo, degree (Diplom) in psychology; training as gestalt therapist, additional training in gestalt dreamwork (IGG Berlin); experience in individual and group therapy, therapeutic and advising activity over several years in a home for mistreated and abused girls, project with homeless young mothers, teaching and supervising activity at the Vocational College for Social Work and the Athletic College in Berlin; lengthy association with Amnesty International and with the Humanistic Union. At the Treatment Center for Torture Victims since 1994; deputy director.

Mechthild Wenk-Ansohn, M.D., born 1952. General practitioner and breathing therapist (Middendorf methodology). Clinical work in internal medicine, surgery, and general practice. Additional training in psychotherapy and physical therapy. Experience in psychosomatic medicine in the clinics of the Theodor-Wenzel-Werk, Berlin, and project work with children and women in Brazil. At the Treatment Center for Torture Victims since 1994.

Library of Congress Cataloging-in-Publication Data

An der Seite der Uberlebenden, Unterstutzung, und
Therapien. English

At the side of torture survivors : treating a terrible assault on
human dignity / edited by Sepp Graessner, Norbert Gurris, and
Christian Pross ; translated by Jeremiah Michael Riemer.

p.   cm.

Includes bibliographical references.

ISBN 0-8018-6627-8 (alk. paper)

1. Torture victims—Rehabilitation. 2. Torture victims—
Mental health. 3. Torture—Psychological aspects. 4. Torture
victims—Counseling of. 5. Torture victims—Medical
care. I. Graessner, Sepp. II. Gurris, Norbert. III. Pross, Christian.
IV. Title.

RC451.4.T67 A5 2001
616.89—dc21   00-048160